THE BRUMBACK LIBRARY
OF VAN WERT COUNTY
VAN WERT, OHIO

The
American
Circus

The
American
Circus

Wilton Eckley

Twayne Publishers
Boston

THE AMERICAN CIRCUS
Wilton Eckley

Copyright © 1984 by G. K. Hall & Company
All Rights Reserved
Published in 1984 by Twayne Publishers
A Division of G. K. Hall & Company
70 Lincoln Street
Boston, Massachusetts 02111

Book Production by Marne B. Sultz
Book Design by Barbara Anderson

This book was typeset in
10 pt. Walbaum by Compset, Inc.,
Beverly, Massachusetts

Printed on permanent/durable acid-free paper
and bound in the United States of America

Library of Congress Cataloging in Publication Data

Eckley, Wilton.
The American circus.

Bibliography: p. 213
Includes index.
1. Circus—United States—History. 1. Title.
GV1807.E25   1984   792.3'0973   84-9010
ISBN 0-8057-9017-9

For Polly and Ernie
Who gave the circus to me

Contents

About the Author

Wilton Eckley is professor of humanities and social sciences and head of the department at Colorado School of Mines. He previously taught at Drake University, at Hollins College, and in Ohio public schools. He received an A.B. degree from Mount Union College (1952), and M.A. degree from the Pennsylvania State University (1955), and the Ph.D. from Case Western Reserve University (1965). He was a John Hay Fellow in the Humanities at Yale University (1961–62) and a senior Fulbright lecturer in American literature at the University of Ljubljana in Yugoslavia (1972–73) and at Cyril and Methodius University in Bulgaria (1981–82). He has published *Harriette Arnow, T.S. Stribling,* and *Herbert Hoover* for the Twayne United States Authors Series, monographs on e.e. cummings and Bret Harte, and a number of articles on science fiction and the short story.

Preface

That all things are temporal is a truism that frequently offers little consolation when a beloved tradition or institution passes away or changes into something noticeably different. Though some may find it unpleasant to contemplate, the American circus has undergone just such a change. Circus history, to be sure, has always been one of change. But for some seventy-five years of that history, change came gradually, sometimes imperceptibly—at least to the layman. The seventy-five years in question cover the period between the birth of the railroad circus in the latter nineteenth century to its demise in 1956. During that period the circus became a familiar part of the American scene, providing color and excitement to millions of people each year. That circus, for better or for worse, is gone—living only in the memories of those who knew it or in the imaginations of those who did not.

This book does not concern itself with what the circus is now or what it will be in the future, but with what the circus *was*—more specifically, with some of those people who made it what it was. The first chapter looks briefly at the beginning of the American circus and covers the careers of P. T. Barnum and the original Ringling brothers, ending with the death of John Ringling. The second chapter describes the logistics of a large railroad circus from its stay in winter quarters through the season itself. The next five chapters focus in turn on a number of outstanding performers who played significant roles in making the circus a theatrical phenomenon and a cultural institution. Among those included are such center-ring stars as Clyde Beatty, the Cristianis, the Wallendas, Lillian Leitzel, Alfredo Codona, and Emmett Kelly. The last chapter, picking up where the first leaves off, covers the decline of the railroad circus and its end. Taken together, these chapters should provide the reader at least a glimpse into one of the more fascinating segments of the American entertainment chronicle.

Wilton Eckley

Colorado School of Mines

Acknowledgments

I should like to extend my appreciation to the following: the Drake University Research Council for a grant to help carry out my research; Professor Max Autrey for editorial assistance; Dave Phipps of the Drake University Educational Media Services for help with illustrations; Bob and Greg Parkinson of the Circus World Museum for books, articles, and much general information; Fred Pfening, Jr., for his generous supply of photographs; Joanne Joys for much information on the wild animal trainer; Rudy Gebhardt, Jr., for information on the Riding Rudynoffs; the many circus historians who have done, and are doing, so much to preserve one of America's great traditions; and finally all those circus people who many years ago helped to plant in the mind of a wide-eyed child the seeds of this book.

1

Circus! Circus!

T O POINT SPECIFICALLY TO A DATE WHEN THE FIRST American circus was started is a bit risky. Even before the Revolution there were menageries of one kind or another that plied the few roads and trails of the Atlantic coast, displaying various exotic animals to the wonder of the inhabitants of the countryside. Itinerant groups of acrobats, jugglers, and clowns also wandered on occasion from village to village, much as they did in the Old World—though they were often looked upon with mistrust and even condemnation in the New. Exhibitions of horsemanship were given in Boston, Philadelphia, and New York by such equestrians as John Sharp, Jacob Bates, and Thomas Poole. If not examples of the circus as one ordinarily thinks of it, such enterprises were certainly forerunners of the American circus. But circus historians generally credit one John Bill Ricketts, an English teacher of horsemanship in Philadelphia, with establishing the first true circus in 1793. In that sense, he heads a rather long line of entertainment entrepreneurs—or perhaps it would be more accurate to say showmen—who made the American circus a unique institution.

Message from Mercury

John Bill Ricketts came to America from England, where he had worked for, and studied under, Charles Hughes, a noted equestrian and owner of a circus of horses, acrobats, clowns, and dogs. The exact date for the opening of his English riding school and show in Philadelphia is a matter of some conjecture, but it would seem safe to say that it was sometime in April 1793. Whatever the exact date, the advertisements for the show were

1

effective enough that President George Washington attended. The latter even agreed to let Ricketts display his old horse Jack, the one he had ridden during the Revolutionary War, in a stall at the circus.

Ricketts himself was the star attraction of his show, as the program for the performance that Washington saw indicates:

> [Ricketts] rides a single horse in full gallop, standing on the saddle at the same time; he will perform a hornpipe on a single horse, with and without the bridle, likewise leaps from his horse to the ground and with the same spring leaps from the ground with one foot on the saddle in the attitude of Mercury, the horse being in full gallop; he rides a single horse, springs from the seat erect without touching the saddle with his hands, then forms the attitude of Mercury without the assistance of the reins; he leaps from the horse to the ground and with the same spring re-mounts with his face towards the horse's tail and throws a somerset backward; the whole to conclude with Mr. Ricketts carrying his young pupil on his shoulders in the attitude of Mercury, standing on two horses in full gallop.[1]

Thus, with his own considerable talent and that of others in his company, Ricketts presented a performance that was generally popular with audiences. So successful was his circus that he decided to take it on the road, first to New York and then to Boston, Hartford, and Charleston, before returning to Philadelphia and a new home for his enterprise.

The first structure that Ricketts utilized in Philadelphia was a simple fenced-in open-air arena. This new building, named Ricketts' New Amphitheater, was a permanent winterized affair, complete with artificial lighting and a figure of Mercury, the Roman messenger god, on the roof. Equipped with both a stage and a circus ring, the amphitheater had seats for 1,200 spectators and presented an overall impressive appearance.[2]

As his circus met with more and more success, Ricketts added more and more to the program, which, writes C. H. Amidon, became "a curious blend of theater and circus."[3] The format generally used was a conventional circus program—equestrians, acrobats, clowns—followed by one or more stage presentations, including numerous pantomimes. "It is," says Amidon, "the number and variety of these afterpieces which is most astonishing. During Ricketts' Philadelphia engagement from 10 October 1796 to 23 February 1797, a total of 48 performances were given. During the run, twenty new afterpieces and thirteen recurring numbers appeared."[4] Thus, with a more-or-less fixed circus program for general appeal and a changing stage program for variety, Ricketts could count on repeat business.

In 1797, when Ricketts's circus was at its height in terms of popularity, three significant events occurred. On 24 January Ricketts again hosted President Washington at a performance, and on 4 March he presented a testimonial program for the president. At about the same time, Lailson and Jaymond, French circus men, erected a large circus building near Ricketts's amphitheater and, presenting basically the same type of program as Ricketts's, began offering competition—even using some of the latter's former performers. Lailson also set up a circus in New York, again near where Ricketts staged his New York performances and again offering competition. Financial problems, however, spelled the demise of Lailson's venture into circus business.

In 1799, Ricketts's amphitheater in Philadelphia was burned to the ground. Although the horses were saved from the flames, Ricketts suffered a considerable monetary loss and, in despair, sailed for England. The gods of misfortune, however, were not finished with John Bill Ricketts. Caught in a violent storm, his ship sank—and with it went America's first circus man.

In commenting on the significance of the Ricketts period of the 1790s, Amidon sees the flirtation between circus and theater as one of its more interesting aspects. He also sees the circus part of that combination as a forerunner to later circus programs:

> Furthermore, the circus performance had not yet developed its full spectrum of variety. Ricketts and his peers did anticipate the mud show treks of the next generation, and for that matter, the present-day existence of auditoriums in major cities. Some of their stage productions anticipated the lavish circus specs of a later time. In England and France the pantomimes developed into elaborate spectacles, during the subsequent century. In this country the birth of the "mud show" necessarily limited the circus program to more basic ingredients. However, the circus constantly searched for new features, and the variety of Ricketts' day eventu-

Courtesy of the San Antonio Public Library.

ally became the "aftershow," with minstrels, variety acts, wrestling, boxing, and the wild west show.[5]

Certainly a far cry from the circus as most people now think of it, Ricketts's circus nevertheless represented a beginning for that institution in America and as such was indeed a "message from Mercury" for those showmen who were to follow in his footsteps.

The Shakespeare of Advertising

John Bill Ricketts was, of course, limited to presenting his circus in the major cities of the Atlantic coast. Even travel between them was painstakingly slow and precarious enough. As the country grew westward in the early decades of the nineteenth century, however, roads become more numerous, making it possible for various kinds of circus troupes to venture further into the hinterlands. The hunger for entertainment on the frontier was strong, and there were many showmen who were daring enough to try to assuage that hunger, some with circuses and some with menageries. The names are legion—including such as Aaron Turner, Hackaliah Bailey, Rufus Welch, John Robinson, Richard Sands, Gilbert Spalding, Dan Rice, and Seth B. Howes.[6] No name, however, looms larger than Phineas T. Barnum; for, along with the Ringling brothers, he is synonymous with the development of the American circus.

Born in Bethel, Connecticut, on 5 July 1810 to Philo and Irena Barnum, Barnum spent his childhood as a farm boy, driving cows, shucking corn, raking hay, and plowing fields. Gifted in arithmetic, he was at the age of twelve "called out of bed one night by my teacher who had wagered with a neighbor that I could calculate the correct number of feet in a load of wood in five minutes."[7] He did it in less than two. Coupled with his arithmetical skills, Barnum had an early penchant for accumulating money. Before he was five, he had saved enough pennies to change them for a silver dollar, "the possession of which made me feel far richer and more independent than I have ever since felt in the world."[8] His acumen for earning money increased as he grew older and was put to work in his father's cash, credit, and barter store, where he drove sharp bargains with those who wanted to trade farm produce for dry goods, nails, or rum.

Barnum learned early that all is not what it might appear to be on the surface, that sharp trades, tricks, dishonesty, and deception are by no means confined to the cities. "More than once," he said, "in cutting open bundles of rags, brought to be exchanged for goods, and warranted to be all linen and cotton, I have discovered in the interior worthless woolen trash and sometimes stones, gravel, or ashes."[9] But Barnum was a shrewd and practical person who did not often get hoodwinked. In 1828, he opened his own small store in Bethel, and when a man asked him to purchase a purse on credit, Barnum responded that he did not mind giving credit but that he did not think it wise to do so for a purse when the man had nothing to put in it. "Later in life," he said, referring to this incident, "I have been credited with the utterance of some sagacious remarks, but this with regard to the pocketbook, trivial as the matter is in itself, seems to me quite as deserving of note as any of my ideas which have created more sensation."[10]

Although Barnum devoted most of his time to his business, which also included selling lottery tickets, he found time to court Charity Hallett, a tailoress, and on 8 November 1829 they were married. Commenting years later on his disapproval of early marriages (his coming when he was just past nineteen), he felt that had "he waited twenty years longer I could not have found another woman so well suited to my disposition and so admirable in every character as a wife, a mother, and a friend."[11]

Shortly after his marriage, Barnum's business career took another direction. Purchasing a printing press and type, he set up his own newspaper, issuing the first number on 19 October 1831. The vigor and vehemence of youth overpowered caution, and Barnum found himself in jail for libel. He continued editing his paper from jail, and upon his release sixty days later, many of his supporters arranged a celebration—a celebration that in one sense can be seen as one of the earliest circus parades in America:

> P. T. Barnum and the band of music took their seats for the coach drawn by six horses, which had been prepared for the occasion. The coach was preceded by forty horsemen, and a marshal, bearing the national standard. Immediately in the rear of the coach was the carriage of the Orator and the President of the day, fol-

lowed by the Committee of Arrangements and sixty carriages of citizens, which joined in escorting the editor to his home in Bethel.

When the procession commenced its march amidst the roar of cannon, three cheers were given by several hundred citizens who did not join in the procession. The band of music continued to play a variety of national airs until their arrival in Bethel, (a distance of three miles,) when they struck up the beautiful and appropriate tune of "Home, Sweet Home!" After giving three hearty cheers, the procession returned to Danbury. The utmost harmony and unanimity of feeling prevailed throughout the day, and we are happy to add that no accident occurred to mar the festivities of the occasion.[12]

In 1834, Barnum sold his newspaper, the *Herald of Freedom,* and his general store. With his wife and new baby daughter, he went to New York to seek his fortune. His first endeavor was a grocery store, but he had outgrown the grocery business, or at least his imagination had. Hearing about an elderly black woman, proclaimed to have been George Washington's nurse, who was on exhibition in Philadelphia, Barnum hurried to see for himself if Joice Heth was real or fake. Purported to be 161 years old, Joice Heth did look to be extraordinarily ancient to Barnum:

> She was apparently in good health and spirits, but from age or disease, or both, was unable to change her position; she could move one arm at will, but her lower limbs could not be straightened; her left arm lay across her breast and she could not remove it; the fingers of her left hand were drawn down so as nearly to close it, and were fixed; the nails on that hand were almost four inches long and extended above her wrist; the nails on her large toes had grown to the thickness of a quarter of an inch; her head was covered with a thick bush of grey hair; but she was toothless and totally blind and her eyes had sunk so deeply in the sockets as to have disappeared altogether.[13]

Barnum was convinced that he had, if not the real thing, at least something that could pass for such, and he purchased Joice Heth. Renting space next to an open-air saloon in New York, Barnum, along with Joice Heth, went into show business. He was truly in his element. Because he knew that success de-

pended upon publicity, he filled the newspapers with advertisements and placed posters in prominent spots. The reception in
New York was such that he took his exhibition to Boston, Philadelphia, and Albany. Joice Heth died less than a year later and
was buried in Bethel. Although an autopsy showed her to be
much less than her advertised age, Barnum maintained that because doctors disagreed on her exact age, the whole question
"will probably always be shrouded in mystery."[14]

Barnum's first contact with the circus came when he joined
Aaron Turner's traveling show in 1836 as a ticket seller. Turner,
too, was a self-made man, having acquired a small fortune
through common sense and industry, a good example of which
occurred on Barnum's first trip with the circus from Danbury,
Connecticut, to West Springfield, Massachusetts. Instead of halting to dine on the first day, Turner merely "regaled the whole
company with three loaves of rye bread and a pound of butter,
bought at a farm house at a cost of fifty cents."[15]

Before long, Barnum decided to break with Turner and start
his own traveling show. With his troupe, he moved through the
South, but soon found that having his own show was not much
better than working for someone else: "The itinerant amusement business is at the bottom of the ladder. I had begun there,
but I had no wish to stay there."[16] Barnum really regarded the
trade of a traveling showman as a means to a better end. Thus,
in 1841, he purchased Scudder's Museum at the corner of
Broadway and Ann Street in New York and christened it Barnum's American Museum, opening it on New Year's Day, 1842.

Barnum took great pride in his museum, and even in his later
and more successful years he always had fond memories of it:
"Whenever I cross Broadway at the head of Vesey Street, and see
the *Herald* building and that gorgeous pile, the Park Bank, my
mind's eye recalls that less solid, more showy edifice which
once occupied the site and was covered with pictures of all manner of beasts, birds and creeping things, and in which were
treasures that brought treasures and notoriety and pleasant
hours to me."[17]

One of the treasures that the museum brought—and that
Barnum greatly appreciated—was money. He soon realized that
to make the million dollars he desired, he merely had to present
wholesome and abundant attractions for a small sum of

money—twenty-five cents, children half price. People thronged to the museum, and Barnum never doubted that he gave them their money's worth:

> Nor do I believe that any man or manager ever labored more industriously to please his patrons. I furnished the most attractive exhibitions which money could procure; I abolished all vulgarity and profanity from the stage, and I prided myself upon the fact that parents and children could attend the dramatic performances in the so-called Lecture Room, and not be shocked or offended by anything they might see or hear; I introduced the "Moral Drama," producing such plays as "The Drunkard," "Uncle Tom's Cabin," "Moses in Egypt," "Joseph and His Brethren," and occasional spectacular melodramas produced with great care and at considerable outlay.[18]

Advertising, of course, was the key, and Barnum knew it. His original plan had been to use all of the first year's profits in publicizing the museum, intending to sow first and reap afterward. But the money came in so rapidly that he was hard pressed to carry out his intention. Still, New York had never seen, and perhaps has never seen again, such ingenious talent for gaining publicity as Barnum displayed. From the paintings of exotic animals that decorated the outside of the museum to pages upon pages of newspaper advertisements to baby contests, flower shows, dog shows, and bird shows, Barnum was ever ready to give "another blast on the trumpet."

From time to time, Barnum exhibited giants in the museum, and he, as well as his patrons, was intrigued by them. But it was a bright-eyed child of five years named Charles Stratton who gave Barnum one of his best opportunities to sound the trumpet. For Charles Stratton stood a mere twenty-five inches high! Securing Stratton's services from his parents, Barnum exhibited him as General Tom Thumb, a dwarf of eleven years of age from England.[19] His explanation for such a billing to Stratton's mother, according to Irving Wallace, was that, in searching for something striking, he "had reached back into history and found the legend of the original Sir Tom Thumb, one of King Arthur's knights, who dwelt in a tiny golden palace with a door one inch wide and rode in a coach drawn by six white mice and was killed in a duel with a spider. Barnum decided that Tom Thumb was infinitely more provocative than Charles Stratton, and so "Tom Thumb" the midget was and would forever remain. As to the pompous military rank of General, the absurdity of it was irresistible."[20]

Barnum spent long hours preparing Tom Thumb for his part in the museum. The youngster was an apt student, and soon his fame had spread throughout the country. It was time, Barnum thought, to sow and reap in other fields. Arranging his business affairs for a long absence, he took Tom Thumb to England, where the little fellow sang "Yankee Doodle" for Queen Victoria and impersonated Napoleon for the Duke of Wellington. Thousands flocked to the Egyptian Hall to see Tom Thumb and his antics, and the money poured in. Leaving London for Paris, Barnum and Tom Thumb had even greater success across the Channel, where again performances were given before royalty.

Barnum's association with Tom Thumb lasted for more than three decades, but as the latter grew older and a bit taller, Barnum began looking for another midget. He found not one but two: George Washington Morrison McNutt and Lavinia Warren Bump. With three midgets, Barnum, in a sense, had a giant of a problem—a love triangle. Both Tom Thumb and McNutt vied for Lavinia's love. Lavinia's mother decided in favor of the General; and so, before two thousand people, Tom Thumb and Lavinia were married, remaining so for twenty years.

Tom Thumb died on 15 July 1883, and ten thousand people attended the funeral in Bridgeport, Connecticut. "These were the people," says Wallace, "who helped to make Barnum big. The showman would never forget that of the eighty-two million tickets sold by his variety attractions, twenty million had been sold by General Tom Thumb alone."[21]

Following Barnum's return to America, his museum became even more renowned, boasting novel curiosities and numerous and valuable specimens in every area of art and natural history. He searched for any new exotic attraction that he could add to his repertoire, such as a bearded lady and Chang and Eng, the Siamese twins (actually Chinese). His next really big attraction, however, did not come from the world of freaks, but rather from that of music—the Swedish soprano Jenny Lind.

Tom Thumb and Lavinia Bump, Barnum's matchless midgets. *Courtesy of the Peabody Museum.*

In October 1849 Barnum conceived the idea of bringing her to America. Despite warnings that he could never make a success of such a venture, Barnum, with his usual flair for the spectacular, laid the publicity groundwork so well that thousands awaited her arrival at the dock in New York. Billing her as the "Swedish Nightingale," Barnum conducted an auction for tickets to her first concert. The first ticket went for $225! Jenny Lind was an instant sensation, and Barnum, not one to permit enthusiasm to wane, took her on a tour of sixty concerts.

Barnum and Jenny Lind got along well enough professionally, but the former must have suspected early on that their relationship was to be shortlived. Noted for giving much to charity, Jenny Lind was, nevertheless, not the easiest person to work with. Barnum's closest comment to criticism was that "she had been petted, almost worshipped, so long, that it would have been strange indeed if her unbounded popularity had not in some degree affected her to her hurt, and it must not be thought extraordinary if she now and then exhibited some phase of human weakness."[22] Their successful relationship was terminated in 1851, having grossed some $712,161. Upon hearing of the singer's death in 1887, Barnum said, "So dies away the last echo of the most glorious voice the world had ever known."[23]

Up to this point, Barnum's life had been one of the greatest success stories of the world, but now he ran into some difficulties. At Iranistan, his estate in Bridgeport, he wrote his first autobiography, *The Life of P. T. Barnum, Written by Himself.* Whether Barnum actually wrote it or had it ghostwritten is a matter of debate, but no matter; the book was ill-received as a kind of confessional of all the ways that Barnum duped the public to amass his fortune. Reviewers characterized him as a swindler and a villain who preyed on the gullibility of innocent people. Some fifteen years later, Barnum published another autobiography, *Struggles and Triumphs; or, Forty Years' Recollections of P. T. Barnum, Written by Himself,* which attempted to present a less crass picture of the showman.

The second misfortune to befall Barnum at this time stemmed from his connection with the Jerome Clock Company. Vouching for loans that the company needed, he ended up owing more than $500,000. "What a dupe had I been!"[24] he said. Everything he had was in the hands of his creditors, and the world-wide publicity he was receiving was at his own expense. "I had notice enough," he said, "to satisfy the most inordinate craving for notoriety."[25]

Finally gaining some financial solvency, Barnum devoted himself to Connecticut politics, winning a Republican seat in the legislature in 1865. Yet another misfortune occurred at this time: the American Museum in New York burned to the ground. Taking his setbacks as he did his successes, Barnum remained in politics for several more years, before his showman side lured him once more to entertaining the public—this time through the vehicle of the circus.

At the urging of William Cameron Coup and Dan Castello, Barnum, at sixty years of age, came out of his retirement from show business to join them in what was to become the largest circus America had yet seen—indeed, the Greatest Show on Earth. Coup was a veteran circus man and just as enterprising as Barnum. Though Barnum said that it was he who overcame Coup's cautious ways to make the circus larger and larger, historians seem agreed that things were really the other way around. It was Coup, for example, who had the idea of transporting the circus on railroad cars during its second season, a season in which it grossed almost $1 million in six months.

The death of his wife, Charity, in 1873 and his subsequent marriage to Nancy Fish, an English girl of twenty-four, a year later did not dim Barnum's interest in his circus. Having bought out Coup and Castello, he now had the circus all to himself, but the competitive International Allied Shows, owned by James E. Cooper, James A. Bailey, and James L. Hutchinson, threatened to overshadow the Barnum circus. With his usual audacity, Barnum proposed a merger, and the two circuses became one. Within six years, Cooper and Hutchinson were bought out, leaving Barnum and the short, thin, nervous Bailey as partners and the circus as Barnum and Bailey's Greatest Show on Earth. And it was that.

The partnership worked well, and the circus prospered. New attractions were added, not the least of which was Jumbo the elephant. A huge African bull elephant, Jumbo stood twelve feet tall at the shoulders and weighed over six tons. Property of the London Zoological Gardens, Jumbo was a favorite of English children. When Barnum purchased the elephant, a huge outcry ensued throughout England. No elephant ever caused so much furor. Thousands were eagerly waiting to greet him in America, and other thousands were tearfully saying goodbye to him in England. Barnum was, of course, in his element. Here was advertising at its highest pitch—and free. Nor was Jumbo to let Barnum down. In return for the $30,000 it cost the showman to buy and bring Jumbo to America, the elephant "drew receipts totaling one million seven hundred and fifty dollars. For three and a half years, ridden by an estimated million children, gulping down endless quantities of peanuts and candy, he enriched the lives of America's young and the pocketbooks of the circus."[26]

Jumbo, however, was no match for a train locomotive. While being led along the tracks back to his rail car on September 15, 1885, he was struck and killed by a speeding freight train unable to stop in time. Even in death, Jumbo was part of the circus.

Barnum had his hide placed over a wood frame and exhibited it in the menagerie. After all, as Barnum himself said, "Long ago I learned that to those who mean right and try to do right, there are no such things as real misfortunes. On the other hand, to such persons, all apparent evils are blessings in disguise."[27]

Six years later, in Bridgeport, on 7 April 1891, a giant in his own right, Barnum followed Jumbo in death. Whether the thousands who attended the funeral matched the number at Tom Thumb's funeral in the same city some eight years earlier can never be known. But all who were there knew that they were mourning the passing of one of the world's great showmen.

Whether P. T. Barnum was really as great as tradition has it is not really so important. Certainly, as far as the circus itself is concerned, there have been other showmen who have made as great, or greater, contributions to that institution as did Barnum. But he had the charisma, the nerve, the sense of the dramatic, and the clear understanding of what people desired for their entertainment that enabled him to live out a legitimate "rags-to-riches" story—and, in the process, to help give to the American circus a character that has made it markedly different from its ancestor, the European circus. Even if Barnum cannot accurately be called the father of the American circus, he surely can be credited with giving it a dimension of brilliance that, combined with James Bailey's managerial skills and daring, brought it to a dazzling level of popular success.

The Boys from Baraboo

Today, when the name Barnum is mentioned, can that of Ringling be far behind? Because of the Ringling Brothers and Barnum and Bailey Circus, which for well over half a century has symbolized the circus in America, the names may seem a bit unnatural if thought of separately. Yet, ironically enough, Barnum and the Ringlings never met. When Barnum died, the Ringling brothers were just beginning to think of venturing out of the small Middle West towns that had been providing their small circus a decent enough sustenance. Still, if they never met literally, they surely did figuratively, in the circus that to this day bears their names.

More than any other world, the circus world is populated by brothers, some real, but many more-or-less fictitious. The Ringlings, however, were indeed real—all seven of them: Al, Gus, Otto, Alf T., Charles, John, and Henry. And for good measure, one sister—Ida.

Descended from August and Marie Salome Rüngeling,[28] the Ringlings grew up in the small upper–Middle West towns of Baraboo, Wisconsin; McGregor, Iowa; Stillwater, Minnesota; and once again Baraboo. Although only Ida completed high school, the boys were all bright and talented musically—the latter characteristic pleasing Marie Salome but not August, who believed only in hard physical labor.

Of the seven sons, only five played any significant part in building the great Ringling circus empire—Al, Alf T., Otto, Charles, and John. Gene Plowden describes these five brothers in *Those Amazing Ringlings and Their Circus:*

> Five of August Ringling's robust sons were like fingers on a hand, each separate but pertinent to the whole; each supporting the other in a remarkable display of coalescence.
>
> Each was strong and versatile but all were apposable and endowed with more connatural capabilities than any other five brothers in America. Stubborn as jackasses, they often argued vociferously and at great length, but once they reached agreement, differences were forgotten and they carried on in complete accord and with enthusiasm.
>
> They could blow horns, stroke strings, or press keys to make music which, likely as not, one of them had composed. They could be clowns or lay out the circus lot, do a Risley act or man the ticket booth, walk a tight-rope or route the show. They could write advertising, put up posters, or talk contracts with merchants and politicians.
>
> Together they formed a powerful fist that could drive their opposition to the wall and smash it, or, with fingers extended, grasp it like an octopus and strangle the life out of it.[29]

A dramatic description to be sure, but an accurate one.

It has been said many times about many people that show business was in their blood, but such a comment has probably never been more applicable than to the Ringlings. Of the various combinations of brothers in the circus, they were to become by far the most successful and the most prominent. From the tiny variety show that they put on in the area around Baraboo in 1882 and 1883, they were to reach heights in the world of the big top

that no one else then or since could challenge. If a P. T. Barnum came along at the right time in American circus history, so too did the Ringlings. But it was not always an easy road, particularly in the beginning.

The first season of their variety show might have been enough to discourage all but the most dedicated showmen. With little money and even less experience, they had to rely on ingenuity, pluck, and an impelling sense of the direction they wanted to go in show business. As Earl Chapin May in *The Circus from Rome to Ringling* points out, they "had their eyeteeth cut on many tough obstacles. Blown out of a night's receipts by the snowstorm which nearly defeated them; gulping hot coffee made by a kindly station agent; riding a slow train behind a snowplow that finally stuck; driving ten miles through heavy drifts in a bobsled not equipped with a heating plant; making the next town just before show time; garnering a few dollars by a hasty performance, the classic and comic concertists who wanted to be circus men learned something about real trouping that season."[30]

The aspiring Ringlings billed their show unabashedly as the funniest and most refined show party on the road—a show for the rich; a show for the poor; a show for the old; a show for the young; a show for everybody. Indeed it was. Organ and cornet solos, dudish delineations, juggling, comedy routines, Irish dances and songs, and dramatic sketches made up the show; and Al, Alf T., Otto, Charles, and John did them all. Still, a circus is what the Ringlings had as a goal—and no doubt had had since the day in 1868 in McGregor, Iowa, when as children they saw Dan Rice's Great Paris Pavillon, a circus that traveled up and down the Mississippi River by steamboat.

Dreaming of a circus and having one, however, were two different things. A circus required animals, equipment, means of transportation, and more than five amateur performers. Undaunted, the Ringlings took the thousand or so dollars they had saved from the proceeds of their little variety show and, using their good name for credit, leaped into the circus business—not auspiciously, but certainly eagerly.

Even though their name might be good for credit, it was not at all known in the circus world, where names were of utmost importance. Fortunately, Al had met the well-known circus im-

presario Yankee Robinson in 1883, and he convinced the then
elderly showman to lend his name and his presence in return
for a share of the receipts. The show was to be called Yankee
Robinson and Ringling Brothers Great Double Shows, Circus
and Caravan. What more impressive sounding name could be
desired?

This early circus was hauled in its entirety on fewer than a
dozen farm wagons, and those hired from various local farmers
around the villages in which the circus showed. Still, it was a
circus, and when it opened in Baraboo on 19 May 1884 it marked
the first step of an entertainment institution that would grow to
become the largest circus that America would ever see. Old Yankee Robinson was not wrong when at the beginning of the performance he would step into the single ring and address the
audience:

> Ladies and gentlemen: I am an old, old man. For forty years I have
> rested my head on a stranger's pillow. I have traveled in every
> state in the Union, and have been associated with every showman
> of prominence in America. I will soon pass to the arena of life that
> knows no ending; and when I do, I want to die in harness and con-
> nected with these boys. If I could have a dying wish granted, it
> would be that my name should remain associated with that of the
> Ringling Brothers; for I tell you [here he raised his hand and his
> voice became solemn and prophetic] the Ringling Brothers are the
> future showmen of America; they are the coming men.[31]

The circus showed a small profit the first year, and the Ringlings increased its size for the 1885 season. By 1887 the show
had grown to considerable size, with sixty horses, other as-
sorted menagerie animals, and many new wagons and chariots
built specially by their wagon-maker cousins, the Moeller
brothers. The name was now Ringling Brothers United Monster
Shows, Great Double Circus, Royal European Menagerie, Museum, Caravan and Congress of Trained Animals. If the earlier
title was impressive, this one almost bordered on the ridiculous
in its ostentation. But then where would any circus be without
ostentation? Circus lights are never hidden under bushels.

In 1888 an elephant was added, and a new big top, but the season was a sore trial to the Ringlings, in terms of both weather
and finances. In a letter to the Bank of Baraboo, asking for a loan
of $1,000, Otto Ringling told of the hardships:

You cannot form any idea of the strain on us with everything at stake in the rain and mud all day and night for over a week. After Reedsburg it was almost unbearable, those clay hills were almost impassable. The wagons would sink down to the hubs and the poor horses could not budge them. We had to hire farmers at their own figure to help us with their horses and we had to put all our men to work with shovels to get the clay away from the wheels. Our repair bills besides were enormous. Wagons continually pulled to pieces, springs broken, etc.[32]

After a better season in 1889, the Ringlings not only went on the road, but on the railroad—with eighteen cars, fifty-four performers, and a greatly expanded menagerie. For the next three years they went out against formidable opposition: Barnum and Bailey's Greatest Show on Earth, Sells Brothers Circus, the Great Wallace Railroad Shows, John Robinson's Big Ten Shows, and others. Nevertheless, they survived and prospered. In 1892, however, disaster struck in the form of three train wrecks, bad weather, and head-on competition from other circuses. Still, they showed on the East Coast that year. Their name was spreading—so much so that in 1893 they opened not in Baraboo, but in Chicago with a three-week stand, turning Tattersall's horse arena into a wonderland of color and rigging. The Ringlings were now real competition, and the circus world knew it.

After several years of rugged competition between the Barnum and Bailey show (then under the control of James Bailey) and the upstart Ringlings, an unwritten agreement was made between the two shows to avoid each other on the road. In 1898, Bailey took his circus to Europe for a five-year tour, a period during which the Ringlings gained supremacy in circusdom. When he returned, another agreement was reached in which the Ringlings bought half interest in Bailey's Forepaugh-Sells Circus—all three shows to steer clear of each other.

When James Bailey died in April 1906, John Ringling, who was the driving force of the Ringlings, began negotiations to purchase the Barnum and Bailey show, the consummation coming in October of the following year. The price was $410,000, a figure that could be more than recouped in a single successful season. The Ringlings were now beyond question the circus kings of America, with their two eighty-four-car circuses towering over the other thirty-odd railroad shows that were touring the country.

Moreover, of all the circuses operating at the time, Ringling Brothers was undisputedly the cleanest-run show, not only in external relationships with the public but also in relationships with its own personnel, as well as with other circuses. Indeed, it was Charles Ringling who espoused an organization of circus owners "to curb unfair competition and eliminate unsavory dealings with the public."[33] In December 1910 agreements were drawn and bonds were posted to insure compliance, but within a year the organization disintegrated, as the competitive realities of the circus world brought about the breaking of virtually every agreement made. Nevertheless, the Ringling show has ever maintained an honest and forthright image in a branch of show business that over the years has had more than its share of chicanery. From the beginning, Al Ringling insisted that they always put on the show advertised, with abbreviations only if necessary to get off the lot on time. And disdaining the general practice of keeping the change from ticket sales, the Ringlings stationed a man at the ticket window admonishing patrons to pick up their change. The Ringlings found the circus business "in the hands of vagabonds and put it into the hands of gentlemen," said George Ade, the humorist. "They started with nothing in a little town up in Wisconsin, and became the circus kings of the world by adopting and observing the simple rule that it is better to be straight than to be crooked."[34]

The year 1918 marked a significant point in Ringling history: two more of the brothers, Henry and Alf T., died (Al having died in 1916), and the decision was made to combine the two circuses into Ringling Brothers and Barnum and Bailey. The war and influenza had cut sharply into business that year, and it was obvious that two operations, including two winter quarters, were economically unsound. So, shipping everything to the Barnum and Bailey quarters in Bridgeport, Connecticut, the remaining brothers bid goodbye to Baraboo—thus closing a colorful chapter in American circus history.[35]

The Big One, as the Ringling show came to be called, was indeed big, made up of the largest aggregation of performers and animals ever brought together in a single unit—a fitting tribute to the efforts of the Ringlings over the years to bring to American circus audiences an entertainment spectacle unmatched in the history of show business. But all was not well between the two remaining brothers, John and Charles. A freewheeler and a self-confident believer in luck, John invested heavily in oil wells, railroads, and Florida land; and his interest in the circus waned. Charles, on the other hand, was envious of his "big brother," yet critical of what he considered John's reckless ways. While Charles's life was centered in the circus, John was present on the lot only occasionally, and then usually to pick up some money from the red wagon (the ticket wagon). By 1925, John was worth $100 million and considered one of the twenty richest men in the world. And that year he built his spectacular Ca'd'Zan (House of John) in Sarasota, Florida—not, according to Henry Ringling North, "to wipe Uncle Charlie's eye, or even to gratify Uncle John's and Aunt Mabel's luxurious tastes. It was part of a long-range plan ... to give the state of Florida a memorial to Mabel and himself that would be at once as magnificent and much more useful than the Pyramids."[36] Included was a museum to house the impressive art collection that he was rapidly increasing.

With Charles Ringling's death in 1926, John saw himself in control of the circus. He also saw Florida languishing in a deep depression caused by the "bust" that resulted from overspeculation in land there. In his own flamboyant fashion, John did his best to revitalize the area around Sarasota. In 1927, he announced that the circus would move its winter quarters from Bridgeport to Sarasota.

While the Ringling circus was riding the crest of continued success, however, there arose increased competition from the American Circus Corporation, headed by Jerry Mugivan, Bert Bowers, and Ed Ballard. Organized in 1921, this corporation owned and operated a number of circuses, including Sells-Floto, Al G. Barnes, Hagenbeck-Wallace, John Robinson, and Sparks. Because of a disagreement with the directors of Madison Square Garden in New York over giving up Friday performances to prize fights, John Ringling lost his lease to open his circus there to the corporation's Hagenbeck-Wallace and Sells-Floto circuses. Refusing to swallow such a bitter pill, he confounded many in the circus world by buying out the American Circus Corporation for $2 million. The purchase gave him a circus empire of 240 railroad cars, herds of horses and elephants, a gigantic menagerie of many species of wild animals, and over four thousand performers and workers. If Barnum's rise to power and fame was impressive, so, too, was John Ringling's—aptly described by the *New York Herald Tribune:*

> How many country boys, admitting the first shy ambition some day to ride the flying trapeze or tame lions, would not rejoice to dream of so glittering a culmination to a splendid career! The circus world is the place, if anywhere, where such things ought happen. Baseball czars or toothpaste dictators have rather a flat, a commercial suggestion; but a circus king, King of Barnum and Bailey's, and Emperor of the Greatest Shows on Earth, risen direct from ring-mastering in the back yard and hard work on the trapeze after school—that is something.
>
> Countless urchins will be more pleased to learn that this brilliant fulfillment is a possibility than to be told that any boy may become President. And the ambitions which Mr. Ringling's career will stir are likely to be less harmful than those aroused by Mr. Hoover's—for the rising generation is far more certain to recover from the former than the latter. But if Mr. Ringling's achievement arouses those who still regard the circus as a splendid wonder, it will have another and an almost equally strong appeal for older people who like to look back to a now-distant past. What does it matter that the circuses are being consolidated like chain grocery stores? Circuses were made to be consolidated, to be the biggest, the best, the most stupendous, the only spectacle in the world. The picture of Mr. Ringling and his brothers, starting out with their "variety performance" from Baraboo through the snows of rural Wisconsin, and growing slowly through the years to the final triumphant, if queerly incongruous, appearance in Madison Square Garden itself, is a picture of so much in American life, of so many memories for so many people.[37]

John Ringling now owned every circus of any note in America, but he was greatly overextended. In 1932, he defaulted on the notes that he had signed in order to purchase the American Circus Corporation, and the circus fell into the hands of Allied Owners, Inc. John remained nominally president but had to relinquish all power to Sam W. Gumpertz, the general manager. So, in one sense, the Ringling show was no longer the Ringling show. The ultimate humiliation came in 1936, when Gumpertz bluntly ordered John from Madison Square Garden, where the circus was opening, telling him that he no longer had anything

to do with the circus. It was over. The last of the original Ringling brothers retreated to his memories, dying of pneumonia on
2 December 1936.

The circus, though, did not die with John Ringling, but went
on as The Greatest Show on Earth. To be sure, change was in
the offing, and the question was to arise as to how the circus
would accommodate to that change. Before examining that
rather sad aspect of circus history, however, we should look in
more detail at the logistics of the circus and the performers
themselves, who, after all, were and are its life blood.

2

Here Today; Gone Tomorrow

T HE TENTED CIRCUS IN ITS HEYDAY WAS, TO EVEN THE most casual of observers, a glamorous and romantic institution. Heralded for several weeks by gaudy posters that stimulated the imagination and aroused the curiosity, it would finally arrive, miraculously transforming a once-familiar vacant lot into a strange world of white canvas and colorful wagons and chariots—a world populated by painted clowns, nimble acrobats, graceful equestrians, daring aerialists, courageous lion trainers, and exotic animals from the far corners of the world. For one entire day, the magic spell lasted; and then, just as miraculously as it had appeared, the circus would disappear, moving on to transform another vacant lot in another town. All of the activities of a circus's coming and going happened so rapidly and apparently so easily that it may almost have seemed as if nothing had really happened at all. In reality, however, a great deal had happened, both before and during the circus's appearance.

Home for the Winter

The circus business is a summer business, at least as far as the spectator is concerned, and at the height of the mighty railroad circuses, each fall would see these shows wending their way home to winter quarters—to Bridgeport, Connecticut; to Baraboo, Wisconsin; to Peru, Indiana; to Rochester, Indiana; to Sarasota, Florida. The last trip of the season was both a happy and a sad occasion. For the owners, if the "nut"[1] had been met and there was some profit, it was happy enough. For the per-

25

formers, it meant an end to the hardships of the road; but it also meant an end, at least for awhile, to the very essence of their existence—the show itself. For the workers, it meant unemployment, unless they were lucky enough to be kept on as part of the winter-quarters crew. But at the moment, it was payday for all, including for the workers a bonus made up of money withheld throughout the season to encourage them to remain to the end. Charles Fox describes such a payday at Baraboo, Wisconsin, the winter quarters for the Ringling show for many years: "The men made three stops—the first was at the barbershop for a shower, shave, and haircut; the second at a clothing store where they bought a new outfit from skin out; and third, the taverns."[2]

For many years, major circuses had their winter quarters in the North, primarily because it put them in proximity to the population centers of the nation, thus affording them ready access to the more lucrative markets when spring came. The small Indiana towns of Peru and Rochester, for example, were winter quarters for a number of circuses—the American Circus Corporation's shows in the former and Cole Brothers Circus in the latter. John Ringling's move to Florida for his show's winter quarters began a trend that saw more and more circuses establish their quarters in the South. The reasons are obvious: not only was the South becoming more densely populated and more industrialized and thus a more fertile field for circuses, but also the climate was more suitable for the work that needed to be done during the winter. But wherever the winter quarters, the work that went on there was essentially the same.

For a month or so, there was little activity in winter quarters, but following Christmas, the pace would pick up. In the three and a half months before time to take to the road again, much needed to be done: tents mended, wagons and railroad cars repaired and painted, wardrobes refurbished, other equipment repaired or replaced, and animals trained. Artists and craftsmen in their own right, the winter-quarters crews, who, in a sense, put the circus back together again, played an unsung but vital role in not only its success, but its very survival. Paid only a few dollars a week, plus board, for a ten-hour day, six days a week, these men worked hard and drank hard. Longtime showman Joe McKennon describes them:

In prohibition days, anything alcoholic from rubbing alcohol to varnish remover and canned heat went down their gullets with relish and sometimes disastrous results. If they had been paid more, these men would not have been able to work more than half time. They drank up their two bucks (the show gave them two packs of Bull Durham or two cans of Snooze Copenhagen snuff along with their pay each week). But they were ready for work at seven AM Monday morning. Given them five, they wouldn't have been able to work before Wednesday, if at all. These men did most of the dirty work of getting the shows rebuilt and back on the road.[5]

Such men as McKennon speaks of were, in short, "with it and for it."

Nor were management and performers idle during the winter months. For management it was the matter of purchasing new equipment and animals, contracting both new and old acts, and deciding upon next season's route. "Any boob can *run* a circus," quipped an old circus man, "but it's a wise showman who knows where to *put* it." For the performers it was practicing old routines and perfecting new ones and, on occasion, breaking in new people for their acts.

Although one might think that winter quarters represented a respite from the dangers of the road, such was not always the case. On the evening of 20 February 1940, for example, disaster in the form of fire struck the quarters of Cole Brothers Circus in Rochester, Indiana. Virtually destroying the main buildings, the fire claimed the lives of two elephants, two zebras, two llamas, a number of monkeys, two tigers, two lions, two lionesses and their cubs, two leopards, a sacred Indian cow, two audads, and a pygmy hippo. The total loss of $150,000 put the future of the show in jeopardy, but Cole Brothers went back on the road in 1940 even larger than it had been the previous year.[4]

Everyone connected with the circus avidly read during the winter—and the summer for that matter—the *Billboard*, for many years the Bible for anyone involved in the amusement business. It was through this weekly publication that they found out what was going on in the circus world and when their respective shows wanted them to report for the new season. The March issues of the *Billboard* would be filled with calls from various circuses. Below is an example of such a call from the 24 March 1928 issue:

CALL   CALL   CALL
All People Engaged for the
HAGENBECK-WALLACE CIRCUS
for the Season of 1928
Report as Follows:

Performers, Clowns, Wild West People, report to Equestrian Director at Cleveland Auditorium Wednesday morning, April 11th. Big Show Band report to Eddie Woeckener at Cleveland Auditorium Wednesday morning, April 11th. Property Men report to H. K. Melhouse at Peru, Indiana, April 2nd. Ring Stock Grooms report to Joe Simmons at Peru, Indiana, April 2nd. Wardrobe People, report to Mrs. La Rue at Peru, Indiana, April 2nd. Trainmen report to Ben Sturgis at Peru, Indiana, April 2nd. Baggage Stock Drivers report to Chas. Rooney at Peru, Indiana, April 7th. Pole Riggers and Canvas Men report to Chas. Brady at Peru, Indiana, April 16th. Light Men report to Thomas Poplin at Peru, Indiana, April 10th. Tractor and Truck Drivers report to Chas. Rooney at Peru, Indiana, April 7th. Candy Butchers report to T. F. Everett at Peru, Indiana, April 7th. Porters report to Henry Robertson at Peru, Indiana, March 26th. Side-Show Workingmen report to Jos. Ross at Peru, Indiana, April 16th. Side-Show Performers report to Pete Staunton at Cincinnati, Ohio, April 22nd. Side-Show Band report to D. C. Officer at Cincinnati, Ohio, April 22nd. Ticket Sellers and Ushers report to Eddie Dowling at Cincinnati, Ohio, April 22nd. Front-Door Men report to Eddie Delevan at Cincinnati, Ohio, April 22nd. Circus Train leaves Peru, Indiana, for Cleveland, Ohio, April 10th. Can use Prima Donnas, also Ballet Girls for entire summer season. Can use for Cleveland engagement four Perch Acts, Feature Wire Acts, Aerial Bar Acts.

Ballyhooing the Show

Work at winter quarters was, of course, vital to the success of the circus. No less vital, however, was the work of the billing crew. Preceding the circuses by two to three weeks, these billers traveled in one or more advance railroad cars, depending upon the size of the show. Up until the 1930s, the Ringling circus used three cars; after that, two. Most other railroad circuses (between fifteen and forty cars) used only one advance car, replacing a second car with trucks.

Carried by regular passenger trains, these brightly painted billing cars were home and shop on wheels for the billers. On each side were long tables with storage lockers for posters below, and sleeping berths above. At one end was a paste-mixing room, complete with water tanks and a boiler, and in the middle or at the other end was a stateroom office for the car manager.[5] Twenty-five or so men lived and worked in such cars, spending one day posting bills in each town where the circus was scheduled to show. The second car (or trucks) would cover whatever the first car missed. If there happened to be a competing circus scheduled to show the same town, an opposition brigade (sometimes a car) was called upon to replace torn posters or to slap up their own over the opposition's.[6]

The mobility of these advance cars was clearly illustrated in 1891, when the Adam Forepaugh Circus found opposition from other shows in thirty-nine towns in the West. Its opposition car, called the Cyclone, left Omaha on 26 May, according to Tom Parkinson and Charles Fox in *The Circus Moves by Rail*, "to combat the rivals on those thirty-nine fronts. Forty-seven days later, on July 2, the car was at Portland, Oregon. It had traveled 5,000 miles and posted 300,000 sheets of lithographs. That evening it headed east out of Portland to resume its usual routing routine. Three days and 2,200 miles later the car was spotted at Marysville, Missouri, and the crew was ready to post the town for the show's appearance three weeks hence."[7]

The billers, too, were mobile and dexterous, often working from high ladders, swinging scaffolds, or bosun's chairs. McKennon aptly describes their skill:

These banner men filled their mouths with big headed billposter tacks and spit them one at a time head first to be caught on their magnet headed hammers. In one smooth movement the hammer swung to the mouth, caught the tack, and drove it into the banner at the desired place. The swing of the hammer was continuous, and was interrupted only by the necessary changing of position on the scaffolds or ladders, or by the tacker swallowing a tack. This was no uncommon occurrence, and the boys usually had a loaf of freshbaked light bread in their aprons. They would spit out the rest of their mouthful, and stuff in a handful of the soft bread to swallow—just like a Russian does his caviar after a big glass of vodka has been bottomed up.[8]

903712

Following the billers was the contracting press agent, who contracted for newspaper space and handed out press releases. He in turn was followed by the advance press agent, who spent a couple of days in the town to be played and then doubled back on show day.

Although billing practices changed little between the latter nineteenth century and the 1930s, circus advertising did evolve during that period. As radio became more widespread as a medium of communication (and thus a way of advertising the circus), less space in newspapers was utilized. And in 1929, the radio advance agent came into being. One aspect of circus advertising that did not change, however, was the penchant for extravagant exaggeration, as evidenced by the following from a 1934 issue of the *Billboard:*

It has often been said that modern circus advertising material lacks the vivid superlative and stirring adjectives of the "golden age of circuses," but is it really true?

Two generations ago the heralds of the Ringling Bros.' Circus described the opening spectacle as "a mighty moving panoramic display of opulence, grandeur, magnificence and splendor, presented by the new invincible monarch of the circus world—Ringling Bros.' Stupendous New Consolidation."

Quite forceful and lavish, 'tis true. But it must be remembered that Roland Butler, general press representative of the Ringling-Barnum combine, is no slouch when it comes to putting together circus publicity copy. Compare the elaborate claims of the 1894 edition of the Big Show with Butler's modest description of the past season's spectacle in those attractive heralds scattered over the length and breadth of the land.

"Ringling Bros. and Barnum & Bailey Combined Circus, this year reaching the zenith of its glorious reign over all amusements, introducing 1,000 amazing new international features and innovations, including the most sublime spectacle of all ages. *The Durbar of Delhi,* by far the most stupendous and dazzlingly beautiful production ever conceived for the delectation of circus audiences."[9]

But why not exaggerate? After all, as William B. Reynolds pointed out in 1928, the circus press agent had a great advantage over his colleagues in other areas:

The material with which the circus press agent has to work is enormously abundant and varied. His performers alone present him endless possibilities for exploitation. Lillian Leitzel is a brilliant instance. Con Colleano and "Poodles" Hanneford are others. There are "aristocrats" of the circus as there are of the films and the stage. The circus, however, has not one "royal family" but a dozen. Among them are men and women, boys and girls, whose fathers, grandfathers and great-grandfathers have been notables of the ring and whose craft has been handed down to them from generation to generation. Among them are the Hannefords, Wirths, Nelsons, Bradnas, Davenports, Lowandes, Hodginis, Ernestos, Costellos, Rieffenachs, Rooneys, Portunas, McCrees and innumerable others.

All with distinguished pedigrees any of us might envy.[10]

Loading Out

Although some circus historians point to earlier experimentation with travel by rail,[11] the consensus is that W. C. Coup inaugurated the railroad circus when he put the Barnum show on rails in 1872. Some showmen, such as Adam Forepaugh, looked askance at the railroad as a mode of circus transportation, but the railroads themselves had made great strides and now dominated the imagination of the country. The advantages of rail travel to circuses, as Parkinson and Fox point out, were readily apparent:

> Circuses took a lead in the rush to rails and in the parallel fad for railroading. The differences were phenomenal. Nearly overnight, showmen could look differently upon the question of territory. Much wider areas became available, and individual jumps from town to town could be a great deal longer than before. Circus horizons were far expanded. The Mississippi Valley was no longer "the West," and railroading circus men were among the first to take advantage of the new transportation to California, Washington, Oregon, and Arizona. The railroad circus was thriving, and it would continue to do so as long as railroads dominated American life.[12]

The railroad also engendered growth among circuses. To be a railroad circus meant status, and the more cars, the more status. The greatest year for the railroad circus came in 1911, when thirty-two shows were on the rails, ranging from the five-car

Bulgar and Cheney Circus to the two giants, Barnum and Bailey and Ringling Brothers, each with eighty-four cars.[13] Never again would there be so many railroad circuses crisscrossing the country. With the improvement in highways and trucks, many circuses in subsequent years disdained railroad transportation for what provided, at least to the smaller circus, more efficient means of movement.[14] By the 1950s, the end for the tented railroad circus had come. Ringling Brothers and Barnum and Bailey closed in the middle of the season of 1956, and the Clyde Beatty show did the same at the end of the season. The Ringling show, of course, still uses a train to get from one indoor-arena date to another, but the circus train of the past is just that.

The trains that those answering the calls of the 1928 Hagenbeck-Wallace Circus and the various other railroad shows of the period were to load out on, however, not only looked like magical carriages of romance and glamour, but also functioned as real vehicles of practicality and efficiency. The flat cars that carried the wagons and the stock cars that carried elephants, horses, and other lead stock were double-lengthed—seventy-two feet—specially built cars (because the railroads charged by the car and not by weight). Animals were loaded in the stock cars sideways and were packed tightly together, not only to save space but to keep them from falling down. A stock car could hold thirteen or fourteen elephants or upwards of thirty horses. Generally, flat cars carried four wagons each. The big-top pole wagon, because of its extra length, took up over half a car itself. The coaches for the personnel were regular railroad coaches that had been stripped inside and refitted with two-high (sometimes three-high) wooden berths. Management and some of the star performers merited comfortable staterooms, but for most the coaches were not a place where one wished to spend any more time than necessary. Particularly unpleasant were the workingmen's cars, called "crum" cars because of the vermin that infested them. On hot nights, it was not unusual for the men to sleep on the flats under the wagons.

Every circus train did have what was called the pie car, a kind of privilege car that served snacks and provided gambling tables and slot machines for those with the show. A popular place for relaxation and companionship late at night, it was also a place where many a showman "gave" back his pay to the circus.

In addition to the ever-present dangers of fires and blow-downs, the railroad circus had to face the possibility of train wrecks. And often the possibilities became realities[15]—but never more tragically than on the early morning of 22 June 1918, when an empty troop train struck the rear of the Hagen-beck-Wallace Circus train near Hammond, Indiana, killing at least eighty-six people and injuring over 175. The circus train had stopped because of a hot box on one of the cars. Although flares were placed at the rear of the train, the engineer of the approaching troop train was apparently asleep. With a shatter-ing roar the locomotive smashed through the caboose of the halted circus train as if it had been made of matchsticks. Unfor-tunately, the sleeping coaches were immediately in front of the caboose, and the locomotive tore through several of these be-fore it came to a halt. Henry Miller, a member of the circus light-ing department, was in the sleeper just ahead of the caboose. He described the experience to the *Chicago Tribune:*

> I was in the last coach, next to the caboose. I woke up to the sound of splintering wood, and then, suddenly, I was sitting up. I thought it was a broken air line. Then there was another crash, and an-other, and another. I was pounded into the corner of my berth. My scalp was split open. The whole car buckled. It parted down the center as clean as though it had been sliced with a giant knife. I felt my section rising as the engine of the troop train ploughed into it.
>
> Then I was away up in the air on top of the wreckage in my shirt and drawers. I put down my head and lay still. A coat came sailing over and landed on top of me. Then everything was quiet. I started to climb down.
>
> I saw a hand waving, just a hand. It was turning in the air, grab-bing for something. I got hold of it and started to pull. Then I saw there was a lot of paint cans on top of the man. I pulled and hauled and got them away. Then I saw that it was "Hickory," a wagonman. I kept jerking, and he kept hollering at me to let him alone. Right then, I saw the fire. It was creeping from the engine. Then the fire started to leap toward us. How I did work on that guy! I pulled him clear. Then we both rolled into the ravine. I got up when I got my breath. The fire was all over the wreck. It seemed that the cars were piled on top of each other. There were blood-chilling screams of men and women. I hung around and did what I could. One woman screamed, "God! O, God! Kill me! Kill me!"

Getting the wagons ready at winter quarters.
Courtesy of the Pfening Collection.

Al G. Barnes Circus train wreck.
Courtesy of the Pfening Collection.

My boss was killed. I guess we will never find him. I've been in three wrecks, but this one is the worst. I don't want anymore.[16]

In a spirit of true showmanship, the Ringling show offered their resources (equipment and performers) to help Hagenbeck-Wallace meet its commitments. As a result, only two stands were lost.

Fifty-six of the total dead were buried in a mass grave at the Showmen's League Rest Plot in Woodlawn Cemetery at Forest Park, Illinois. Of these, reports Warren Reeder in *No Performances Today,* the identity of only thirteen was known.[17] He also describes the grim stoicism of those who made the show go on:

> Those who were still able in body went about their respective duties with grim determination. The foremen rarely spoke to crewmen. Work of erection of facilities for the afternoon and evening performances progressed rapidly and smoothly. The big tents, as well as the smaller ones, from the cook tent to the big top rose rapidly into position following the machine-gun-like staccato of sledges landing on anchoring pegs sunken deeply into the turf. The teamsters maneuvered their heavy draft horses quietly and efficiently to raise main poles and the various canvases.
>
> The entire atmosphere of the circus grounds before and after performances seemed to reflect the sombre feeling of those who survived but "must carry on." Disaster, quietly, had made brothers of all.[18]

Putting It Up

Even without disasters, keeping the show going certainly took stamina and dedication from performers and workingmen alike. It also took a significant amount of planning and ingenuity. Circus day to the townsman was a one-and-only kind of day; to the showman it was every day. Each town was the same yet different, and each lot posed its own peculiar problems to those whose job it was to "put it up."

While most of the town was still asleep, perhaps even before the gray of dawn, the first section of the circus train would be spotted, and unloading would begin. A day prior to the show's arrival, the twenty-four-hour man had marked off the route from where the train would unload to the circus lot with white arrows chalked on telephone poles and had got word to the boss canvas man as to the condition of the lot. If it was muddy or un- even, he would have arranged for dirt or ashes to be spread. He also would have checked previously and made arrangements for any necessary permits and for hay and straw for the animals, as well as bread for the cookhouse. His was indeed a most im- portant job.

The typical railroad circus would have among its tents a big top, a menagerie, a side show, a cookhouse (dining tent), a bag- gage-stock tent (for working horses), a ring-stock tent (for performing horses) called the pad room, and a dressing tent. Sometimes the pad room was under the same roof as the dress- ing tent. There were, of course, many smaller tents—blacksmith shop, physician, private dressing tents, and so forth. The largest of the tents was the mammoth big top, which might be as long as 510 feet and as wide as 210. In circus terms such a tent would be a 210 round with five sixty-foot middles. The menagerie would be the next largest, with the sideshow or cookhouse next.

From the moment that the boss canvas man set foot on the lot in the morning, activity was at a feverish pace, but it was a pre- cisely organized activity. While work proceeded on laying out the big top and the other tents, the cookhouse was already up, and the cooks were preparing breakfast for the small army of hungry workingmen that would soon descend upon it. This tent was divided in the middle by a curtain into the long side (for workingmen and their bosses) and the short side (for manage- ment, ticket sellers, candy butchers, front-door men, ushers, performers, band, and sideshow freaks). These two sides were the same size; long and short simply meant the length of tables used. No better picture of circus hierarchy could be had than in the cookhouse. Ticket sellers, candy butchers, and front-door men were high in the caste system because they often were pro- moted to management positions. The performers, too, had their positions of status—equestrians, aerialists, animal trainers, ac- robats, clowns, and sideshow freaks—in that order. The band was more or less an entity in itself. Democracy ruled only in the food served; all got the same and as much of it as they wanted.[19] Perhaps the most romantic description of a circus cookhouse occurs in Thomas Wolfe's "Circus at Dawn":

> We could see the circus performers eating tremendous breakfasts, with all the savage relish of their power and strength: they ate big

fried steaks, pork chops, rashers of bacon, a half dozen eggs, great slabs of fried ham and great stacks of wheat cakes which a cook kept flipping in the air with the skill of a juggler, and which a husky-looking waitress kept rushing to their tables on loaded trays held high and balanced marvellously on the fingers of a brawny hand. And above all the maddening odors of the wholesome and succulent food, there brooded forever the sultry and delicious fragrance—that somehow seemed to add a zest and sharpness to the all powerful and thrilling life of morning—of strong boiling coffee, which we could see sending off clouds of steam from an enormous polished urn, and which the circus performers gulped down, cup after cup.[20]

One of the more interesting activities to have witnessed in the setting up of the circus was the raising of the big top itself. This huge canvas structure was supported by six—or four, as the case might have been—sixty-two-foot center poles, each weighing approximately one ton and costing almost $1,900 apiece. Raising them was no easy feat and took the combined efforts of men and elephants.[21] Once these poles were raised and the great rolls of canvas spread and laced together, elephants began hoisting the tremendous weight up to the top. At the same time, men slid the two rows of quarter poles that circled the center poles into place. Now the seat wagons entered, and the deafening racket of putting up some eight to ten thousand seats could be heard all over the lot.[22] At the same time, riggers were putting up the intricate array of ropes and steel bars that would be used in the various aerial and trapeze acts. By the time the big-top work was completed, the miracle was performed: a city of canvas had been constructed in a matter of a few hours.

Hold Your Horses

"Hold your horses, the elephants are coming!" is a cry not heard since early in the century. But for anyone interested in the circus, it conjures up the color and pageantry of the great street parades that were one of the highlights of a circus's visit to a town. In the early days of the American circus, when shows traveled by horse and wagon, the very arrival of a circus was in itself a parade. Later, however, circuses developed the parade into an integral part of their programs. After getting set up on the lot, virtually the entire company would regale themselves in costume and uniform and, with the roar of animals and the blare of bands, would parade through the streets of the town and back to the lot.

As the publicity value of the parades became more and more apparent, circuses began using wagons, floats, and chariots designed specially for the parade, with the result that the "circus parade was brought to a pitch of magnificence in America that eclipsed anything achieved elsewhere, providing perhaps the finest free spectacle since the triumphal processions of imperial Rome."[23] Just as circuses were judged by the number of railroad cars it took to transport them, so too were they judged on the elaborateness of their street parades.

"The golden era of the free street parade started in 1872," according to Charles Fox and Beverly Kelley, "when the big circuses started to move about the country on railroad cars. This immediately gave showmen an opportunity to develop even bigger and longer parades and bigger and more magnificent wagons, some reaching a length of 28 feet. Bigger teams were used. Eight and 10-horse hitches were commonplace, with many using 12- to 24-horse teams just for the effect it had on the townspeople. A dozen circuses used 40-horse teams on the No. 1 bandwagons."[24]

The most elaborate of the bandwagons was the Two Hemispheres bandwagon, a twenty-eight-foot affair with the Eastern hemisphere on one side and the Western on the other. It was built by the Sebastian Wagon Works in New York in 1903 for the Barnum and Bailey Circus. Circus wagons are an entire subject in themselves—from the plain baggage wagons to the elaborately designed cage and band wagons.

No circus parade was complete without the shrieking tunes of the steam calliope (pronounced calli-ope, as in *hope*, by circus people). It usually came at the end of the parade and was often followed by children and adults alike to the circus lot. One of the few working calliopes left today is at the Circus World Museum in Baraboo, Wisconsin, where on summer days one can hear its nostalgic whistle floating over the town.

While words cannot adequately depict a circus parade, the following parade order of the 1928 Sparks Circus will give some idea as to what was included in a typical parade:

The interior of the big top of a large railroad circus
presented a maze of poles and rigging.
Courtesy of the Pfening Collection.

The 1934 Ringling Brothers and Barnum and Bailey
family. *Courtesy of the Pfening Collection.*

1 — Mounted parade marshall and two flag bearers.

2 — Dancing-Girls tableau wagon with eight musicians from the big show band pulled by eight dapple gray horses.

3 — Cage of monkeys pulled by four black horses.

4 — Cage with carved corner statues holding five polar bears pulled by six dapple gray horses.

5 — One man and twelve ladies mounted wearing English riding costumes.

6 — Cage with carved corner statues holding five lions pulled by six dapple gray horses.

7 — Cage of spotted deer pulled by dapple gray horses.

8 — Air calliope pulled by eight black ponies.

9 — Cage of lions pulled by four dapple gray horses.

10 — Cage of tigers pulled by four dapple gray horses.

11 — Dolphin tableau wagon with eight musicians from the big show band pulled by eight dapple gray horses.

12 — Cage of four leopards pulled by four dapple gray horses.

13 — Cage of kangaroos and two ostriches pulled by four dapple gray horses.

14 — Horses Head tableau wagon with clown band pulled by six dapple gray horses.

15 — Cage of four leopards pulled by four dapple gray horses.

16 — Cage with carved corner statues holding three tigers pulled by six dapple gray horses.

17 — Dolphin tableau wagon with the side show band pulled by six dapple gray horses.

18 — Cage of hyenas and two black leopards pulled by four dapple gray horses.

19 — Cage of three sea lions pulled by four dapple gray horses.

20 — Wild West contingent of twelve mounted people.

21 — Five camels in single file with grooms dressed in Turkish costumes.

22 — Three zebras with one groom dressed in Turkish costume.

23 — Three llamas led by three grooms.

24 — Nine elephants in single file, a mahout on the head of each, the lead bull carrying a girl in a howdah.

25 — Steam calliope pulled by six dapple gray horses.[25]

The increase of automotive traffic and the congested streets that resulted signaled the demise of the street parade. Some smaller circuses paraded as late as the 1940s, but by then the parade was essentially a thing of the past. For the performers and the others who had to "do" the parade, its passing was a blessing; but to the circus lover, it was just one more nail in the coffin being fashioned for the tented railroad circus itself.

This Way to the Big Show

The midway (in circus jargon the front yard) of the circus consisted of the sideshow (often called kid show) and its intriguing, sometimes grotesque, banner line on one side and a number of concession stands on the other, with the ticket wagon and entrance marquee (front door) to the menagerie at one end. The circusgoer, after a visit to the sideshow, should he have chosen to view "the world's largest collection of freaks and oddities," bought his ticket and entered the menagerie, which was connected to the big top by a side-wall passageway.

The ticket sellers themselves, as mentioned previously, were well up in the caste system of the circus. In addition to those at the front door, there were a couple of reserved-seat ticket sellers in the connection between the menagerie and the big top, as well as about half a dozen around the hippodrome track of the big top. Because of the possibilities of promotion to top management that were open to ticket sellers, many sought jobs in that department. More than that, however, at least to one ticket seller, there was "a certain fascination connected with this job. To witness the mighty rush for tickets of admission and to help gather in a goodly harvest of the shiny shekels of the realm is quite irresistible."[26]

The performances of the major railroad circuses were fairly standard, usually opening with a spec (spectacular), an elaborate procession around the hippodrome track of floats and chariots, elephants, horses, and virtually all of the performers and many of the workingmen—the latter wearing Arabic or some other exotic costumes over their working clothes. In some cases, the spec was a dramatic or musical spectacle, presented on stages, in the rings, and on the track. One of the high points of the spec came in 1889, when James Bailey employed Imre

Kiralfy, the famous ballet master, to produce "Nero, or the Destruction of Rome." A. Morton Smith describes this spec: "The stage on which the pantomimic drama, with accompanying musical score, was presented ran nearly half the length of the big top. In addition to the regular members of the circus personnel, who were principals and supernumeraries, 200 persons were carried to participate only in the spec as singing and dancing artists. These included six principal singers, a mixed chorus of 45, a ballet of 96 dancing girls and 48 male dancers."[27]

This extravagant production had considerable influence on the specs of other circuses of the time. Ringling Brothers countered with "Caesar's Triumphal Entry into Rome," and the Great Wallace Show presented "Triumphal Entry of Augustus into Rome." Many roads, it seems, converged on Rome. Other specs with themes drawn from history were used by such shows as Hagenbeck-Wallace, John Robinson, and Sparks. After World War I, the processional spec gained ascendancy over those presented on stages or in rings, and the sources for themes were expanded to include nursery rhymes, fairy tales, and myths.

The program of the Ringling Brothers and Barnum and Bailey Circus of 1938 is a typical example of that offered by the major railroad shows of the period:

DISPLAY 1
NEPAL, a spectacular processional.

DISPLAY 2
The Pallenberg Wonder Bears in rings 1 and 3 performing feats of skating, tight-rope walking, and bicycle and motorcycle riding. Dollie Jacobs and performing black leopards in the center ring.

DISPLAY 3
The Walter Guice Troupe performing on aerial bars.

DISPLAY 4
Terrell Jacobs and his performing African lions.

DISPLAY 5
Parade of the freaks.

DISPLAY 6
Scores of girls on swinging ladders.

DISPLAY 7
Performing elephants in three rings.

DISPLAY 8
Clowns.
Harry Ritteley and his toppling tables; Nelson and Nelson on high stilts; The Mirador Troupe in acrobatic feats; The Budanos and the DuBells in tumbling acts.

DISPLAY 9
The Cristiani Troupe in a bareback riding act.

DISPLAY 10
Bearto, the frog-legged contortionist and Frederico on the unsupported ladder in ring 1; The Maysy-Brach Troupe on the unicycle on stage 1; The Wen Troupe of Chinese Gymnasts in ring 2; The Spurgats in head and hand balancing feats on stage 2; The Mikados in equilibristic feats and the Keltans in a Risley act in ring 3.

DISPLAY 11
William Heyer presents in three rings and on the track a display of high-school horses and their riders—Tamara Heyer, Rudy and Erna Rudynoff, and Ella Bradna.

DISPLAY 12
The Naitto Troupe on the tight wire.

DISPLAY 13
Alf Loyal and his trained dogs in ring 1; Captain John Tiebor and his educated sea lions in ring 3.

DISPLAY 14
Gargantua the Great.

DISPLAY 15
The Antaleks, The Walkmir Trio, and The Davisos in high perch acts on stages 1 and 2 and in the center ring; The Torrence-Victoria Duo, Edward and Jennie Rooney, and The Great Dearo give aerial performances.

DISPLAY 16
Liberty Horses presented in rings 1, 2, and 3 by Adolph Delbosq, Rudy Rudyoff and Gordon Orton.

DISPLAY 17
The Sandoval Troupes in living art creations on stages 1 and 2.

DISPLAY 18
The Paroof Trio on unsupported ladders atop a tiny platform on the top of a high perch.

DISPLAY 19
International congress of hippodrome sensations.

DISPLAY 20
Parade of clowns.

DISPLAY 21
The Flying Comets, The Flying Concellos, and The Flying Randolls in sensational flying feats.

DISPLAY 22
The Walters Troupe, the Loyal-Repenski Family, and the Angelo Troupe doing trick riding.

DISPLAY 23
Acrobatic feats by the Maschinos, the Yacopi Troupe, the Uyeno Troupe, the Magyars, and the Cannestrellis.

DISPLAY 24
The Grotefent Troupe and the Wallenda Troupe in feats on the high wire.

DISPLAY 25
High-spirited jumping horses on the hippodrome track.

DISPLAY 26
The Hippodrome Races.

While the Ringling show of 1938 did not have an after-show—or concert, as it was called—many shows did. This was often a miniature Wild West show, complete with cowboys and Indians. Often a cowboy movie star was featured—e.g., Ken Maynard, Hoot Gibson, Buck Jones.

The entire program was under the direction of the equestrian director (ringmaster) and ran like clockwork. It was his job to see that it did. But he had to be more than just a program director, as Fred Bradna, famous equestrian director of Ringling Brothers and Barnum and Bailey, points out:

> He must be at once a showman, a stage director, a martinet, a diplomat, a family counselor, a musician, a psychologist, an animal keeper and a weather prophet. Since horses are the keystone of circus entertainment, he should be an accomplished equestrian. He must know sufficient about all circus techniques: tumbling, leaping, flying, catching, casting, juggling, clowning, ballet, animal training (which varies greatly between seals, bears, tigers, dogs, horses, chimpanzees and elephants), slack and tight wire, and even being shot from a cannon, to discern at a glance whether specialists in these arts are shirking and, in the case of animal acts, whether the sin of commission or omission is the fault of the human or animal star.[28]

In the Back Yard

What the audience saw in the "big show" was really only one facet of the circus. In many ways more interesting than the show itself was what went on, as it were, behind the scenes—that is, in the back yard. For here was where those with the circus lived—at least during the day. Between shows the back yard was where performers relaxed and conversed among themselves; where they washed and mended costumes and clothing; where they cared for and educated their children; where they received and wrote letters; where they planned their futures; in short, where they carried on their private lives as best they could.

The circus world, cosmopolitan though it has always been, with many nations and languages represented, has also always been a world unto itself—and this was never more true than in the days of the tented circus. Loyal and understanding among themselves, the inhabitants of the back yard maintained an aloofness from anyone or anything not circus. Of course they recognized the importance of audiences, because without such there would be no need for a performance. But they also recognized that of even more significance was the integrity of the show and especially of the act itself. To the performer, his act was indeed his life. And because most of the great acts were family acts, more or less, the domestic family was held in the highest regard. One generation trained the next, so that as the show went on, so too did the act.

While to the casual observer the tented circus might have seemed a setting that would encourage loose morals and various kinds of vices, such was far from the case. Closely knit and moving much like a solitary ship on the sea, the circus had very definite rules—some written, but most unwritten. For one thing, circus performing required both a sound mind and body; lives depended upon such. For another, the success of the show depended upon everyone's doing his part promptly and efficiently. Personal problems and frictions had to be warded off, or at least kept in the background. The original Ringling brothers, always concerned that their show be above reproach, early laid down over fifty specific rules (in writing) to be followed by their personnel. Below is a random sampling of those rules:

> Be clean and neat in dress and avoid loud display.
> No smoking in cars at any time.

Do not bring liquors or intoxicants into the dressing rooms.

Do not take strangers or friends into dressing rooms without permission.

In going from dressing tents to dining tents do not pass through the menagerie or circus tents, and never pass through the main entrance.

Do not chew gum while taking part in spectacle.

Male performers are not to visit with ballet girls. The excuse of "accidental" meetings on Sunday, in parks, at picture shows, etc., will not be accepted.

Do not sit cross-legged on floats or tableaux wagons.

Absolutely do not chew (gum or tobacco) or smoke in parade.

Do not loiter about the front of the show grounds.

Do not nod to friends or acquaintances who may be in the audience.

Avoid arguments with other employees. Be agreeable and promote harmony.

Since you have chosen to travel with the circus, it is evident that your success depends upon the success of circuses in general, and the one by which you are employed in particular. Therefore, the greater the success of the circus and especially the part of that success to which you contribute, the better it is for you and the more valuable you will be in your profession.

For the ballet girls, there were some special rules:

Do not dress in a flashy, loud style; be neat and modest in appearance.

You are required to be in the sleeping car and register your name not later than 11 P.M. and not to leave car after registering.

Girls must not stop at hotels at any time.

You are not permitted to talk with male members of the Show Company, excepting the management, and under no circumstances with residents of the cities visited.

The excuse of "accidental" meetings will not be accepted.

You must be in the ballet dressing room at 1 o'clock for matinee and at 7 o'clock P.M. for night performance.

You must not go into the big dressing tent.[29]

Show business of any kind seems much more glamorous to the spectator than it is in reality. For six months or so of the year, constantly moving from town to town—yet really always the same town—those who trouped with the tented circus were indeed nomads. Their home, such as it was, consisted of a berth on the train and about twenty square feet of dirt under the dressing top. Their furniture—a square-edged circus trunk, a canvas chair, and two buckets of water. Their place of business—the big top itself. Is it any wonder, then, if a clown, who so quickly brought laughter to people in the big top, might have abruptly and curtly dismissed a youngster who approached him outside? Or if many of the other daring and graceful performers, if they could have been seen up close, might have appeared bored and tired? The spectator went home with his spirits lifted by the magic of the circus and with an admiration and envy of those who were with it, while the latter stumbled through the darkness back to the cars, which often were a long way off and not easy to find. The words of Courtney Ryley Cooper quickly strip away the magic of the circus and describe it with a brutal realism:

> Perhaps you still imagine a circus to be solely a place of spangles and tinsel and gold and lace; of blaring bands and funny clowns; of beautiful equestriennes and sleek, graceful "rosinbacks"; of swirling, fairylike aerialists, and shimmering beaty everywhere? That's only the veneer! A circus is a fighting machine of grueling work, of long, hard hours which begin in the gray of dawn and do not cease until the last torch has been extinguished down at the railroad yards late at night; a thing which fights constantly for its very life against the demons of adversity, of accident, of fire and flood and storm; a great, primitive, determined organization that meets defeat every day, yet will not recognize it; that faces disaster time and again during its season, and yet refuses to countenance it; a place where death stalks for those who paint the bright hues of that veneer which is shown the public,—a driving, dogged, almost desperate thing which forces its way forward, through the sheer grit and determination of the men and women who can laugh in the face of fatigue, bodily discomfort, and sometimes in the leering features of Death itself! That's a circus![30]

One story, whether apocryphal or not, tells of a bareback rider who fell from her horse during a performance and was fatally injured. Her husband, a clown, ran to her side, picked her up, and, flinging her over his shoulder, made a grimace to the audience as he ran off with her. He paused once and, with a comical gesture, seized her hand and waved it. The audience, thinking it all a part of the act, applauded loudly. He was bound, he later said, to see that she left the arena in an artistic fashion.[31]

Circus life required strong people to live it. But if the lot of the performer was hard, that of the workingman (sometimes called roustabout) was even harder. And railroad circuses required a large number of unskilled workingmen—as many as a thousand for the Ringling show. The permanent employees were "with it" and could be counted on at all times. The great mass of workingmen, however, was culled from the lowest levels of society— drifters, criminals of one kind or another, dropouts from life, drunks. "Rootless, reckless, and feckless," according to Henry Ringling North, "they were a tough anonymous lot—a sort of Foreign Legion of the Labor Army."[32] Such men would come to the circus from nowhere and just as quickly disappear. John Francis O'Connell, a veteran showman, had great praise for those who stuck with the circus in rain or shine, but he gave short shrift to those who deserted when the going got tough: "As far as these men were concerned it was all right for them to help as best they could to put it up in the morning, but they could not grasp the idea of tearing it down at night. And it is best illustrated by the story of one of the bosses who met an Englishman, a worker with the show, drinking in a saloon. He asked the Englishman what he was doing away from his work. 'Well, by golly, old captain, I'm working in the day gang [there was no such thing], y'know . . . . and, anyway, I have just helped to move the bloody world.'"[33]

The true showman might have pointed an accusing finger at the workers who deserted the show when circumstances became trying, but the fact remains that the circuses themselves did little to make the lot of the workers more than bearable. Indeed, not only did they hold back a portion of workers' wages in order to "encourage" them to remain to the end of the season, but in some instances they practiced "red lighting"—that is, throwing someone from a moving train. If he was lucky enough still to be alive, all he could see were the disappearing red lights of the caboose. The Robbins Brothers Circus was accused of red lighting in 1927 to avoid paying some workers the money owed them.[34]

Tearing Down

Movement was beyond question the essence of the tented circus, not only in its fast-paced, precise performance but also in its daily coming and going. Between the time the first tent went up in the morning until the last one went down at night, there was never a period of more than several hours when everything was in place on the lot—and during most of that time the afternoon performance was going on.

The first up in the morning, the cookhouse was the first down in the evening. Shortly after the matinee, everyone was fed supper (usually by 5:30), and the dining department was dismantled and sent off to the train. As soon as the evening performance was underway, the same was done with the sideshow and the menagerie. And so on. Indeed, by the end of the performance, there was very little left standing but the big top itself—and it did not remain so for long. Even before the last of the audience was out the front door, rings, rigging, and seats were being dismantled. To say that a sense of urgency permeated the whole scene would be an understatement, because, inevitably, the "bloody world" had to be moved again.

If, to the observer in the early morning hours, the putting up of the circus had been marked by excitement and anticipation, its tearing down at night in the weird shadows cast by flares and spotlights was marked by a kind of melancholia. Part of it perhaps was the result of envy of those strange nomads who would soon be traveling through the night to practice their magic in another place. And part perhaps was the somber reminder that all things of this earth are temporal. But by the time that one might have brought such thoughts to a clear focus, the circus lot was once again a vacant lot, stripped clean of the sights, sounds, and smells that, for a day, had made it a world of wonder and amusement. And the circus? It was moving.

3

Lions 'n Tigers 'n Everything

JUST WHEN THE FIRST PERSON TRAINED LIONS OR tigers as part of a circus performance in America is open to conjecture. The earliest practitioners simply did nothing more than enter a cage of one or more beasts, and to call them trainers (or tamers, their early title) would be something of an exaggeration. Joanne Joys points to William Sherman, who in 1829 broke a lion and a lioness and presented them to President Andrew Jackson, as probably the first American actually to enter a cage with such animals as trainer.[1] Most circus historians, however, would agree that Isaac A. Van Amburgh was the first wild-animal trainer of note in America. Or at least he was the first to receive widespread publicity. In 1833, on the stage of New York's Richmond Hill Theater, Van Amburgh, then only twenty-two years old, dressed "to convey the impression that man, in accordance with the decree of God, should be the monarch of the Universe," entered a cage containing a lion, a tiger, a panther, and a leopard—with the following result: "The Lion halted and stood transfixed. The Tiger crouched. The Panther with a suppressed growl of rage sprang back, while the Leopard receded gradually from its master. The spectators were overwhelmed with wonder. . . . Then came the most effective tableaux of all. Van Amburgh with his strong will bade them come to him while he reclined in the back of the cage—the proud king of animal creation."[2]

While Van Amburgh's biographer was guilty of good old-fashioned circus hyperbole, and while halting, crouching, and springing back hardly constitute a performance, Van Amburgh's efforts were a signal step toward the more sophisticated wild-animal acts that by the 1890s were becoming part of many circus programs. Colonel Edgar Daniel Boone and Miss Carlotta of the Adam Forpaugh Show, for example, presented an act described by an Iowa newspaper in 1891:

> After the imposing entree came a startling novelty. In a steel bound ring forty feet in diameter and of sufficient height to prevent the escape of the animals that might be confined within it, appeared a gentleman and a lady, Col. Edgar Daniel Boone and Miss Carlotta, and two hounds. A moment later a big elephant came walking into the tent pushing a cage of three lions. The cage was backed up to the entrance to the steel ring. The door was opened and the three kings of the forest came bounding down into the enclosure. The people were startled; but apprehension soon gave way to the admiration and wonder at the exhibition of the lion trainers' supremacy over their monster pets. The lions formed pedestals, held ropes for the hounds to jump over, played seesaw, rode a tricycle, fired a pistol, romped with Col. Boone and seemed to enjoy the whole performance.[3]

Apparently the larger shows of the period had little interest in wild-animal acts. Barnum and Bailey, for instance, had only one such act between 1871 and 1918—that of Mlle Adgies and her ten lions in 1915; and Ringling Brothers had none at all.[4] For John Ringling, wild-animal acts were not only dangerous, they were also a nuisance to transport and set up.

Between the late 1880s and 1910, according to Fred Pfening, Jr., the wild-animal act was a rarity in circuses; but, by 1910, many of the smaller railroad shows were using them again. By the 1920s, such acts were featured attractions on virtually all the major shows. Even John Ringling gave in in 1921, presenting in the second display three arenas of wild animals—though, as Pfening suggests, it may have been brother Charles who "exerted the authority."[5] Whoever was responsible, these Ringling acts proved quite popular with circusgoers, just as they did on every show that had them.

Their sensational aspect, of course, was a strong reason for featuring wild-animal acts; but, according to two circus press agents, Gardner Wilson and Robert Hickey, the high costs of putting a circus on the road, especially those associated with circus acts themselves, caused shows to turn to animal acts as a way of "cutting down the nut."[6] Proof of this was the newly sprung-up Al G. Barnes Circus, which, despite performers' increased salary demands and rising railroad rates, was making profits as a wild-animal show. After all, anyone could see that wild animals, beyond their initial cost, were cheaper to maintain than a corresponding number of acrobats, aerialists, equestrians, or ballet girls. Moreover, they presented none of the personality conflicts that were so prevalent among primadonna performers.

To the circusgoer who sat on the edge of his seat as the fearless trainer entered the steel arena to put his charges through their paces, the wild-animal act may well have been one of the high points of the whole circus performance. But there were those who spoke strongly against such acts because of the inhumane methods that many trainers were suspected of using in breaking the animals. As early as the first decade of this century, magazine articles and newspaper editorials castigated the use of wild animals in circuses—specifically cats, bears, and elephants. An article in 1908 by Maurice B. Kirby, for example, graphically describes the methods used to train a tiger to sit on a pedestal. After having been jabbed by a steel fork and beaten on the nose with the butt end of a whip, the tiger was ready for the next step:

> Fifteen feet of slack rope were permitted the animal as the trainer directed him once more to the seat and once more he failed to understand. Then the order to hoist was given, and, as the men pulled, the tiger felt the collar tighten about his neck. His head gradually was lifted up, until his fore legs left the ground and he pranced on his hind paws. With the fear of strangulation and the instinct of self-preservation his brain became a mental mud-puddle. He beat the air with his forepaws, whirled, squirmed, and wriggled, in a vain effort to get out of the collar that clutched his throat. Every movement of his body brought him nearer to the seat over which hung the block and tackle. When he reached it an assistant grabbed his tail through the bars and pulled him toward the little stool, while the trainer punched him against it with the iron bar.[7]

Jack London, in his novel *Michael, Brother of Jerry* (1917), did much to arouse further the sympathies for animals subjected to training for circus acts. The protagonist, Harris Collins, though physically unimposing, is a vicious animal trainer who seems to get a devilish delight in the torture-training of his animals. Joys questions whether or not London ever witnessed such brutal training procedures and points to the similarity of London's descriptions and those of Kirby.[8] Either way, the book was influential enough to cause the formation of Jack London Clubs around the country—clubs whose purpose was to protest against animal acts.

In the 30 June 1923 issue of the *Billboard,* two articles appeared refuting the charges of cruelty leveled against animal acts and animal training. In one, Peter Taylor, an expert trainer in his own right, argues that the truly knowledgeable trainer need not rely on cruel means to achieve his ends, though occasional harsh methods might be necessary to establish and sustain the trainer's authority. He goes on to say that performing animals lead a better life than their counterparts in zoos or in the wild and that their performing provides them wholesome exercise unavailable to caged zoo animals.[9] In the other article, Courtney Ryley Cooper explains that training techniques had improved and that there was a new relationship between the man and the beast:

> There was a time when animals were only animals, to be taken from their cages, pushed thru their tricks, then shunted back into their cages and forgotten. Things are different now. The average menagerie has become more an animal hotel, with conveniences. The superintendent must be a person who has studied not only the beasts themselves, but their anatomy, in other words, a jungle veterinarian.
>
> The boss of the circus menagerie of today doesn't merely content himself with seeing that his charges are well fed. By the glance at the coat of a lion or tiger he can tell whether that beast has indigestion; ventilation is watched carefully to dispell the ammonia smell of the cat animals and thereby prevent headaches on the part of the animals; teeth are pulled, ingrown toenails doctored, operations performed, and every disease from rickets to pneumonia cured. And the fact that man at last has learned that beasts possess temperaments, individuality, emotions and a good many things that humans brag about, has seemed to place them on a different plane. Where there once was cruelty there now is often affection, both on the part of the trainer and also on that of the animal![10]

Cooper was realist enough to recognize that "the training of animals does not simply mean that they're given food in return for which, by some magical process, they realize they are to do certain work."[11] On the contrary, much time and patience were required to get the cats to do even the simplest tricks. Moreover, he goes on,

> there are times when the cats seem to realize that they are no longer protected by intervening bars, and the old instincts of fright and self-preservation overcome them. One by one they attempt to rush their trainer. The answer is a swift, accurately placed blow of the whip, usually on the nostrils. In force it corresponds to a sharp slap on the lips, such as happens to more than one child, stinging it for the moment and causing it to recoil. Unless the beast is intractable, an inbred or "bad actor," about two of these blows are sufficient to teach the animal its first combined lesson: that a whip hurts, that the man in the arena commands that whip, but, most important of all, he only uses it as a means of self-protection.[12]

Although the Ringling show dropped cat acts from its program in 1925 and gained plaudits from various corners for such an action, Al G. Barnes, Hagenbeck-Wallace, and others continued featuring performing cats. "The high point," writes Joys, "was reached during the 'Jazz Age' when over fifty animal trainers plied their trade. This fierce competition forced ... exceptionally reckless and daring performances with a new feeling of excitement and spontaneity. The popularity of these daredevils caused the domination of the wild-animal act over 'pure' circus turns. They became the mainstay and feature in all [major] American shows, including Ringling Bros.–Barnum & Bailey."[13]

Of all the trainers who entered the steel arena to face the big cats during the height of the tented circus, three stand out from the crowd: Alfred Court, Mabel Stark, and Clyde Beatty.

From Horizontal Bars to Arena Bars

Born on New Year's Day, 1883, in Marseilles, France, Alfred Court would have seemed a most unlikely candidate for the life of a circus trouper. His parents, both from the French aristocracy, certainly had no such intentions for him. Indeed, like many of his social class, he was sent to a very strict Jesuit school, where the future trainer was himself to be "trained" for his niche in French society.

While studies in such a school were demanding, young Court found time to pursue his interest in gymnastics, so much so that he became the best in Marseilles. This success nurtured his dream of being a circus performer, and at the age of fifteen he ran away with a traveling show to begin his career. This first attempt was cut short by the police, who, sent by his father, appeared on the scene to return him to Marseilles. The next year, however, Court once more ran away, and this time he made good on his promise to himself to become a circus acrobat. His success was notable, and in 1914 he appeared in America with the Ringling show. Returning to Europe the following year, he never dreamed that some twenty-five years later he would return to that show as a center-ring cat trainer—or, for that matter, that he would ever enter a cage of cats. As he says in his autobiography, "On the day that I first wielded a chair and whip within the cage I had already toured most of Europe and the United States as an acrobat and a performer on the horizontal bars. I had traveled with circuses from Marseilles, my birthplace, to Copenhagen, from Madrid to Cuba, and yet in all the rough and tumble of that life there had been no hint of the career which was to be thrust upon me so suddenly—that career that was to fill my days, and many of my nights, for the rest of my life."[14]

The day in question was in March 1917, when Court was directing a small circus that was touring Mexico. Because the lion trainer with the show was wont to ease his cares with whiskey, Court checked into the possibility of obtaining the services of another trainer. Meeting with no success, he decided that he would watch the act closely to learn what he could, in the event that he himself might have to substitute for the trainer. Watching not only performances but practice sessions as well, he caught the eye of the trainer, who "came over and asked if I would like to come in [the arena] for a moment. He had no idea how pleased I was. Amazingly enough, I found myself eager to accept his invitation."[15] And that entrance into the arena began a new career for Alfred Court, for he discovered that lion training was an occupation that he thought he would enjoy. Nor was it long before he was to find out for sure.

In a few days, Sam, the trainer, was again drunk, and Court had no choice but to fire him. Thus, he found himself "suprisingly and suddenly a lion trainer. I had the lions and their equipment; I had the costumes and the whips. At least I *looked* like a trainer!"[16] Dressed in Sam's extravagant cowboy outfit, with its black and silver spangles, Court began his journey back to the Greatest Show on Earth. He was thirty-five years old.

Because of the boiling political conditions in Mexico, Court returned to France after a year. His passion for animal training, however, did not slacken. Working as a press agent for his uncle's soap factory, he dreamed "nightly of the excitement of the big top" and filled his "working hours with thoughts of my lions."[17] And it was not long before he and his brother Jules put together a zoo-circus and went on tour.

Perhaps if there had been no Second World War, Court would have remained in Europe, where he had over the years built up a considerable fortune in wild-animal acts, owning five of the largest ones on the Continent. But there was a war; and, fortunately, there was also an invitation from John Ringling North to join Ringling Brothers and Barnum and Bailey Circus—an invitation that Court did not hesitate to accept. And so the diminutive, aristocratic, fifty-seven-year-old Frenchman made his second voyage to America.

Because his act had an air of sophistication—almost gentility—about it, it stood in marked contrast to the typical "fighting lion" acts of the American circuses. How was it to be advertised? "There was no difficulty," writes Joys, "in promoting a Clyde Beatty, whose fifteen-minute battles in the big cage gave youngsters summer long dreams of running away to join the circus and made every dog and cat in the neighborhood the subject of souvenir whip and cap pistol training sessions."[18] A new approach was needed for Court, and the Ringling ad men were up to the challenge:

First Time in America Dangerous Man-Killing Wild Animals That Are Really Educated! Direct from Europe—Three Great Mixed Groups of the Most Bloodthirsty Savage Beasts Ever Assembled— All Perfectly Schooled and Inculcated with Inconceivable Intelligence, Presented Under the Personal Direction of the Incomparable ALFRED COURT Master Trainer of the Ages. Polar Bears,

Alfred Court working a dangerous combination of two
leopards and a black panther. *Courtesy of the Pfening Collection.*

Tigers, Lions, Himalayan Bears, Siberian Snow Leopards and Great Dane Dogs—Natural Enemies Since the Dawn of Creation, Taught with Understanding, Kindness, and Patience, combined with Gray Matter—Performing Together in the Most Hazardous and Exciting Exhibitions in History—WITHOUT USE OF GUN-FIRE, CROWBARS, ELECTRIC PERSUADERS, PYROTECHNICS, OR DRAMATIC PRETENSE on the part of Court or his Retinue of Experts. A SIGHT THAT MAKES ALL OTHER WILD ANIMAL TRAINERS FEEL LIKE NINCOMPOOPS![19]

Court brought with him his Indian assistant Damoo Dohtre, Fritz Schultz, and Harry and May Kovar—along with three mixed acts of wild animals (sixty in all), including lions, tigers, black jaguars, snow leopards, black panthers, pumas, cougars, Great Dane dogs, polar bears, Himalayan bears, spotted leopards, mountain lions, spotted jaguars, ocelots, and black leopards. It was truly a Noah's ark of cats and was, says Pfening, "without question the greatest variety of trained wild animals ever presented in America."[20] Harry and May Kovar would alternate in ring one; Fritz Schultz would work ring three; and Court and Damoo would alternate in the center ring.

The image conveyed in the above ad of the humane, patient master-trainer, at all times in complete command of his charges in the arena, was not false. If one can believe Court himself and such people as Henry Ringling North and Fred Bradna, then he was indeed that kind of trainer. Rejecting the use of choking collars, blank-firing pistols, and iron forks, Court followed a strategy of gaining an animal's confidence before beginning training. "He did start off with animals collared and chained to their pedestals," writes Henry Ringling North, "but he began by making friends with them. He went into the training ring with a leather pouch full of beef on the end of a sharp stick and offered it to the animal, whatever it was. Then he would talk to it, coming closer until he was along side. The next thing you knew he was stroking it."[21]

Such a technique worked well for Court, even to the extent of getting Rajah, a tiger, to let the Frenchman plant a kiss on his salty muzzle as part of the act. This particular trick, though, was not without its dangers. On one occasion, Court ignored the fact that Rajah was sulking during the act, and when the moment for the kiss came (without the usual purring invitation from Rajah), the tiger responded with a slap to the "kisser," so to speak, drawing blood from Court, as well as applause from the audience. Undeterred, Court showed up for the next performance, his head swathed in bandages, and put his cats through their act. As for Rajah, he "felt it would be better for once to handle the fierce Rajah and his nerves as gently as possible. When the crucial moment came for our kiss I admit frankly that I hesitated. Facing Rajah, I seemed to hear the pounding of his heart more distinctly than his purring. Rajah had to increase and intensify his purr, and even put into it an undercurrent of insistence, before I was convinced that the invitation was in good faith. Then and only then, did I put my lips once more to the tiger's muzzle."[22]

"You can train 'em, but they never really are tamed," is an axiom that Court never forgot. He carefully scrutinized new animals he hoped to fit into one of his acts, fully aware that many cats are not intelligent enough to respond to training. Cats born in captivity, moreover, present a greater challenge to a trainer than do those born in the wild. Those that are jungle bred never lose their fear of man and are thus more receptive to training, whereas those cage bred, having observed man's fear and studied his habits, are quick to take advantage of his weaknesses whenever they can. "All cats," points out Fred Bradna, the famed Ringling equestrian director, "are moody. A bee sting, a sudden noise, an exploding flash bulb, a toothache, an attack of indigestion, may cause sudden violent rages with them. For such outbursts the trainer must be on the alert. A lion fiercely snarling on a pedestal is merely having fun. When he quietly lays back his ears and slinks or crouches, he has become deadly."[23] But Court, a master of animal psychology, made sure that he knew and understood his animals. It was, to him,

> absolutely essential to learn to understand each cat, not to be mistaken in the character of any of them, to observe their friendliness and animosities, and, finally, to know how to exploit this knowledge for the success of the act you plan. In addition one must be perceptive enough to discover as rapidly as possible what I call the "keys" to training. The discovery of these different "keys" constitutes the real problem, and I admit that this process is difficult to put into words. The clearest way that I can phrase it is to say that a polar bear, for example, does not behave like a bear from Tibet, which, in turn, is not at all like a Russian bear; and all three differ from the grizzly or giant Kodiak. Each type has, naturally, well-

defined characteristics, and therefore the natural disposition of each must be studied so that it may be used to advantage. This is true, of course, of the cats as well—lions, tigers, leopards, jaguars. One must find the special "key" to each and use it to make the animal understand what is required of him.[24]

Understanding, kindness, patience—all were salient characteristics of Court's training methods, but they did not preclude the necessity for instant punishment for disobedience. Early on an animal under his tutelage was made to realize that the trainer was the stronger of the two. And in any struggle to the death, there was no question in Court's mind as to how it should go: "Although I love animals as much as any man, and although I have several times in my life wept for grief at the death of one of my cats, I have never gone about my work in a suicidal frame of mind. On the rare occasions when I have had to fight for my life, I have always thought that if one of us had to be killed, it had better not be the trainer."[25]

By this last comment, Court certainly intended no bravado. His whole demeanor in the performing arena, as well as in the practice arena, was one antithetical to that of the daredevil trainer. Courage to him was necessary, but, ironically enough, a great deal of it was not of prime importance. Braggarts made him nervous, because often as not they ended up in the hospital. In short, caution to Alfred Court was a virtue, and scars were not badges of honor. On the contrary, they were to him clear evidence that somehow he, as the trainer, had committed an error.

While Court had his share of close encounters in the arena, some resulting in scars, he was never really seriously hurt. One particular incident, however, came close to unnerving him. When his zoo-circus was playing in Spain, Court on one occasion needed someone to handle one of the two animal acts, and he sent for a young man named Mollier, who was an understudy trainer with the French Zoo-Circus. On the morning of his debut, Mollier was holding a dress rehearsal, when Bengali, one of the tigers, seized one of his legs and began dragging him across the arena. Court dashed into the arena empty handed, shouting at the tiger, who dropped Mollier's leg and momentarily retreated. But Mollier, instead of trying to protect himself with his whip and his stick, began to hop toward Court. Bengali sprang again, this time fastening his jaws on the nape of Mollier's neck.

At this moment, another tiger attacked. Frantically, Court worked to force the tiger away from Mollier, receiving a gash on his shoulder in the melee. He finally succeeded in dragging Mollier from the arena, and quickly drove the mortally injured young trainer to the hospital. Mollier died on the operating table, and Court was overwhelmed at the tragedy:

> I spent the hours that followed wandering around the circus, staring unseeingly at animals and people, haunted by the black series of accidents that had been visited on the circus in the past month: Vargas in the hospital in Madrid, a child crushed to death the day before, and now Mollier's death. . . . Many times reporters have asked me, "Between ourselves, isn't your job really very dangerous?" I have always answered, "My job is no more dangerous than any other." That day I was less certain that my usual answer was correct; and an entirely different question pounded in my ear: "When will it be your turn?"[26]

Court's turn never came, however, and he completed a remarkable career in 1945, when he retired from the Ringling show and from his beloved animals. Though other trainers may have presented more sensational acts, none had any better rapport with animals than did Court or was more in control of himself and his cats during a performance. His master act of three polar bears, two black bears, eight lions, two leopards, two tigers, a jaguar, two wolves, and two dogs still stands as probably the greatest mixed act in circus history.

The Lady or the Tiger

Women were far from unknown in the steel arena, but few were featured stars, and those who were were mostly in the smaller shows. Mabel Stark was the most noted exception to the rule. Generally recognized as the greatest woman cat trainer of all time, she rose to stardom in the Al G. Barnes Circus and later on with Ringling Brothers and Barnum and Bailey.

Born in Toronto, Canada, in 1889, Stark was reared on a small tobacco farm in Kentucky. Seeking a career that would take her out of the back hills of that state, she entered nursing school. A nervous breakdown following graduation, however, sent her to California for recuperation. Visiting the Selig Zoo in Los Angeles one day in 1911, she saw a Hollywood stuntman wrestling a tiger. Her fascination for the striped beast was such that she immediately arranged to purchase a tiger for herself from the zoo for $350 and was soon busy attempting to train it. Within six months, through trial and error, she had, according to Bill Ballantine, "a passably trained tiger."[27] But more than that, she had a job with the Al G. Barnes Circus as an exerciser of horses. Thus, at twenty-two, she was embarked on a circus career that would bring her not only fame but also a very real sense of personal satisfaction in her relationship with her beloved tigers.

One half-trained tiger and a great deal of nerve, however, did not in themselves suffice to open the door of the steel arena to Stark. Most women trainers of the period had had some connection with the circus, often through marriage to a menagerie man or a trainer. Cooper describes such a situation: "She knows nothing of acrobatics, she is unable to accomplish the trapeze or riding feats which require bodily training from childhood, and yet she has the ambition to do something more than merely ride in parade or to form a part of the 'grand, glittering and magnificent introductory spectacle.' And so she naturally turns to the menagerie, where her husband works."[28] Stark had no such connection, but she did have the ambition, and she was in a circus that could certainly provide more opportunities than many others.

Alpheus George Barnes Stonehouse (Al G. Barnes) was one of the leading proponents of the wild-animal circus. From 1895, when he started his one small wagon show, to 1909, he migrated among carnivals, fairs, and small circuses with his trained-animal act. In 1909, the Al G. Barnes Trained Wild Animal Circus went out on rails to the West Coast and began to build a reputation for having some of the best animal acts presented by American circuses. Barnes demanded high-quality performances from his trainers and tolerated no cruel training methods. He was himself, writes Ballantine, "attuned to even the commonest of animals and possessed a decidedly uncanny ability to make all four-footed beasts understand him. For Mr. Barnes, pouting parrots became eager to recite their entire vocabularies, to sing their most squawking arias, to whisper their most shocking profanities. Even the shy desert coyote carried on moonlight conversations with Mr. Barnes. He once taught a jackass to bray on cue; and balky horses, even those not circus trained, obeyed his every soft-spoken word."[29] While there may be some exaggeration here, Barnes's feeling toward animals was not lost on those around him—and certainly not on the young Stark.

Barnes's ability to find the best among trainers was well illustrated in the fall of 1909, when he hired Louis Roth, a Hungarian immigrant who had put together several interesting combination-animal acts. For twenty years Roth was to be the chief trainer and menagerie superintendent for the Al G. Barnes Circus. It was to him that Stark directed her pleas for an opportunity to work with tigers on the show. Finally, Joys reports, "Hoping to get rid of her, the circus press agent cleared the way for her to enter the arena, not really caring if she were killed or not. He had her sign a release, and she went in. Incredibly, she survived. Roth, who had thought that she would surely be killed, took her as his pupil."[30] Stark was once again a student; a more serious and dedicated one could not be found.

Unlike so many other performers, who might be said to be born to their art—e.g., equestrians, aerialists, acrobats, wirewalkers—the animal trainer is made. Again relating such a situation to the woman trainer, Cooper talks of the contrast:

> You will find in the equestrienne the descendant of a long line of riders. Her mother before her was a rider, and her grandmother, even back to the fourth and fifth generations. She is trained on the "rosin-back," as the ring horse is called, from the moment she is large enough to sit upon it. From her birth she is destined to become a rider; her thoughts are never elsewhere. It is the same with the acrobat; stroll into the big top of the circus following the matinee performance and you will find every ring clustered with fathers and mothers teaching their offspring the tricks and stunts which have given them a living beneath the canvas tents, training them from youth that the children may take their places and carry on the family name. But with the animal trainer all this is different. She steps into the game in maturity; she trains for it as one would take a college course for some profession.[31]

Roth was the best of teachers; and though no one can deny that Stark learned much simply from her own study of, and experience with, the big cats, he surely did much to smooth out the edges. Her impatience to be in the arena with tigers was obvious to all who knew her, but Roth brought her along slowly, giving her minor acts in the Barnes performance. One of the earliest, the "Aviation Lion," she did with Roth. The two of them and a lion were hoisted in a cage to the top of the big top, whereupon fireworks were shot off. Spectacular, but hardly what Stark was after. Eventually she was given a small tiger act, and by 1916 she was working the show's feature tiger act—this at a time when there were few tiger acts among the country's circuses, and none handled by women.[32]

A petite blond, Stark seemed physically to be out of her element in an arena full of tigers. But she seemed even more so when, for several years, in a featured act on the Barnes show, she wrestled Rajah, a huge 350-pound Bengal tiger. A real show-stopper for the audience, the act seemed also to be a pleasure for Rajah. Other than a few unintentionally given scratches, Stark was never injured by her wrestling partner. When Stark left for the Ringling show, however, and a new woman trainer took over the wrestling act, Rajah injured her seriously in the very first rehearsal. After a second trainer was mauled in the same fashion, Rajah was sold to a zoo, where, according to Francis Beverly Kelley, he sorely missed the glamour of the big arena and the fun he had wrestling with Stark:

> He became stupid and irritable and spent his time sleeping in a corner of his den. But Rajah remembered the days when he was part of a great portable city that pitched its billowing white tops among strange noises, strange faces and in all sorts of weather. His plight was similar to that of the fire department horse that was sold to the milk man. Rajah was hitched to the "milk wagon" as compared to the former life under circus canvas. The zoo was too quiet and nothing interested him.
>
> But whenever a blond head appeared, he would bound out of his corner and pace up and down, purring joyously, his amber eyes peering anxiously through the bars in search of the one thing he loved. When he was satisfied that the blond head did not belong to the object of all his savage affection, he would return to his corner and whimper like a hurt kitten.
>
> Rajah's health failed rapidly and one morning he did not respond to the attendant who pushed him a pan of milk and raw meat. Where is there anyone in all circusdom who will say that Rajah did not die of a broken heart?[33]

While to some it may seem more than strange for a woman, especially one who never weighed more than 114 pounds and who was not particularly strong, to wrestle with a tiger, Stark never thought it so. Not only did she simply like tigers, she wanted to do something that would reflect her strong spirit of individualism. "I grew tired," she once said, "of having people say, 'A woman cannot do this,' or 'A woman cannot do that.' I determined to do the thing I am now doing because it had not been done and people said it could not be done."[34] There was nothing of the daredevil in Stark; it was essentially a quiet, fearless confidence, a kind, even temperament, a clear mind, and above all a love of her charges that enabled Stark to master the most treacherous of the big cat family. "I love these big cats as a mother loves her children, even when they are most wayward," she said. "They are killers because they know their strength. They can be subdued but never conquered, except by love. And that is the secret of all successful animal training. I have learned it at the risk of my life."[35]

Some animal trainers might question whether love is the most salient factor in training the big cats, but no one would question that Stark, love or no love, risked her life following her profession. There is an oft-told story of a young woman who, visiting Stark in her dressing tent, asked what it took to be a great tiger trainer. Stark calmly parted her dressing gown, showed a pair of legs cruelly scarred from ankle to thigh, and quietly said, "This." Another incident, which shows that Stark, despite her many close brushes with death, never lost her sense of humor, occurred one day on the Ringling show when she was seated in the canvas connection between the menagerie and the big top talking to friends. A pet badger escaped his leash and came near her. Appearing a bit nervous, she started to leave. When asked how she could face tigers if she was afraid of a pet badger, she shrugged and said, "The tigers wouldn't hurt anyone."

One of Stark's early close calls came during an Al G. Barnes parade. She was riding in a cage with four lions when a frightened farm horse bolted and fell beside the wagon she and the lions were occupying. The lions began leaping at the bars to get at the horse. Failing in their frenzied efforts, they turned on Stark. Fortunately, with the help of the wagon driver, she was able to crawl into a safety cage at the end of the wagon. Taken to

Mabel Stark loved her tigers.
Courtesy of the Pfening Collection.

the hospital with a mangled leg, she vehemently refused an anesthetic during the stitching process. For three days she fought delirium as the circus traveled its route. She was again taken to a hospital, where the doctors at first thought that the leg would have to be amputated. "Don't you dare cut my leg off! If you do, I'll kill myself!" she cried. The doctors removed a sliver of bone that had been causing the infection and scraped the leg bone. In eleven days she was back with the show.[36]

Probably her worst mauling came in 1928 in Bangor, Maine, when she slipped in a muddy arena and was jumped by two tigers. Only quick action by Terrell Jacobs, a lion trainer, saved her life; but, as Ballantine notes, "not before Miss Stark had suffered a badly mangled leg, a torn and mashed face, an ankle that remained stiff for many months, a deep hole in her shoulder, a torn deltoid muscle and a hole in her neck uncomfortably close to the jugular vein."[37] It took several hours for the doctors to complete the stitching, and Stark was unable to perform for some two months.

To some, it may seem that maulings of animal trainers are no more than happenstance or the result of a cat's decision to go after its human master. For Stark, however, every effect had its cause. Every time that she lay in a hospital bed recovering from her wounds, she was always able to reconstruct just what had happened to put her there. Perhaps it was only through such concentration, both in and out of the arena, that she was able to follow her career to its completion. Never one to blame her animals for injuries that she received, she, as most good trainers would, saw her own errors of omission or commission as the cause.

One thing, however, that Stark, or any other trainer, could hardly hold herself responsible for were fights between cats in the arena. Stark felt that fights were a bad business, "not merely because the combatants may decide to get together and turn on the trainer, but more especially because they hold grudges. They are like naughty schoolboys who lie in wait for each other. I have seen two cats break down bars in cage wagons or turn on each other in a narrow runway to fight out an old grudge. Once one of these cats gets a throat hold he will hang on until one of them is dead. Iron prods and even a stream of water enough to drown him have no effect."[38] Stark would rather have had her tigers take their peevishness out on her, because she felt that she could handle such a situation: "If he is contemplating a spring I jump aside and shout at him. My voice startles him. By stepping out of his direct vision I can generally arrest that impulse and bring him up short."[39]

After ten years with the Barnes show, six as a center-ring star, Stark got her chance to go to Ringling Brothers in 1922. A move up in terms of circuses, it was a move down in terms of visibility. Relegated to an end ring, she presented her act of five tigers and a black panther at the Ringling opening in Madison Square Garden. In what in previous times would have been an annoying incident, Nigger, a black panther, was a recalcitrant performer and fought Stark for several minutes, refusing to obey any of her commands. On this occasion, it was exactly what Stark needed. Not only did it draw the attention of virtually all the audience, it also gained her a very favorable notice in the *New York Times* coverage of the Ringling opening. The result was that Stark was moved to center ring, staying there until 1925, when the Ringling show dropped cat acts from its program.

Leaving Ringling, Stark, after spending a year in Europe, worked with the John Robinson Circus in 1929. The next year she returned to the Al G. Barnes show and remained there through 1936, after which she spent a number of years with smaller circuses. In the 1950s, she toured Japan with her tigers and then wound down her career at the World Jungle Compound at Thousand Oaks, California, where she performed up until a few months before her death on 20 April 1968.

Mabel Stark's contribution to wild-animal acts in America would be difficult to overestimate. Choosing perhaps the most dangerous cat to train, the tiger, she proved that through a combination of sheer determination and a keen insight into the personalities of her striped charges, a mere wisp of a woman could consistently present an act worthy of the center ring in any circus. She loved her tigers, and she loved the circus. She herself puts it best in her autobiography, *Hold That Tiger:*

> But I would not trade my profession for any other. The smell of the circus is in my blood. I love the acrid pungence of the menagerie tent with its strange animals from many lands. I like the grease paint, and the powder that comes in clouds from the dressing tents

of the equestriennes and show girls and mingles with the tang of the horse and elephant tents. Over it all floats the odor of smoke and grease from the cook tent, where ham and eggs and coffee satisfy the outdoor appetites of the circus family. This is a land of thrill and glamour that gets into the blood and holds performers, not only for a lifetime but for generation after generation.[40]

The Boy from Bainbridge

For over forty years, Clyde Beatty—a muscular, 145-pound man who stood just under five and a half feet tall—stood very tall indeed in the steel arena. Some, such as Fred Bradna, may point to Alfred Court as the greatest cat trainer; or some, not so well acquainted with the circuses of yesteryear, may see Gunther Gebel-Williams of the current Ringling show as the foremost in that field. But the great majority of circus aficionados would not hesitate to proclaim Clyde Raymond Beatty the greatest of all wild-animal trainers.

Born in 1903 in the village of Bainbridge, Ohio, a short distance from Chillicothe, Beatty had an early affinity for animals, raising rabbits, guinea pigs, and skunks. He saw his first circus at the age of nine, when Sun Brothers World Progressive Shows played Chillicothe. Though he was, like most boys that age, awed by the wonders of the circus, it is doubtful that he foresaw that in a few years he himself would be part of the world of spangles and sawdust. But the year 1921 found him working as a cage boy with Howe's Great London Shows—and beginning a career that would truly make him a legend in his time.[41]

With Howe's Great London Shows at the time was menagerie boss Louis Roth, the same trainer who some years before had tutored Mabel Stark in the fundamentals of cat training. How close a relationship Beatty and the Hungarian had is open to speculation, but in any case the youngster set for himself the goal of being a wild-animal trainer. His first chance came, according to his own recounting, when, upon learning that the regular polar-bear trainer had asked for a leave of absence, he approached Roth about substituting in the act. "To my astonishment," he says in *Facing the Big Cats,* "Roth replied that he had been thinking of making that very suggestion himself. He had noticed that I regularly watched the bear act, even making notes of some of the things the trainer did, and that whenever he

[Roth] had discussed the different tricks and formations with me, I had sounded as if I knew what it was all about."[42] So into the arena Beatty went, cutting a rather humorous figure:

> I must have been a strange sight when I put on the uniform of the man I was supplanting—he was very tall and somewhat on the portly side, though he preferred to be known as "stocky." He wore one of those ornate outfits that resembled the dress uniform of a high-ranking general in a mythical musical-comedy kingdom, and when I put on the jacket it looked like an overcoat on me. I was slender and a little under average height, so when I tried on the trousers I found myself flopping around in them as though they were part of a clown's get-up. That fancy jacket came down so far I figured I could wear my own pants without anyone being the wiser.[43]

In 1922, Beatty was with Golmar Brothers Circus (really Howe's show with a different title[44]) and there, under the tutelage of John Gilfoye, worked an act of four or five polar bears. In 1923, the corporation combined a large part of the Golmar show with the John Robinson Circus. For two years, Beatty worked a bear act and served as an assistant to the well-known trainer Peter Taylor—"the one man who surely had more influence on Beatty's style than all others."[45] (According to Dave Price, the two must have got along well together because Taylor let the neophyte trainer handle his [Taylor's] own big cat act in winter quarters.)[46] When Taylor was sent to the Hagenbeck-Wallace Circus (another corporation show) in 1925, Beatty went with him and not only worked a bear act but also his first cat act—a mixed act consisting of lions, pumas, leopards, and bears. Just how he got the cat act is not clear. One story has it that Pete Taylor collapsed in the safety cage prior to entering the arena and that Beatty carried him from the cage and then worked the act to the audience's admiration and great appreciation. Or, as another story goes, he got the act because Taylor was preoccupied with romantic considerations and was gone. Either way, he got the act and had, in a manner of speaking, found a home; he was to stay with the Wallace show for the next ten years, during which time his reputation would grow to the point where he was considered the premier cat trainer in America.

After the 1925 season, Beatty turned his efforts entirely to training lions and tigers. But more than that, he became a heavily featured and billed center-ring attraction, a position he was to maintain for the remainder of his career.

Perhaps it would be fruitful to pause here for a moment and look at the man Clyde Beatty. While his personal life was, and still is, a topic of considerable gossip and speculation and awaits treatment in some future definitive biographical study, certain of his attributes are clear enough. With relatively little formal education, he became one of the most knowledgeable persons regarding the physical and psychological traits of the animals he trained. An intuitive naturalist whose favorite subjects were zoology[47] and natural history, he was also a master showman who understood audience psychology as much as he did that of animals. Neither a smoker nor a drinker (except for an occasional beer), he was always physically fit. Like many men of small stature, he had a feisty cockiness about him that did much to establish his battling arena image. He was well aware of the demands of his profession and the qualities needed to meet them. "I'd like nothing better," he once said, "than to turn over my years of experience to some kid. I'll never stop looking, but I don't think I'll ever find one with what it takes; raw guts, steady nerve, real endurance, a feeling for animals—and he's gotta be just plain cussed crazy about circuses."[48] That he accomplished all that he did, as E. W. Ritchey puts it, "by the sheer strength of his talent, aggressiveness, will to succeed, and fine public image is a great tribute to Beatty's ability as a performer and as a business man. To do this alone and single-handed from a humble beginning is a great achievement to me. He was a very gifted man and made his mark in the circus field where his name will be very highly regarded by future historians."[49]

Like Mabel Stark, Beatty approached his animals with patience and understanding, both of which derived not from love but from a sincere respect and an unending fascination for the elemental strength and beauty they possessed. His experience taught him that cats can never be trusted. "You can never be certain that a lion or tiger won't hook you if it has the opportunity," he once said. "Big cats are wild by nature, even if they're born in captivity. They never develop any affection for their trainer, no matter how gentle he may be with them."[50] Thus, he could also say that he had no "friends" among the lions and tigers in his act, "although some are more dependable than others."[51]

One of those more dependable, at least so in Beatty folklore, was Nero, a lion who, when Beatty was bowled over by a tiger and in danger of being clawed to death, leaped on the tiger—thus probably saving the trainer's life. But as Beatty himself admitted, Nero was more than likely simply taking advantage of an opportunity to get his teeth into a preoccupied tiger.

Like most trainers, Beatty preferred his animals to be jungle bred, because, unlike those born in captivity, they were not spoiled as cubs and thus never got over their fear of man. Such animals, however, were expensive—$500 to $1,500 in the 1930s—and difficult to obtain. Zoo-bred animals, on the other hand, were a glut on the market and could be had for as low as $100.

Taking his animals when they were about two and a half years old, Beatty would begin their training with seat-breaking, that is, teaching them to get up on a block seat, which would later be replaced by a pedestal. The idea was to get the animals ultimately to leap from pedestal to pedestal with no fear. From that point on, each animal would be evaluated in terms of his intelligence and his receptiveness to further learning. Beatty, writes Ballantine, "never found a 'born performer.' According to him there is no such animal—and not many that have the spark of arena genius, a built-in responsiveness that can be developed to make a good circus performer."[52] But when he found one of the latter, Beatty would set out to make him in some way a feature of the act—e.g., globe rolling, hoop jumping, rope walking. In *Facing the Big Cats,* he comments on the problems facing the trainer as he tries to decide which animal is best suited for a particular stunt:

> Suppose you try out three different cats for the role you are trying to fill. Candidate A, who is cooperative in the beginning and seems a cinch to learn the trick fast, may bog down as the lessons proceed and develop a dislike for this particular assignment (and later on prove a happy and dynamic performer in another). Candidate B may develop a liking for the role but may perform so slowly and methodically in these training sessions that it is easy to appraise him in advance as a performer who will not excite the audiences. Candidate C, who at the start fights me every inch of the way to the accompaniment of his angriest snarls, roars and black looks, may, after I have solved the riddle of how to

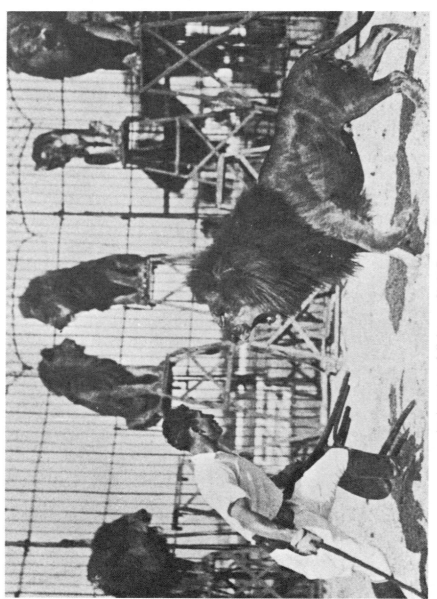

An American folk hero—Clyde Beatty at work.
Courtesy of the Circus World Museum.

communicate with him, prove to be the best and most reliable performer.[53]

Again like most of his contemporaries in the cat-training business, Beatty gave short shrift to the idea that trainers relied on cruel tactics in order to bring their animals to heel. "No one," he said, regarding the tales of animals being prodded by sharp lances, "who wants to live long ever pokes a big cat with a pointed lance. No jungle animal can be trained successfully by cruelty. It'll take the maltreatment for awhile, then whammy! One day the cat explodes into a raving maniac, and you're done for."[54] Beatty knew well that far more effective in training cats than any kind of cruelty were a "kindly approach and a capacity for taking pains, plus a reasonably cheerful disposition."[55]

If one were to place Beatty's act side by side with Alfred Court's, he would notice a distinct difference. From the more effete European school, Court aimed to have the audience's attention focused almost entirely on the animals themselves. His role as trainer was made to appear almost an incidental one; he, too, seemed more or less a spectator. Thus, Court stressed tableaux; that is, he posed the animals in various formations, like a series of still lifes. In Beatty's act, on the other hand, the focus was virtually always on Beatty himself. Learning from his early mentors, he adopted the American "fighting act" as a trademark—indeed, developed it to its highest level. If Court took pains to make his act appear smooth, almost easy, Beatty took just as many pains to make his look difficult—an elemental battle between man and beast. With the sleeves of his white shirt rolled up, chair in one hand and whip in the other and pistol holstered at his side, he entered the arena as a gladiator ready to battle to the death.

Beatty's act was, of course, considerably "hoked up," what with his crouching, pivoting, poking the chair toward an animal, generously cracking his whip, and occasionally firing his blank-filled pistol.[56] Such antics and such noise, combined with the roar of forty lions and tigers, presented a spectacle that kept many a patron in nervous suspense and did much to enhance Beatty's image as the foremost animal trainer of all time. He himself was the first to admit that much of the drama of his act was carefully staged:

> One of the features of my act which always receives a tremendous burst of applause from the crowd is the apparent cowing of a big Nubian lion, after it has cornered and disarmed me, by the last resort of staring it into submission.
>
> The lion suddenly charges, striking viciously. To be perfectly frank, I assist in the disarming process by deliberately releasing the chair when it is struck. The whip and pistol are sent flying from my grasp by another lunge.
>
> I have backed against the bars—can retreat from the roaring fury no farther. Then I stop the lion's charge by suddenly taking a step toward him, leaning forward until my face is within a foot of his own, and staring him into submission.[57]

Beatty's act was a natural for press-agent "hype," and it got more than its share of same. But no matter how elaborately Beatty staged his act or how much press agents worked to make him into an American folk hero, what he was doing for a livelihood was, to say the least, dangerous. His basic idea was to get a cat to fight the chair so that he could then maneuver him around the arena in order for the audience to see "his majestic look, his speed, the suggestion of great power. When I am in good form the animal is really fighting the chair, not me."[58] Sometimes, however, the chair was ignored, and Beatty became the target.

Perhaps the most sensational of Beatty's accidents with his cats, though at the time it seemed not to be so, occurred in the Hagenbeck-Wallace winter quarters on 23 January 1932. In practicing his trick of outstaring a lion—Nero in this case—the trainer tripped over a dropped chair, falling to the arena floor. At that moment, Nero fastened his jaws on Beatty's right leg. An assistant drove Nero off and got Beatty out. Doctors at first thought the painful wound relatively minor, but a mysterious infection set in, driving Beatty's temperature to 105 degrees and sending him into delirium. The doctors' frantic efforts to identify the infection attracted the attention of the national press, giving Beatty nation-wide publicity. Finally, as a last resort, Dr. S. D. Malouf operated and found the source of the poison in a small pocket of pus on the leg bone. With this removed, Beatty began weeks of recuperation. Publicity-wise, this accident was timely, for Beatty was scheduled to open with the Ringling show in the spring in Madison Square Garden.[59] With his name appearing in lights outside the Garden, he entered the arena as a true hero to the thousands who came to see and to applaud the gritty young daredevil who had not only escaped the jaws of a lion, but also the mysterious germs of infection.

All was not well, however, between Beatty and the Ringling organization. Sam Gumpertz had taken over the management of the show in the struggle that effectively removed John Ringling from his position of power. Beatty and Gumpertz disagreed about a number of things, but primarily about Beatty's activities in Hollywood. Because of his growing acclaim, Beatty had been sought after by Universal Studios for movie work. Two movies, *The Big Cage* (1933) and *The Lost Jungle* (1934), resulted, but Gumpertz felt that such movies were detracting from Beatty's image as a circus star.[60] So, when Jesse Adkins, the manager of Hagenbeck-Wallace, and Zack Terrell decided in 1934 to put together a new circus, Beatty joined them as the featured act; and his name was added to the title in the billing. Thus was Cole Brothers Circus born.

The Cole show, with winter quarters in Rochester, Indiana, was slated to take to the road in 1935. Since the animals Beatty had worked in his act on the Wallace show belonged to the Ringling interests, he was faced with the enormous task of purchasing animals and training them in a short period of time. He speaks of his efforts in *Facing the Big Cats:*

> Racing the clock while putting together a whole new animal act is not good for the nerves. Mine are pretty steady, but I doubt it was ever intended that I should put them to the test of working night and day at the difficult business of teaching wild animals to perform.
>
> There were times when I was so exhausted I wondered whether I could go on. Then a nap would revive me. When you're really tired you can rest anywhere—even on a cement floor if you soften it up first with whatever happens to be handy as padding. You can't be very elegant around training quarters. Practically every square foot of space is in use and the only way you can create any room for a quick snooze is to push things out of the way.
>
> I had accomplished a great deal in a few weeks, and while I had a long way to go, my natural optimism routed my doubts and I was betting on myself to finish on time unless illness interfered.[61]

Had anyone taken Beatty up on the bet, he would have lost. Cole Brothers Circus, featuring Clyde Beatty, opened the 1935 season on schedule. It was then, and continued to be for the years that it operated, a first-class show. Beatty was, of course, the major attraction. His newly acquired wife (his second), Harriett, a stunning blonde, also did a stint in the arena with a lion, a tiger, and an elephant. The Cole show's best year was 1937, when it challenged Ringling in New York City. Beatty, too, was at the height of his fame.

The next year, however, was a bleak one for American circuses. More will be said about this in the final chapter. Cole Brothers closed early, and some of the acts, including Beatty, were sent to Robbins Brothers, Adkins and Terrell's second unit. But it was time, Beatty thought, to strike out on his own. Following a season at the Steel Pier in Atlantic City, he directed his efforts toward building the Clyde Beatty Jungle Zoo in Fort Lauderdale, Florida, the idea for which he got on an earlier trip to Florida. He purchased the McKillop-Hutton lion farm, along with some additional land, and began building what was to be one of the finest zoos anywhere. Beatty's own description hardly does justice to it:

> Located two miles north of Fort Lauderdale, it is encircled by a high bamboo fence. As you enter from the highway you see black and white swans swimming gracefully in several shaded pools. Animal and bird life is all around. Steps rise on either side of a huge waterfall, and at the top you can look down on the entire zoo. Across the way flamingos stand motionless. Lions and tigers pace up and down in the barless dens behind moats. Leopards and bears range about in separate grottos. Monkeys of all species chatter and scold. The elephants weave and beg for peanuts. Pheasants, peacocks, and demoiselle cranes wander about garden paths. Cockatoos and macaws flit among the palm trees. Passing down the long walkway through the zoo you come to my animal arena, circus ring, and grandstand. Here we give several performances a day. We also have a special exhibit of Florida wild life: little black bears, alligators, pumas, snakes, raccoons, opossums, and other products of the Everglades. All of which adds up to twenty-five acres.[62]

During the tourist season, performances consisted of ten acts, climaxed by Beatty's cat act. In the summer, the Clyde Beatty

Wild Animal Circus toured the country, usually as part of other circuses or carnivals. All in all, it was a good arrangement for Beatty for five years. But then progress, in one sense, spelled the end of Beatty's zoological paradise. As Fort Lauderdale changed from a rather sleepy coastal town to a growing city, houses and apartments were built around the zoo. And, writes Charles Sprague, "City Hall was suddenly besieged by complaints from that area. 'The lions roared at night. . . . Monkeys escaped and terrified the neighborhood. . . . The blare of the loudspeakers was irritating. . . . Even the peacock cries were too loud.'"[63] Despite Beatty's efforts to appease his neighbors, he was forced to close the zoo in 1945.

Turning his full energies back to the circus, Beatty put out his own full-fledged railroad circus—the Clyde Beatty Circus. Though he sold the show to Frank McClosky and Walter Kernan after the 1956 season, he remained the featured performer until his death in 1965.

Beatty once said, "I want people to see me close—close enough to smell the cats. When I'm in there, I don't know if there are a hundred or a thousand in the audience. It doesn't matter. I'll give them anything; I'll give them everything."[64] That he did just that over his forty-year career is documented by the some 30,000 performances to over 40 million people that he gave; the million miles he traveled in the process; the thousand lions and about the same number of tigers he trained; and the nearly one hundred trips to the hospital he made.[65] Few circus historians, to be sure, would hesitate to label Beatty a super-showman—for surely he was. But he was, in a very real sense, more than that.

Representing the epitome of the wild-animal trainer—fear-less, almost reckless—Clyde Beatty had all the trappings of a folk-hero. Like Jay Gatsby in F. Scott Fitzgerald's *The Great Gatsby,* Beatty "sprang from his own conception of himself." From his more-or-less purposely obscured beginnings in a small Ohio village through his whole career, he consciously cultivated the image of the self-confident, unbeatable, bigger-than-life cat trainer who faced death twice a day—in the evening, as well as at the matinee—asking no quarter and giving none. It really did not matter if his act was "hoked up" or if, as some say, he really did not train his own animals. After all, Beatty was smart enough to know that it is not what *really* happens that is important, but what people *think* happens.

While to some purists the wild-animal act was not true circus, to the majority of the audiences who watched it, it had an attraction that other acts did not have. That attraction was the element of conflict. The trapeze artist or the aerialist had only to be concerned with his own skill, and perhaps that of a cooperating companion. The wild-animal trainer, on the other hand, had to overcome a savage adversary—to impose human will on nature. There was no rhythm or beauty of form to this conflict; it was noisy and violent and fought out in the dust of the arena. Alfred Court, as an example of the European school of wild-animal training, may have had a dimension of decorum or gentility in his act—but, like it or not, the American spirit, nurtured as it was by the frontier, seems to thrive on violence, or at least the witnessing of it.

The American experience from the very beginning has been one based on both a physical and a spiritual relationship with nature. Nature on the one hand has been something to conquer and, on the other, something with which to be in an almost mystical unity. These two relationships are at times in harmony and at other times in diametric opposition. Beatty, when he outstared Leo at the climax of his act, certainly could be seen as a symbol of man's dominion over nature. Yet, in that stare, staged as it may have been, was a ritualistic relationship between man and beast that had nothing to do with domination—or with an audience. It was, for an instant, man and beast come to the bottom of themselves, in an understanding that defies objective analysis.

During his time, then, Beatty did become a kind of folk-hero. As time passes, however, so often do folk-heroes. When a recent class of some fifty university students were asked about Beatty, only one admitted to having heard of him—and that one only because of a recent visit to the Circus World Museum in Baraboo, Wisconsin. The new hero—though he will never achieve the status that Beatty did—is the Ringling show's Gunther Gebel-Williams. A talented, even if also a bit "hoked up," performer, Gebel-Williams exhibits the macho aspect of a man unafraid of wild beasts with a strong element of almost primitive sex appeal. But none of this detracts from what Beatty accomplished in his life. He earned his place in the list of circus greats and in the minds of all those who were fortunate enough to see him go "one on one" with a snarling big cat. Of such people is history, circus or otherwise, made.

4

Equine "Escapades"

A LION'S ROAR MAY BE MORE SPINE TINGLING THAN A
horse's neigh, and the trainer of the former may well be
seen as a symbol of man's power over the savage beast—but the
fact remains that the horse has ever been central to the circus
performance in both Europe and America. And the equestrians
and equestriennes, moreover, have ever been among the elite of
circus society. From the early days when John Bill Ricketts captivated audiences with his sundry riding tricks, to the numerous
dog and pony shows that slogged their way over country roads,
to the mighty railroad shows that epitomized the golden age of
the American circus, circuses took great pride in their horses
and in those who trained them and performed with them. A circus without horses would have been no circus at all. The strings
of liberty horses with their jingling bells and jaunty feathers, the
prancing high-school horses, the rhythmic rosinbacks, the frol-
icking ponies—all cast their own kind of magic in the big top.

Such magic, however, did not occur by accident. Circus
performing horses were carefully chosen and painstakingly
trained. While the beautifully rugged baggage stock that pulled
the cumbersome red wagons to and from the lot and in the parade were primarily native American horses—coming mainly
from the states of Ohio, Indiana, Illinois, and Iowa—the ring
stock came from virtually everywhere. Some, of course, were
the property of the various performing troupes; others belonged
to the circus. Either way, the search for circus horses was ever a
constant and wide-ranging one. Nor was the search limited to
horse shows or horse farms. One might have been just as apt to
find a likely candidate for the circus ring on the front end of a

trash wagon. What then were the criteria used in the selection process?

To begin with, each act needed its own kind of horse. The manège, or high-school, act needed saddle horses or show horses. These horses and their riders performed on the hippodrome track in what some saw as the only real horse act in the circus. There were two forms of high school: *Hoche Schule über die Erde,* in which the tricks were performed essentially with the horse's front feet in the air; and *Hoche Schule auf die Erde,* in which the horse's hooves were often in contact with the ground.[1] The former was, as might be expected, much more difficult than the latter. Because most horses could usually master only one trick in either school, close attention was paid to discern that for which he exhibited the most talent. A really exceptional high-school horse could, according to Bradna, "walk, trot, canter, gallop, do a controlled canter obliquely or sidewise, march (called the Spanish Walk), high trot (passage), gallop on three legs while changing leads, gallop standing still (en place), trot on one spot (piaffe), gallop backwards, sit down (pesade), hootchy-kootchy (balloter des hances), waltz, one-step and, today, rhumba."[2] Perhaps the greatest manège rider and trainer was William Heyer, a former Dutch cavalry officer, who during the 1930s was a star with the Ringling show. A big man, he had perfect seat and sensitive hands—qualities that contributed to a masterful and complicated act with his sixteen-hand horse, Starless Night.

The liberty act, a ring act in which a number of riderless horses ran through various formations under the direction of a trainer, demanded showy stallions, usually of identical color. In this act, the trainer stood in the center of the ring, with the horses circling him at a gallop. While not so demanding as the high school, the liberty act, nevertheless, required an astuteness on the part of the trainer. The ideal was to use as little motion and as few verbal commands as possible. Heyer, too, worked liberty acts, maintaining that he actually mesmerized his horses, "establishing connection with one of them and then having that animal transmit the ray of influence to the others."[3] Interestingly enough, it was not unusual for one horse in a liberty act to be more or less the leader and to keep the more recalcitrant of his equine companions in line.

The last of the major equestrian acts—the bareback-riding act—required a large broad-backed horse, such as a Percheron, with a keen sense of rhythm. The rosinbacks, so called because of the resin rubbed generously on their backs to provide sure footing for the performer, were usually white or dapple gray, so that the resin would be unnoticable. The unchanging, monotonous gait of the rosinbacks as they moved around the ring was essential to the safety of the bareback rider. The slightest change in a horse's movement during a trick could have meant (and often did) serious injury or even death to the performer. While the same could be said of all circus horses, the rosinbacks especially had to be of a temperament that would inure them to the noises and confusion of a circus tent filled with thousands of people and arrayed with elaborate rigging and equipment. Theirs was not to master a clever trick, but to be as steady and even-gaited as a mechanical horse would be—one who would, in Cooper's words, "keep right on loping in that same jerky, springy pace, no matter if the tent blows down. Of curiosity he must have none; and when it is realized that the ordinary horse is as curious as the proverbial cat, one can understand the catastrophe when a rider announces the necessity for new ring stock."[4]

Cooper tells of the Hobson family, husband and wife bareback riders, who needed a new horse for their act, because their two young sons were about to be worked in. Homer Hobson wanted a horse with a long back, so that all four of the troupe could stand on it. During the parade one day, a clown saw just the horse Hobson needed—hitched to a scavenger cart. He offered the owner ten dollars to drive his cart to the circus lot, where Hobson paid him $150 on the spot for the horse. "Four years later," says Cooper, "Long Nile—he's one of the longest shortest-legged horses in the circus business—carries the four Hobsons on his back for the finish of the act, while somewhere a scavenger-wagon driver wonders whatever became of that fool circus man who paid $150 for a $75 horse without even batting an eye."[5]

All circus horses, too, had to have good, strong legs, with bodies that were not too heavy—usually not over fourteen hands high—because training and performing were demanding physically. If there were any infirmities in a horse, they showed up quickly. But even a horse with the required physical qualifications and a look of intelligence in his eyes did not guarantee a good circus horse. As with all performing animals, these horses required an abundance of patience on the part of their trainers. After a month of two training sessions a day, according to the noted trainer Adolph Hess, one would know whether or not he had a circus horse. Any more efforts after that were, he felt, fruitless. John Agee, equestrian director of the Ringling show in the early 1920s, recalled training an important group of vicious stallions that had killed three previous trainers in Europe:

> When the horses came over, and after I had an opportunity to get acquainted with them, I found out that they were all bad. That is to say, they would take any opportunity afforded them to attack their trainer. So I decided that if I was going to work the act successfully I would have to secure their confidence and affection.
>
> I commenced by starting early in the morning and having the horses brought out singly. Then I would dismiss the groom and bolt the door of the training barn so that I might be free of any interruption. I always brought a carrot or some green succulent dainty with me. Then I would sit down on the ring bank and simply talk to my pupil.
>
> So far as I could judge, these horses had lost all confidence in human educators. So at first I did not try to put them through any of their regular stunts. I would talk to them and try to coax them to come up to me and receive a carrot or whatever I happened to have. Then I would cross over to the other side of the ring, sit down as before, but always keeping up my line of conversation.
>
> I never carried a whip or any other weapon, and when they began to come to me without much persuasion I never tried to take hold of them or to detain them—just let them wander around and go and come as they would; a pretty tedious operation.
>
> I imagine that over there they had several different trainers, who all probably employed different methods, and they were really at a loss as to who was their master. There are a thousand different ways of working a horse, and you can lay down so many rules; but when all is said and done the universal one is kindness.
>
> After awhile I allowed them to come into the ring together. The moment I called them they came flocking around me like children who had been invited to partake of a sack of candy.[6]

Agee went on to train the horses to perform very difficult feats in the ring.

Important as they were, the horses, of course, were only part of the equestrian acts; equestrians and equestriennes were the other. And of these, the bareback riders were surely the most popular and the most featured; both as individuals and as troupes.

From Rompers to Ringling

Along with aerialist Lillian Leitzel and tight-wire walker Bird Millman, May Wirth is considered one of the three great women stars of the American circus. The only woman to do a forward somersault on a horse's back, she was unrivaled as a bareback equestrienne during the second and third decades of this century. Her physical beauty alone was enough to make her a famed attraction. That beauty, coupled with her daring and graceful acrobatics on the back of a horse, legitimately earned for her acclamation as the finest equestrienne in the world.

Her early years, like those of Leitzel, are somewhat obscure. Born possibly in 1896 in Australia, she was, at about age five, taken by Marizel Wirth as a foster daughter and as an apprentice in a riding act on the Wirth Circus. This circus, started by Marizel's husband, John, was truly a world-toured show—visiting South Africa, South America, England, Europe, and India during the years 1893 through 1899. A precocious youngster, Wirth was performing with the circus by the time she was five, appearing in the ring in rompers and with a large pink bow in her hair. Marizel, herself an expert equestrienne, provided not only excellent teaching, but also the encouragement to excel. And excel Wirth did, performing by age ten five different acts— riding, wire-walking, contortions on a high pedestal, acrobatics, and even feats on the trapeze. Before long, as John Draper reports, "she could throw seven cleancut somersaults on the back of a running horse while once encircling the ring, and, as a finish, she could dash around the ring on, over, and under the horse, clinging in Mazeppa fashion with loosened, tangled hair floating to the winds with the form of a Venus."[7] By this time, there was little question that she was destined for stardom.

Following her formal debut as a bareback rider in Europe in 1911, she came to America with Marizel and Stella Wirth and Frank White to join the Barnum and Bailey Circus. The troupe made their American debut when the show opened its 1912 sea-

son in Madison Square Garden. May Wirth was an instant success both with the audience and with the critics, who hailed her
abilities as an equestrienne with superlatives usually reserved
for older and more established performers. For the remainder
of that year and through the next, Wirth was heavily billed and
featured on the Barnum and Bailey show.

Proclaimed in 1913 as a somersault rider in a class by herself,
Wirth proved that year that she was indeed "Marvelous May."
Her backward somersaults and an extraordinary forward somersault from her knees had drawn enthusiastic plaudits from
audiences in 1912. Now she added a double backward somersault from one horse to another—the first such trick ever
presented by a woman in public. Eventually, she did this trick
blindfolded. An article in the *Billboard* that year extolled her
performance:

> May Wirth is one of the greatest features of Barnum and Bailey.
> When this most marvelous lady rider of all times makes her en-
> trance, the audience gives her a general round of applause show-
> ing that her sensational riding last year is not forgotten. To be
> remembered in the circus from one season to another is the high-
> est possible proof of greatness. Her somersault riding is flawless
> and she performs with seemingly ridiculous ease feats that have
> been regarded as impossible for a female rider. Her youth and
> dainty prettiness have an irrestible appeal. In her spangled ring
> costume with her two snow white horses, Joe and Kitty, May pre-
> sents a picture that is lovely to behold. She is as game as they make
> them. Though suffering severely from a bruised foot, she goes on
> with her work as though nothing had happened, making three
> clean jumps, two forwards, a dozen backs and three somersaults
> over banners around the ring. No such riding as May Wirth's has
> ever been seen in the Garden or is likely to be seen again until May
> Wirth returns.[8]

Early in the 1913 season, Wirth's gameness was clearly evident again when she had a near tragic accident caused by her
horse's stumbling. As she fell, she was caught in the horse's
trappings and was dragged around the ring with her head vio-
lently bouncing off the curbing. Bruised, bleeding, and unconscious, she was carried from the ring by anxious attendants. Her
injuries, however, did not deter her, and before long she had re-

Courtesy of the San Antonio Public Library.

covered enough to carry on her act. Like all bareback riders, Wirth knew the dangers of the ring; she lived with them and accepted them.

The year 1914 found the Wirth troupe back in Europe. The outbreak of hostilities, unfortunately, made Europe a precarious place for circuses, and the troupe returned to Australia. For the next two years, Wirth was with her foster-father's show again, honing to an even greater sharpness her riding skills. When she returned to America in 1917—to Ringling Brothers this time—her "somersaults and handsprings on the horse's back were," says Draper, "being declared as perfect as if she was performing on solid ground. The climax came when she affixed two market baskets to her feet and leaped to the back of a running horse. With this feat of strength as well as her forward somersaults and somersault from one horse to another she was stopping the show."[9] Symbolic of her star position was her Chandler touring car, one of the very few motor cars carried on the Ringling show trains.

Many circus performers, naturally enough, played to the audience, often making their tricks look more difficult than they were or doing tricks that were more spectacular than they were difficult. Wirth, however, delighted in doing what Bradna called "performers' tricks"—those that involved degrees of difficulty and risk that, while not appreciated by the audience, were remarkable to other equestrians. Her back backward somersault was one such trick. Facing the rear of the horse, she would throw herself contrary to its forward motion, somersaulting and simultaneously twisting so that she lit facing forward. Also, she jumped from the ground to the back of a galloping horse—even on occasion doing this trick with the baskets mentioned by Draper. "She was," in Bradna's estimation, "a fascinating showman, delighting the audience with her daintiness and graciousness and, in the backyard, was one of the best loved of all the stars. Her like will never be seen again, for the tradition is now lost and no one will have the opportunity to learn the act."[10]

Wirth continued performing regularly with various circuses through 1931. After that, she performed occasionally at fairs and the like, but her career as a premier equestrienne was essentially over. She and her husband, Frank White, whom she married in 1919 and who took the name Wirth as his own, established a booking agency for show people. She died on 18 October 1978 in Sarasota, Florida. Perhaps Bradna was right, and there will never be another like her. She was born to be a bareback rider—if ever anyone was. She said when she was still a young girl that her "idea of heaven would be to ride horseback all the time, to have her meals brought to her that way when she was hungry and to sleep while jogging along when she got tired."[11]

Equestrienne—Equestrian Director

If May Wirth was the greatest of gymnastic horsewomen, then surely Ella Bradna, the wife of the Ringling show's distinguished equestrian director Fred Bradna, was not far behind. This Bohemian beauty, the daughter of Johan and Katha Bradna, grew up in her father's circus as it wandered through Bohemia, Austria, and Hungary during the late nineteenth century.

Along with her four brothers and one sister, Ella learned many of the basics of circus performing, ranging from ballet to slackwire-walking. Her primary interest, however, was bareback riding; and it was in perfecting her techniques in that area that she spent many long hours in the practice ring. By age ten, she was accomplished on the slackwire and on horseback, but Johan did not want to exhibit her skills in bareback riding until that moment when "she could burst on the world as a spectacular performer."[12] So Ella was more or less relegated to performing ballet—experience that was later to be invaluable when she donned ballet slippers and toe danced on the back of a horse. But for the time being, she could only watch, admire, and copy her sister Beata, who had developed into a celebrated rider and whose beauty and showmanship captivated every audience—especially the male segment.

Ella's moment came in Pilsen when she was eleven years old. Beata broke both legs in a fall from her horse, and Johan needed an immediate replacement. Bradna describes the occasion:

> Out of the backyard came all of Ella's tricks. Pilsen was enchanted by the long-haired blonde child. It applauded when, on her sister's horse, she participated in the family jockey act. But Ella's biggest success was her slack-wire turn. Without the use of umbrella or balancing pole she picked up a handkerchief with her teeth. She

also swung on the wire with great speed. These stunts had been done before, but Ella's performance was set apart by an extra quality: showmanship. All of her life a lover of birds, Ella had trained a dozen pigeons to come at her call and settle on her arms. Now she put them into her act, calling them to her as she took her bow. Pilsen loved it.[13]

Ella Bradna was now embarked on her performing career. Concentrating primarily on bareback riding, she performed dancing, tumbling, and balancing tricks on the broad back of a white horse. Like that on any traveling circus, life with Circus Bradna was a test of will and endurance. Ella performed twice each day, studied her school lessons, practiced her act, helped washing dishes for the company of fifty, and took her turn at night driving a wagon to the next town. She was, in Bradna's words, "too busy to think. She welcomed Sunday as the one day when everything stopped while Johan Bradna led his family to Mass, after which she had a little time to herself. Then she repaired her wardrobe and thought about her future."[14]

Like any talented and beautiful circus performer, Ella was deluged with attentions and gifts from men—some eligible and some not—who saw in her the glamour and mystery of a captivating young girl and an exotic way of life. When she was only fourteen, the elderly mayor of Newbyzow, through Johan, proposed marriage to Ella. Johan felt she was too young, and, though the mayor promised to wait awhile, his death ended any possibilities of matrimony.

Political problems in 1887 made it virtually impossible for the Circus Bradna to cross Eastern European borders without incident; consequently, Johan closed the show, and the family split up, with various members joining various circuses. Ella, along with her father and her brother Charles, went with Circus Drexler. Her star continued to rise in the circus world, and she became the featured equestrienne of Germany's greatest circus—Circus Schumann. In 1900 she joined her brother Josephy, himself a highly accomplished bareback rider, with the Circus Salamonsky in Moscow. There she was often entertained by Smirnoff, the noted vodka king. To Josephy's objections that it was not appropriate for a married man to pay so much attention to Ella, the Russian "protested that his interest was one of admiration only, and promptly sent Josephy a sleigh full of champagne, cognac, and vodka, and presented a gold whip to Ella. But he stopped visiting the circus."[15]

Josephy proved more than a protector for Ella. He gave her valuable advice regarding the horse as a performer and convinced her that she should break and train her own horses—since only in that way could she establish the necessary rapport. She became an expert trainer, and for the remainder of her career she trained her own mounts, one of the few women to do so. So well were her horses trained that, unlike most bareback riders, she eventually worked without a ringmaster during her act.

In 1901 Ella's path crossed with that of Frederick Ferber, a young cavalryman in the German army. She was with the Nouveau Cirque in Paris, and Ferber, paying an unauthorized visit to that city, saw the show—and Ella. She not only dazzled the entire audience, she almost hypnotized young Ferber with her beauty and grace. When, at one point, her horse shied and she was thrown into the box he occupied, Ferber found himself with his arms around the small girl. Explaining to him that she was not hurt, she returned to the ring and continued her performance. Ferber, however, was truly smitten and vowed that he would marry her—which he did three years later when his enlistment was up.

Ferber's courtship of Ella, however, was not an easy one. Johan raised objections, as did Ferber's father, a well-to-do brewer in Strasbourg. Undaunted, the young suitor followed Ella across Europe, finally catching up with her in London, where he persuaded her to marry him. Disowned by his own father but finally accepted by Johan, Ferber adopted the name Bradna. Thus, in 1903, Fred and Ella Bradna embarked for America and the Barnum and Bailey Circus. Ella was to perform, and Fred was to assist her. The transition from the European circus to the larger and more garish American circus was not an easy one for the Bradnas. Not only the living conditions caused some consternation, but also the fact that Ella was relegated to ring three in the performance. The young couple learned, as Bradna relates, that "the big show did something to people. Temperament developed with importance, athletes became artistes, suspicion and indignation supplanted cooperation and good will, the struggling novice of yesterday either was the favorite of today or gone. I have seen the greatest arrive and depart, and I must admit that few of them were strong enough to remain aloof from the intrigues of competition."[16] To the credit of Ella and Fred, they did remain aloof from such intrigues. Ella devoted her energies to her performance; and, in a very short time, James Bailey notified Bradna that Ella was to go into the center ring.

While Ella's career was developing in positive directions, Fred's was at a standstill. In a sense, he had no career at all. He was simply Mr. Bradna—and that name borrowed. Thus, when he was offered a position of equestrian director with a small one-ring circus in Central America, he and Ella left the Barnum and Bailey show and headed south. This interlude proved to be a productive one. Fred polished his skills as equestrian director, and Ella developed a new act in conjunction with Fred Derrick, another rider who had once been with Barnum and Bailey. When the Bradnas and Derrick returned to that show in 1906, this act was made a center-ring attraction and remained so for twelve seasons.

When the Ringling organization bought the Barnum and Bailey show, Fred was becoming more and more valuable as assistant to equestrian director William Gorman. He remained in that position until 1915, when John Ringling made him equestrian director of Barnum and Bailey. Eventually moving to the Ringling show, Fred Bradna was ever the classic equestrian director—regaled in black boots, white pants, formal coat, and top hat. A master at running a circus program and handling the plethora of temperaments among the performers, he was himself center-ring until he was injured in a tent blowdown on 12 September 1945 and went into retirement.

Fred and Ella Bradna shared center ring for twenty-nine years. Fred himself totaled forty-two years with the circus, thirty-one of them as equestrian director. Following his injury in 1945, the Bradnas retired to Sarasota, Florida. Fred died in 1955 and Ella, two years later. They were, in all respects, true circus.

The Riding Rudynoffs

When, on a summer day in 1913, Erna Seiffart, a pretty fifteen-year-old ballet dancer with the opera company of Zurich, Switzerland, went with some of the other dancers out behind the

Ella Bradna and Fred Bradna in the back yard.
Courtesy of the Pfening Collection.

opera house—where the Circus Knie had pitched its tents—to watch some of the circus performers practice their acts, she had no idea that she was about to move from the conservative, middle-class Swiss life that she knew so well to a vastly different one. But neither did she know that she was going to meet Rudolph Gebhardt, a twenty-year-old, talented, debonair bareback rider with the circus. "He was," as she recalled in 1981, "very handsome and could fly through the air like an airplane."[17] What more could a fifteen-year-old girl ask? It was simply love at first sight, and the fact that at the time she was engaged to a German aristocrat was no barrier to a heart so taken. Rudolph's feelings were the same, and a year later, when the circus returned, they were married.

To say that the last life-style that Erna's parents had in mind for their daughter was that of the circus would be an understatement. Indeed, they could not understand why she would even consider giving up a future of living in aristocratic luxury and status for that of traveling with a circus. "My father," she said, "thought I was marrying a gypsy. I was almost disowned, but we were in love."[18]

Born in Stuttgart, Germany, Rudolph himself came from a circus background, his father having been a bareback rider and his mother a wardrobe mistress with the Circus Schumann. A saddle chest was his bed "until I was ten years old. I've been a bareback rider, trapeze artist, tumbler, contortionist and ballet dancer. I've even played in the circus band. They taught you everything in those days."[19] By the age of six, he was performing daring tricks on the back of a horse in circuses in Russia, and it was with horses that he was destined to spend his life—performing on them or training them. And when he married Erna Seiffart, that was to be her destiny also.

Following their marriage, Rudy left the Circus Knie; and Erna, the ballet company. After Rudy taught Erna some Russian dances, they formed a dancing act, calling themselves Rudy and Erna Ernavitch—later changing that to Rudynoff, the name that was to be their professional identity for the remainder of their performing careers. Dancing in vaudeville houses, however, was not what Rudy had in mind for a permanent vocation. Like any good equestrian, he loved horses, and, leaving the vaudeville stage, he purchased some and returned to bareback riding.

Within six weeks, he taught Erna enough so that she could be part of the act. Standing on a jogging horse was quite a change from dancing on a firm floor, but Erna learned how to do it—so well, in fact, that Rudy would jump from a trampoline to her shoulders as the 104-pound girl stood on the rump of the moving horse. Her ballet-strong legs stood her, as it were, in good stead for this trick, as did Rudy's ability "to make himself very light."[20] Thus, in 1919, they joined the Circus Knie. For the next four years, they toured throughout Europe with their act.

In 1923, as happened with so many European performers at one time or another, the Rudynoffs got the opportunity to come to America to join Ringling Brothers. That first year, unfortunately, was not so pleasant as it might have been, because Erna, in a nasty fall from her horse, broke her leg in five places. On this occasion she was able to return to the act after a reasonable period of recuperation. In 1928, however, when the Rudynoffs were with the John Robinson Circus, Erna was performing a jump onto a fast-running horse when the horse stumbled and fell on her, breaking her arm and causing severe compound fractures of her right leg. The fractures were such that, even after numerous operations, doctors were unable to repair the damage—and the leg was amputated. At the time, it was feared that Erna's performing days were finished, and for five years they were.

Those years were trying indeed for the Rudynoffs. Erna's accident dimmed Rudy's desire to continue bareback riding, and he turned his efforts to training liberty horses for American Circus Corporation shows. Erna, in the meantime, remained in the winter-quarters town of Peru, Indiana, painfully learning the use of an artificial leg and caring for Rudy, Jr., who had been born in 1925. Finally, Erna decided that she "had to find something that I could do to get back into the act. I was afraid that if I didn't, Rudy might forget about me."[21] She need have had no worries there, but she did want to return to the ring. As plucky as she was beautiful, she did just that. In the summer of 1934, while Rudy was out with the now Ringling-owned Sells-Floto Circus, Erna found an old circus horse left in retirement at winter quarters and, piling up some boxes, managed to mount the aged steed. To her glee, she found she could ride—perhaps not as a daring bareback equestrienne, but certainly as a high-school or manège performer. More than that, however, she also taught two Great Danes to dance to music. Rudy, upon his return in the fall, was so pleased and proud that he bought her a five-gaited black thoroughbred stallion named Prince Dare.

This spectacular-looking horse, which Erna and Rudy trained to dance in step with the dogs, lived to be thirty-three years old—a life span equal to 115 years for a human. As he grew older, the hair around his eyes turned white. Erna would use mascara to blacken it and thus make Prince Dare look younger. One day, however, "everything was going wrong and we were late getting our act ready, so I had to go on without blackening his eyes. An old farmer in a seat near the entrance to the ring saw Dare and I heard him say, 'That horse has seen better days.' I said, 'You look like you've seen better days, too.'"[22]

The next season both Rudy and Erna went out with the Ringling show, he with his liberty act and she with Prince Dare and the dogs. In addition to his twelve-horse act, Rudy also trained sixty other horses, camels, and ponies that performed simultaneously in three rings. "Rudy found it harder to train the 24 girls that rode the horses than to train the horses," Erna recalled. "And to get the girls to practice. The horses would listen and do what he told them. The girls sometimes didn't, so he had to be strict with them. Sometimes they complained. But you don't see acts like that anymore."[23]

In the early spring of 1937, as the Ringling show was conducting its final rehearsals at Sarasota, Florida, fate once more dealt a blow to Erna. Helping Rudy train his horse Sir Lindy to dance with her dogs, she mounted the horse without changing Rudy's saddle for hers. Because the stirrups were longer than she was used to, her artifical leg slipped out and she fell once more, this time breaking her neck. Again her career was threatened, but even the waist-to-chin cast that she had to wear did not deter her from announcing that she would be riding within two months. After seventeen days in the hospital, she rushed to New York to join Rudy and the show, which was in its Madison Square Garden stand. Because of the radical climate change, she contracted a severe sore throat—almost a blessing in disguise. To treat her throat, the doctor removed the cast. With that out of the way, her next goal, of course, was to ride again. But Rudy had ordered all the grooms not to saddle a horse for her lest they be fired. Undeterred, Erna managed to get herself on horseback and to shock Rudy one day when she rode into the ring. It was barely eight weeks after her accident.

When labor problems forced the Ringling show to close in mid-season at Scranton, Pennsylvania, that year (1937), Rudy and Erna rented a huge stone barn in the Wisconsin river town of Cassville and began training new liberty and high-school acts. The old structure was filled daily with the rhythmic thud of horses' hooves and the sharp crack of Rudy's whip. But what really impressed the local gentry who came to witness the activities was the flaxen-haired Erna limping over to her horse, mounting it, and being transformed into what a Milwaukee newspaper called "a thing of grace and beauty" as she put the horse and the two Great Danes through their paces.

Unlike most circus families, neither Rudy nor Erna was particularly eager to have Rudy, Jr., join the act, but the inevitable happened. When the Ringling show was opening in Madison Square Garden in 1938, the management asked if the youngster could work an act of six little stallions. So, dressed in a bellhop's uniform, Rudy, Jr., became a performing part of the Riding Rudynoffs. And he was to remain a part of the act as long as they existed as a troupe. His own reminiscence of his early circus days provides insight into the life of a performer in the tented circus:

> In the circus we were always working, although we loved what we did. We never conceived of regulated time as most people do, watching the clock until quitting time. We practiced mornings, performed evenings, took care of the animals and equipment and had our big meal of the day late at night.
>
> During the time the circus was off the road, we developed new routines, repaired or prepared new costumes, changed props or equipment and practiced some more. We never had time for a vacation, but we didn't really need one because we were doing what we wanted. And no one ever talked about retiring. Circus people don't retire. Still, I did think about what it would be like to have some time all to myself.[24]

In 1956, Rudy, Jr., married Beverly Mueller, a member of a teeterboard act with the circus. Like his parents, Rudy, Jr., and Beverly knew immediately that they were for each other. Five days after their meeting, they were engaged, and nine months later they were married—making the Riding Rudynoffs four.

Two years later, the Rudynoffs decided to leave the Ringling show and form their own act, arranging their own schedules and bookings. After their first child was born, Rudy, Jr., and Beverly decided to leave show business. It had been a good life, but perhaps they, too, realized that the real circus was a thing of the past and that it had no part in their future. In quite a switch from the back of a horse or the center of a ring in a big top, Rudy, Jr., eventually became a vice president with the Maryland National Bank—where he is now.

Rudy and Erna continued performing, the latter riding until she was sixty-five; but mostly Rudy was training horses for others—circuses, other types of horse shows, and wealthy stable owners. "My father," says Rudy, Jr., "could have made a lot of money if he would have been a little less particular about where the horses performed. But he was a very proud man and thought more of his animals than of himself."[25] As befitted such a talented troupe, the Riding Rudynoffs were enshrined in 1969 in the Circus Hall of Fame in Sarasota—though it was left to Erna to make the acceptance. Rudy had died in 1968.

Erna enjoyed her later years, living an active life with Rudy, Jr., and Beverly and their children until her death in 1982. Asked on one occasion about her disability, she said, "Frankly, losing a part of your physical make up is a handicap at times. But I must point out that the world has denied me nothing on one leg that it would have given me on two. It's pretty much up to the individual."[26]

A Circus in Themselves

Of all the families that have performed in American and European circuses, none can surpass in talent, number, or longevity the Cristianis. Along with the Wallendas (see the next chapter), they are the only troupe covered in this book that still has members performing. But, like the tented circus, the Cristianis, too, have passed the zenith of their fame. When they were at their peak, however, they were truly the Royal Family of the circus—excelling in bareback riding, tumbling, juggling, performing on the high trapeze, and even clowning. There will, in all probability, never be another family, in the circus or out, quite like them.

Their rise began in nineteenth-century Italy, during the reign of King Victor Emmanuel II, with Emilio Cristiani, blacksmith to the king, and his oldest son, Pilade. Emilio found relaxation from his forge in gymnastics, and he taught what skills he knew to his small army of children and to anyone else interested. Pilade early caught the circus "bug," occasionally doing a strongman exhibition for touring companies passing through. Like many men, his eye was caught one day by a pretty bareback rider and trapeze artist, Anna Bottari. After an abbreviated courtship, they were married, planning to travel with the circus in which she performed. Emilio, however, had other plans: a Cristiani family circus. With what money he could muster and with animals from the royal zoo, courtesy of Prince Humbert, he and Pilade began Il Circo Cristiani—a circus that was eventually to become one of Italy's largest and best, with two shows on the road and a permanent arena in Modena. Many of Pilade's twenty-six children went on to achieve fame in the circus world, but it was Ernesto, his third eldest, who did most to further the Cristiani name—ultimately carrying it throughout Europe and America. In 1919, with his wife, Emma, he began his own small wagon show and continued propagating the Cristiani line with seven sons—Oscar, Daviso, Lucio, Benito, Belmonte, Mogador (Paul), and Parieto (Pete); and three daughters—Chita, Ortans, and Corcaito (Corky). (Three other girls died in infancy.) These were to become the foundation of the American branch of the Cristianis.

While Papa Ernesto ran his family with an iron hand, it was Mama Emma who was the invisible glue that kept the family together and functioning—once in later years referring to herself as "big chicken" and to Ernesto as "little rooster." Each member was possessed with his own individuality and his own share of Latin temper—and more than that, his own exceptional talent. Under the harshly disciplined training of Ernesto, they were to become, in the words of Richard Hubler, "a symbol of the circus in more than proliferation. Though they are a family, they have their outstanding individual stars. Lucio Cristiani is famous for his unmatched backward flip to a third horse; Belmonte has no peer in his adroit stunt riding; Daviso is noted for his training and dressage; Adolpho for his tumbling; Chita for her ballet; Ortans is the only girl in the world to accomplish the triple somersault into a chair."[27] Ernesto knew well that talent may be a birthright, but he knew, too, that it takes hard work to bring talent to fruition.

By the mid-1920s, the Cristianis' circus was so renowned that Ernesto had every reason to be proud of what he and the family had accomplished. Italian political affairs, unfortunately, were not running as smoothly as the Cristianis' circus. Benito Mussolini and Giacomo Matteotti were contesting against each other as would-be saviors of Italy, with the result that the nation was rocked with riots and unrest. Like so many others of the time, Ernesto cast his lot with Mussolini—if for no other reason than that circuses, if they were to be successful, needed order. Within two years, however, the whole problem would become academic, for the Cristianis would follow the pattern of so many European troupes and go to America.

By 1925, Lucio and Chita were probably the stars of the family, in terms of both talent and showmanship. When the circus was virtually destroyed by a strong wind in Sicily, Ernesto succeeded in getting his family booked by the Medrano Circus of Paris. There Lucio unveiled a new act that he had been preparing—a backward somersault from one horse over a second one to a third one. He knew tumbling well, of course, because Ernesto had demanded it; but horses were his primary interest. And in this act, the two came together—tumbling and horsemanship. Skillful as this first exhibition was, Lucio "improved it as time went on until at his height of performance a few years later he had the ring virtually filled with horses, caracoling and bouncing from one to the other, horse-to-horse, ground-to-horse, horse-to-ground, with what seemed to be insane energy and inspired direction."[28]

Like Lucio, Chita felt most alive on the back of a horse, where she was "in my own kingdom, my own boss, and no one could tell me what to do."[29] As happened to so many feminine circus stars, Chita became the object of fawning, gift-laden men of means, from cheese brokers to counts. Only one of her suitors reached any level of success—an engagement that lasted two years, before Chita broke it off in 1932. Many of those who sought her company were fended off by her ever-watchful brothers, not always to her liking. Still, her talent and beauty could not but awaken admiration and more in the minds of those who saw her perform. Paul Gallico wrote in 1948 that Chita was, when he first saw her about 1935,

> a circus queen, the star of the famous and wonderful family of rid-ing Cristianis and I was a nobody. She performed on the back of a milk-white horse. She had jet-black hair and two of the largest and most beautifully luminous black eyes ever set in a human face. She was as light and airy as thistledown, and when she poised on her toes on the rump of the big, lumbering circus horse, all in white, she was like a silver-and-black hovering dragonfly. Everybody who saw her fell in love with her. She was probably never aware of how many dreams she visited.[30]

From Paris, the Cristianis went to England, where they were an immediate hit with audiences and reviewers. Both Lucio and Chita were singled out for special praise. John Clarke, a Glas-gow reviewer, wrote in the most glowing terms of Lucio:

> Lucio first leaps and lands upright upon a trotting rosinback. He turns forward and backward somersaults (one of these somer-saults is thrown with both ankles tied) until a groom brings in a second horse.
>
> As the two horses career around the ring, Lucio performs an amazingly difficult trick. He lifts a hoop in his right hand, makes a backward somersault from the back of the first horse, passes his body through the hoop, and lands with beautiful precision and bolt upright upon the back of the second horse.
>
> While awaiting for the applause which the audience is appar-ently too thrilled to give, a third horse is brought into the ring. Now follows the *bonne-bouche* of the act. The three horses have been perfectly trained in synchronization. They trot with a rhythm of hoofbeat that causes their croups to rise and fall in unison. They are not this time, however, tail to tail but neck to flank. In other words, the third horse is rather more than a horse width to the left of the first horse.
>
> Twice around the forty-two-foot ring and—hold your breath! It happens. Lucio gives a glance backwards and leftwards, grace-fully somersaults and *lands upright on the back of the third horse.*[31]

This last trick, as mentioned previously, was Lucio's most famous.

The Loyal-Repensky troupe in a spectacular and
dangerous exhibition of bareback riding.
Courtesy of the Pfening Collection.

Three somersaulting Cristianis. From left to right:
Lucio, Belmont, and Paul.
Courtesy of the Pfening Collection.

Because they possessed such great talent and displayed it in such daring fashion, the Cristianis did not have to wait long for recognition from the Greatest Show on Earth. Having left England, they had gone to Belgium, where the Ringling organization's Pat Valdo signed them to a contract in 1933. They opened with the Big One the next year in Madison Square Garden, beginning long and illustrious careers with American circuses.

Although relegated to end rings at the beginning, their superb skills, particularly those of Lucio and Chita, did not go unnoticed—and they were soon center-ring. As one might expect, some jealousy was directed by other performers of the show toward the newly imported Cristianis. This jealousy occasionally manifested itself in efforts to distract the Cristianis during their acts or to turn the audience's attention away from them at crucial moments. It got so bad, says Hubler, that at one point, "the Cristianis simply ceased to perform in the middle of their show. They walked en masse to the next ring curb, sat down, and for five minutes applauded the other act with ironic enthusiasm."[32] Their greatest competition (and rivalry) came from the Loyal-Repensky troupe, a bareback-riding act of six girls. Though friends in Europe, the two families were anything but that in America.

Following the Ringling show's stay in New York, the Cristianis were sent to the Hagenbeck-Wallace Circus, one of the former corporation shows then under Ringling control, for the remainder of the 1934 season. This show was in all ways an excellent one—well managed and well stocked with talent. And the Cristianis, of course, did much to enhance its performances, with Lucio eventually becoming heavily billed and featured. The 1935 season was also spent with Hagenbeck-Wallace, but the next year the family was assigned to another Ringling-owned show, Al G. Barnes. Because this show toured primarily in the West, the Cristianis got to spend much time in California, an experience that they greatly enjoyed. Their reputation by this time was such that they were the feature of a short-subject film by Metro-Goldwyn-Mayer.

The next season, 1937, however, was a most unfortunate one for a number of American circuses (see the last chapter of this work). The Ringling show returned to quarters in the middle of the season, sending some of its best acts out to the Barnes show in South Dakota. When the latter closed a bit later, Ernesto took the family back to England and the Olympia in London for the 1938–39 winter season. The noted Bertram Mills, manager of the Olympia, commented on their success: "All the acts were good but I should say that their riding act was outstanding, as one of the brothers, Lucio, was in my opinion quite the best bareback rider in the world at that time and I should have to think very hard to be able to name anyone since who has been better."[33]

Back in America for the 1939 season, the Cristianis joined the Ringling show itself, where they remained through 1942, when their contract was mutually canceled. After an unsuccessful try at a Broadway show and some tours of army camps on an individual basis, the family came together again in 1944— twenty-one strong by that time—with the Cole Brothers Circus, a first-rate show that gave keen competition to Ringling. They remained with Cole Brothers until 1946, when they mounted their own truck circus. Playing upwards of 180 towns a season, this thirty-three-truck circus enjoyed profitable years through the 1950s. Disdaining John Ringling North's ideas of moderniz- ing the circus performance with Broadway trimmings (see the last chapter of this work), Lucio Cristiani, the manager and star performer, felt that children went to the circus for excitement and grown-ups for nostalgia. "If the grownups don't find what they remember from childhood," he said, "they feel cheated."[34] Thus, emphasizing classic circus acts of clowning and daredev- iltry, the Cristiani show, as described by John Kobler, "eschews chorines, balletic extravaganzas, fancy lighting effects and air conditioning. It prints no programs. The top price of admission ranges between one dollar and one dollar and a quarter, de- pending upon local entertainment taxes (children under twelve, fifty cents). Its windjammers (musicians)—five brassy virtuosos . . . play in shirt sleeves."[35]

Of the sixty performers with the show, thirty-six were mem- bers of the family; these included Ernesto's older brother Pie- tro's branch, who had come to America shortly after Ernesto's. That, more than anything else, probably best explains the suc- cess the circus enjoyed. Each had his or her own specialty, and each worked to sharpen that specialty to show-stopping form. While Lucio's backward somersault to a third horse was usually the *pièce de résistance* of the performance, no Cristiani act could ever have been called second rate.

In 1954, the Cristiani show did what no other circus had ever done—they went to Alaska, where they presented thirty-six performances, each of which was reported on the front page of the *Anchorage Times*. Hungry for a circus—much like Americans of earlier frontier days—the Alaskans flocked to see the show, with the result that the Cristianis cleared $100,000 for the tour. As good as it was, however, the Cristianis' show, like many others, could not maintain the necessary margin of profit and, after 1965, faded from the American circus scene. Belmonte Cristiani was right when, commenting on what the circus was coming to in America, he said that ultimately "the circus as the Cristianis have known it for generations will be dead."[36]

As mentioned earlier, it is highly unlikely that another family will ever duplicate the achievements of the Cristianis. The very change that brought the end of the tented railroad circus also brought an end to the kind of unrelenting family discipline and gnawing hunger to excel that was so much a hallmark of the Cristianis and that gave to thousands of circusgoers performances that were unsurpassed in skill and daring.

5

A Walk on the High Side

E VERY CIRCUS AERIAL ACT HAS ITS DANGERS, THOUGH perhaps none more than that of the equilibrist or wire-walker—especially the high-wire walker. Anyone who has ever tried to walk a fence rail or the iron rail of a railroad track knows the difficulty of maintaining his balance for any distance. If that strip of wood or iron is replaced by a strand of five-eighths-inch steel wire and then raised some thirty-five to forty feet in the air, to walk on it seems more than merely difficult; it seems virtually impossible, not to mention foolhardy. Yet, some of the performers mentioned in this chapter walked many miles during their careers on just such wires—and usually without nets. Not only courage, but strength, agility, and balance were signal characteristics of those who walked on the highwire in the big tops of the tented circus.

Tightrope-walking can be traced back to the early Romans, but, according to Vivienne Mars, the earliest written records begin about 1385, when M. Froissart, a Parisian, described a tightrope performance on the occasion of the marriage of Charles VI to Isabel of Bavaria:

> He tyed a cord upon the hyest house on the brydge of Saint Mychell over all the houses, and the outer ende was tyed to the hyest tower of Our Ladye's Church [Notre Dame]; and as the Queen passed by and was in the great strete, called Our Ladye's Strete [Rue Notre Dame], this sayd Master, with two brynninge candells in his hands, issued out of a little stage that he has made on the heyght of Our Ladye's Tower, synginge as he went upon the corde all alonge the great strete, so that all that sawe hym marvaille how it might be; and he bore still in hys hands the two brynninge candells so that he might be sene all over Parys, and two miles without the citie.[1]

Mars also points to performers in sixteenth- and seventeenth-century England. Still, it was Jean Francois Gravelet (1824–1897)—better known as the Great Blondin—who is generally considered as the first great wire-walker (manila rope, in his case). He is even credited by the *Encyclopaedia Britannica* with having turned a somersault on a rope stretched across the central transept of London's Crystal Palace while wearing stilts—a rather sensational trick, if indeed he did it. His fame, though, rests on his crossing Niagara Falls on a tight rope, the first time in 1859. The rope stretched some 1,100 feet between the United States and Canada, 160 feet high on one side and 270 on the other. He left from the American side, somersaulting and lying down on the way. Then, he retraced his steps; only this time he had a camera and tripod strapped to his back. Vincent Starrett describes the scene:

> Advancing upon the cable to a point some two hundred feet from shore, he lashed his balance pole to the rope, unstrapped his burden, adjusted it in front of him, and took a picture of the crowded shore line. This achieved, he shouldered his machine, unlashed his balance pole, and returned whence he had come, quickly to reappear again with another and heavier burden.
> "What under the sun?" asked the gaping people.
> In no time at all, the little man was seen coming toward America with a lumbering chair. When about a third of the distance had been covered, he placed his chair upon the rope, seated himself, and, crossing his legs, gazed around him with magnificent unconcern. A moment later he had adjusted two legs of the chair upon the rope and again seated himself. Coming closer to the American shore, he readjusted his chair and stood upright on it. At this point women began to faint.[2]

Blondin later repeated this feat a number of times, once blindfolded; once carrying a man, Henry Colcord, on his back; and once on stilts. A master of showmanship, Blondin would deck himself out in gaudy costumes, string his rope in all manner of improbable places, and then proceed to dance on it with baskets tied to his feet, play a fiddle, set up a small stove and cook an omelet, and even take his daughter across it in a wheelbarrow. He was truly the Prince of Manila.

While Blondin's antics on the tightrope were greatly applauded in America, such was not the case in England. The 22 November 1862 issue of *Punch* attacked both Blondin and Jules Leotard (a flyer) as imitators of monkeys:

> The taste for seeing fellow creatures put their lives and limbs in danger we cannot call romantic, but view rather as disgusting. It is not so much the skill of the performer that attracts audiences, as the peril he is placed in and the chance of seeing his neck broken. If monkeys could be trained to do the tightrope and trapeze business, they would soon eclipse the feats of Blondin and Leotard. Monkeys are by nature better fit for such achievements and having fewer brains than men, have no fear of falling. Surely, we repeat, it would be a good thing for humanity if acrobatic monkeys could be trained and exhibited. The lives of human beings then need not be endangered, and the public might be weaned from its present brutal taste for seeing men imperil their existence by attempting feats which monkeys could achieve with perfect safety, and far more ease and skill.[3]

The author of the above piece, of course, missed the point entirely as to what Blondin and Leotard were doing. That monkeys could do most acrobatics better than men was hardly at question. The question was how far could man push his own abilities back through the eons of evolution, as it were, to achieve feats that defied both reason and probability. The performers covered in this chapter, like Blondin and Leotard, did precisely that.

Three Stars of the Silver Thread

Although, to most spectators who witnessed wire acts under the big top, those acts performed on the highwire probably held more drama, there were, nevertheless, acts staged closer to the ground that required as much skill as those higher up. These acts were done on slackwires (wires with a lot of give), tightwires (wires with no give), and boundingwires (a more-or-less tight wire with a spring at one end). These wires were ten to twelve feet from the ground, and the acts themselves were usually done by single performers. Three of the more famous of these in America were the incomparable Bird Millman, Con Colleano, and Hubert Castle.

Bird Millman, though perhaps not the best woman performer on the tightwire in terms of technique and skill, was nevertheless a show-stopper in her own right. A vivacious slip of a girl, she had beauty and charm that, combined with the captivating personality that she projected, put her in the same class with Lillian Leitzel and May Wirth.

Born in 1888 in Canon City, Colorado, Millman came to know the circus at a tender age. Her parents had trapeze and wire acts in a small circus; and though, during her earlier years, she remained with her grandmother while her parents were on the road, Millman joined the circus and gave her first performance at the age of six. Resplendent in a silk dress and blue slippers, she made her debut with an act of trained ponies. Four years later, the family joined a carnival and presented a program of circus acts—ponies, iron jaw, trapeze, and wire. When her father was injured in a fall during his stint on the highwire one day, ending up in the hospital, Millman was the only member of the troupe available to perform, her mother having gone with her father to the hospital. After much persuasion on the part of the carnival manager, Millman mustered what tricks she could and presented a solo performance.

By the time she was twelve, Millman was doing nothing but her wire act, the act that would carry her to stardom. On the wire, "she didn't walk," writes Dixie Willson, "she danced! Laughed aloud as she bounded in the air with dancing toes that came down to whirl and waltz and pirouette so fast across the silver thread that it took your breath away! The weeks were few until her work on wire overshadowed everything else in the act."[4] Millman perfected her skills on the wire during two years of touring Europe with her parents—the culmination of which was a command performance before Kaiser Wilhelm of Germany in 1912:

> The performance was at twelve noon, under that famous Winter Garden sky, a dark blue ceiling specked with stars, the performance quite like any other excepting for the colorful and spectacular audience, men striking in military uniform, women in the smartest of afternoon dress, the Kaiser very solemn about it all, though most gracious and appreciative. I remember best, a tall quiet man standing in the wings beside the stage manager and carrying a full bloom American Beauty rose. As I passed him,

Bird Millman, a perfect picture of beauty, charm, and skill. *Courtesy of the San Antonio Public Library.*

going to my dressing room upon completing my act, he stripped the petals and dropped them in a shower over my head. I came to know him later. He was Franz Layhar.[5]

Signed by John Ringling, Millman returned to America and became an established center-ring attraction with Ringling Brothers in 1914 and later with the combined Ringling Brothers and Barnum and Bailey show. The first American tightwire artist to rely on no umbrella for balance, Millman presented a spectacular act as she danced and ran back and forth on a wire thirty-six feet long (instead of the usual eighteen), accompanied by songs from a chorus of eight voices. She, too, sang at certain points in the act. "To appreciate her act," says Bradna, "you had to see her imitators; they did the same tricks—but lacked that distinguishing asset of the true star, hypnotic charm."[6]

During the winter seasons, Millman performed at the famed Zeigfeld Roof in New York, as well as with the Greenwich Village Follies. It was at a performance of the Follies in Boston that she met Joseph O'Day, a Harvard graduate, who was to become her husband. For Millman, marriage and the circus were not compatible, and, at the height of her fame, she gave it all up one June day in Boston, not quite a year after she met O'Day:

> As I came out of the dressing tent after the afternoon show, getting together my courage to begin good-byes, a little crowd began gathering, performers, working men, band boys, officials from the front door, and presently little May Wirth, the world's greatest bare back rider, was presenting me with a silver plate, a gift from the show, a huge hand-carved silver flower, the names of the stars engraved on the petals, my name in the center; certainly my proudest possession and one I shall cherish always as a very real symbol of all the glad days and the sad ones between that first day in blue china silk, and that last day with the six foot boy of Boston.[7]

Millman lived a quiet, domestic life in Boston until O'Day died in 1931, at which time she returned to Canon City. She remained there until her own death on 5 August 1940.

Con Colleano was born in Australia (1904) of an Irish circus family named Sullivan. He later changed his name to Colleano. Like May Wirth, he loved horses as a child and was an accomplished equestrian before he was twelve, the age at which he began performing in his father's circus as a bareback rider and acrobat.

During these early years, he developed and performed a number of unusual stunts—the most notable being running double forward and backward somersaults and a running forward somersault to the back of a horse. At the same time, his sister Winnie was displaying considerable skill and daring on the single trapeze with her heel-catch act. Hanging on to the trapeze with her hands while it swung in a wide arc, she would let go and fling her body upward in a somersault and a simultaneous half twist, catching the bar with her heels. With stunts like these, it is not surprising that both Con and Winnie came to the Ringling show in 1925, where they began long and illustrious careers under American big tops.

No sooner did Colleano make his appearance on the Ringling lot than he performed, on a bet, a sequence of stunts that, though their difficulty might not have been fully appreciated by a circus audience, certainly impressed Colleano's fellow performers. These stunts included a roundoff, flipflop, and double back somersault; running double forward somersault; one-half twisting double somersault; back somersault with double twist; and jerk, flipflop, and back somersault onto a horse. On another occasion, he ran through twenty-eight complete units of acrobatics—each requiring a change of movement, a start, and a stop—in eight seconds. Even for someone who could run the hundred-yard dash in eleven seconds (as it is claimed Colleano could), this was an astonishing feat.[8]

But it was on the wire that Colleano made his greatest contribution to the circus performance—and that, the forward somersault. Having mastered virtually all of the tricks known on the tightwire, he decided to attempt what everyone said could not be done: the forward somersault. The difficulty with this trick is that it is impossible to see the wire when coming out of the somersault until just an instant before the feet hit it. A miscalculation meant the very real possibility of hitting the thin steel wire headfirst and receiving a brutally slashing cut. Colleano first tried the trick at the Hippodrome in New York City, and he very nearly ended his career:

The drummer rolled crescendo as Con bounced delicately for balance and confidence. His feet left the wire and he turned over. One foot touched the wire as he came out of the somersault, but he couldn't hold the balance and he had to jump to the ground. Twice more he tried it and twice more he missed. Something in the youth's expression communicated his grim determination to the orchestra and to the audience itself. In the wings the stagehands prayed silently for the fool with that impossible trick. They hoped he'd stop before he killed himself.

On the fourth try, Colleano struck the wire full with his chest and blood spurted forth. He had slashed himself on the saber-like steel cable—deadly springboard to oblivion or fame. The curtain rang down as the tightwire acrobat regained his feet and stood, bloody and dejected, looking at the rigging. The audience applauded his courage.

The orchestra struck up the music for the next act. They played it twice through, for Colleano was begging the stage manager to ring up the curtain and let him try it once more. The stagehands were pulling for him and so were other actors on the bill. At last the stage manager consented and the curtain lifted to reveal the tight-wire rigging outlined against a Spanish backdrop.

Colleano, like a determined athlete and without fanfare of any kind, climbed the framework and danced out onto the wire. His legs gave him the momentum and his head went over and his feet found the wire. A tense moment followed, while the acrobat fought to hold his balance and then the knowledge of his accomplishment broke over the whole theatre in a frenzied wave of shouting and applause.[9]

Like Bird Millman, Colleano disdained the use of the balancing umbrella, the first man to do so. For someone who has never walked a tightwire, the value of an umbrella may be difficult to appreciate; but its absence forced Colleano, as it did Millman, to rely exclusively on his own sense of balance. His bodily control, however, was extraordinary and his sense of style and showmanship unrivaled. Even when he missed the forward somersault, notes Bradna, "the audience did not know it, for he seized the wire in falling, turned a giant swing completely over it, and lit on his feet; it looked like another trick."[10]

After ten consecutive years with the Ringling show, Colleano performed with various American circuses until 1960, returning on two occasions to Ringling. Considering the tricks that he did on the wire, it is remarkable that Colleano was never seriously injured. A twisted back, a broken bone in his heel, and a fractured hand were the only injuries that caused him to miss performances: not a bad record for someone who, at one time, aspired to be a musical comedy star. What a loss to the circus that would have been.

Unlike Colleano and Millman, Hubert Castle did not perform on the tightwire, but rather on the boundingwire. This wire would give about ten inches under a man's weight, and the spring attached to one end made it rather unforgiving. Landing on it incorrectly would cause the performer to be shot off it like an arrow from a bow.

A country kid out of Enid, Oklahoma, as he referred to himself, Castle saw Bird Millman perform when the Ringling show played Enid in 1919. At the time he was seven years old, and his name was Hal Smith. In the next two months he learned not only how to walk the length of the clothes wire in his backyard, but also how to balance a chair on the wire and sit in it. Within five years, he and his childhood friend Bunny Dryden were being paid to perform at various gatherings in Enid. And it was, of course, only a matter of growing a bit older before the boys joined a circus. Two years older was enough, and in the summer of 1926, Hal and Bunny, at fourteen and fifteen years of age, respectively, signed a contract with Orton Brothers Circus for several acts twice a day—for sixty dollars a week, good pay for two youngsters in those days. Billed as Smith and Dryden, the boys did wire-walking, acrobatics, horizontal bar feats, and strongmen exhibitions.

In 1928, Smith and Dryden joined the small show that Hal's father had bought. This show failed before the season was over, financially wiping out the elder Smith. Hal finished the season with the John S. Silver Circus, changing his name to Hal Silver— a name that he felt more in keeping with his performance on the wire. There followed tours with various circuses until he finally joined the Ringling organization, performing with the Al G. Barnes-Sells-Floto combine. It was at that time that John Ringling, wanting to feature him as an import from England, convinced him to change his name to Hubert Castle.

In 1935, when he was with the Tom Mix Circus, Castle met and married Mary Tanner—about the same time that he and

Bunny Dryden split up. The latter had switched to the highwire and was, at least in Castle's mind, "the best high-wire performer that ever lived."[11] Whether he was or was not, Dryden met his death when he fell while doing giant swings over and under the highwire. "He was still spinning when he hit the ground," said Castle. "Some scissorbill, old Bunny."[12]

Castle himself was some kind of "scissorbill." He duplicated Colleano's forward somersault; he stood on his hands on the wire, then sprang back to his feet, facing the other direction; he did a back somersault through a hoop; and he did various tricks with a unicycle on the wire—just to mention a few of his feats.

Though he never reached the level of Con Colleano, Castle did not lack skill or daring. The many fractures that he suffered in falls—left arm (twice), ribs, collar bone, a leg, a wrist, an elbow, and a shoulder—attest to the latter. He never worried about serious injury, according to J. Ryan, until he incorporated a full gainer from the bar to the wire into his act. The closest call he had, reports Ryan, was in Houston, Texas: "He used to make his entrance as a drunk—stagger along the wire, lurch around, and finally take a fourteen-foot fall on the back of his neck in the ring. That night he lit half a degree crooked and smacked himself silly. He finished the act by instinct, but his strained neck muscles wouldn't let him sleep for three weeks."[13]

For Castle, it was worth it, broken bones and all. His trouping took him over almost half the world—not bad for a country kid out of Enid, Oklahoma. "And besides," he said, "when I step on my kid's roller skates in the dark, I know how to spill."[14]

Millman, Colleano, and Castle, with their escapades on the tightwire, did much to liven the programs of the shows with which they performed. Anyone who ever saw them would vouch for that. But, difficult and dangerous as they were, those acts did not catch the circusgoer's breath in his throat as did the acts of those troupes that risked their lives on the highwire. An additional twenty-five or thirty feet made all the difference.

Skirting Eternity's Brink

"You're gonna come down," Harold Alzana said quietly to this author as we stood by an eight-foot-high practice wire in his spacious backyard in Sarasota, Florida, on a warm March day in 1981. He was referring to anyone who has the nerve to be a highwire-walker, or any other aerialist for that matter. This matter-of-fact statement was not meant to be anything other than that—for during his colorful career, Alzana "came down" enough times that he should know.

Born Harold Davis in the coal fields of Yorkshire, England, Alzana joined his father Charles in the Maltby Main Collier at fifteen. A short but extremely powerful man, Charles was a frustrated acrobat and tumbler who saw his life being wasted in the depths of the mine because his wife had objected to the vagaries of a performing career. He took much pleasure, however, in teaching Harold and his other children various acrobatic and tumbling tricks. Possessing the same stocky build as his father, Harold's muscular strength grew as he did—until at eighteen he could hop down a flight of stairs on one hand and could lower his body parallel to the ground in a two-hand balance.

Charles saw in his son the possibility of becoming what he himself had yearned so much to be—a performing acrobat. Harold, too, had the desire and the ambition to use his bodily skills as a vehicle of escape from the mines. The problem was that, grim though it might be, mining provided a more-or-less dependable income; performing as an acrobat or a tumbler was not so dependable and certainly not so remunerative. Still, Harold carried on with his training, eventually putting up a wire in the backyard to try to imitate what the Great Blondin had done. After two years of practice on the wire, Harold felt that he was good enough to give performing a serious try. Thus, with his sisters Elsie and Hilda, who also could walk the wire, he began contracting for performances at various fairs and celebrations around Sheffield—billing the troupe as the Great Alzanas. The name came from Harold's nickname, Al, and Elsie's middle name, Annie. "If you didn't sport a foreign name in England," he pointed out, "you couldn't get a job."[15] Enthusiastic for, and proud of, his children, Charles accompanied them as their net. If they fell, he would break their fall with his own body—a feat that he eventually did have occasion to perform.

In 1939, Alzana convinced a neighbor girl who often practiced with the troupe that she would be safe perched on his shoulders as he walked a fifty-foot-high wire in Kent. She was—and in 1941 she married him, becoming a permanent part of the Great Alzanas. Unlike many wives, Minnie Alzana never feared for her husband's life. "His sisters don't like to watch him," she said. "I'm just the opposite. I don't want him killed, but if it happens, I guess I'll just watch it."[16]

World War II forced the Alzanas to reduce their performances drastically. Harold was called upon to work seven shifts a week in the mines and thus had little time, not to mention energy, for wire-walking. Still, he found time to practice—even occasionally performing for special morale-boosting affairs.

Following the war, the family regrouped and began performing on a more regular basis. Because their act was getting better, the Alzanas, especially Harold, gained favorable notice throughout England, and they were signed by the Blackpool Tower Circus. In the meantime, Harold had sent some photographs of the troupe to John Ringling North in hopes that the latter might consider them for his show. North was interested enough to send Hans Lederer, one of his agents in Europe, to see the Alzanas perform. The performance he saw was carried out in the Davis backyard on a winter afternoon, but he was impressed—so much so that he signed the troupe on the spot. Thus, the Alzanas joined the vast pilgrimage of European circus performers to America and the Greatest Show on Earth—opening with Ringling in Madison Square Garden for the start of the 1947 season.

The act that impressed the agent was, according to Greg Parkinson, "full of treachery and novelty."[17] Alzana opened the act by walking up a forty-five-degree incline cable to his five-eighths-inch highwire, where he immediately proceeded to dance the Charleston, turn cartwheels, do a handstand on one arm, and finish up that segment of the act with giant swings around the wire. These swings were not as easy as they might have appeared. The whip of the wire was quite strong enough to send Alzana flying had he lost his grip—something that he did do once in an Aberdeen, Scotland, theater, ending up in the orchestra pit on top of a microphone, and with a nasty cut on his head to show for his effort.

Alzana had never done the walk-up in a real performance, and he was not intending to in New York. North, however, had seen him practice it in Sarasota, so on opening night he asked Alzana about it, hinting strongly that it would be an eye-catching feat. Never one to back away from a challenge, Alzana donned

The Alzanas display a unique bit of daring on the high
wire. *Courtesy of the Pfening Collection.*

rubber shoes, and up he went. "I slipped off about six times," he
recalled. "But it was a pretty good idea that just cropped up, like.
It was one of the biggest thrills they'd ever seen here."[18] Indeed
it was, and it continued to be as Alzana made it a regular part of
his act. He embellished it by adding a parasol that he would
wave around and sometimes drop to add a bit more drama. The
rubber shoes gave way to elkskin boots, not only because of
looks but also because they permitted a better feel for the cable.

Like others who traded the more leisurely life of the European circus for that of the more frenetic American variety, Alzana found the pace more taxing than what he had known
before. Two shows a day, day after day, could become a grind
even to the most dedicated performer. Whether it was weari-
ness or just carelessness, Alzana made an almost fatal mistake
in Marion, Ohio, that first season. He reached for a rope behind
his pedestal, with the intention of returning to the ground—
which he did, but much more quickly than he had planned. The

rope was not secured to anything, and Alzana felt a deep thrill, "like going down a fast elevator," he said.[19] He fell forty feet, landing squarely on his feet and breaking both heel bones. Within six weeks, he hobbled to the ring on crutches, climbed to the wire, performed, climbed down, and departed on the crutches—explaining later that he used only his instep on the wire, never the heel.

Alzana became a sensation that first year in America. John Ringling North could not have been more pleased with the new addition to the show, referring to Harold as "the greatest and most foolhardy high-wire artist who ever lived."[20] On the wire, without the benefit of a balancing pole, Alzana would walk, hop, run, pivot, leap, skip rope, and whatever else would come to his mind—a whirling dervish of the highwire, whose whole performance, in Edward Peyton's view, was "punctuated by agonizing moments of suspense as what seem almost certain falls are nipped by split-second recovery. Even the most fatalistic observers find their palms wet and their emotions stampeded. Thrills, after all, are what they've come for, and Alzana's no man to let them down."[21]

Some of those near falls were planned and others were not. One never knew for sure whether Alzana was faking it or whether he really had made a mistake and was fighting for his life. Either way, he was strong enough and agile enough that as long as the wire was within reach, he would grasp it somehow—with hands, armpits, or hooked knees—and hang on. On the last day of the 1947 season in Miami, however, Alzana could not grasp the wire and hang on—with the result that the audience did indeed receive a thrill and Harold and Hilda Alzana were nearly killed.

One of the highlights of the Alzanas' act saw Harold riding a bicycle, with his sister Hilda standing on the rear of the bicycle and his wife, Minnie, and his other sister, Elsie, swinging on two trapezes hanging from the wheels of the bicycle. The whole configuration added up to six hundred pounds of weight that Alzana had to propel across the wire. This was the one instance when he used a balance pole. And it was the balance pole, ironically, that almost did them in. As they were moving slowly across the wire, Harold felt the pole catch on something. Glancing to the side, he saw a loose rope hanging from the top of the tent entangling the pole. Minnie and Elsie were safe because the bicycle had a safety clip that held its wheels to the wire. As the bicycle swung down under the wire, however, Harold and Hilda fell. In such a situation, the first thing any wire-walker does is to go for the wire and try to hang on. Although Harold could not reach the wire because the pole got in the way, he thought that Hilda would get hold of it. She did not. "Going by," he said, "I saw Minnie's face. She was white as a ghost. 'You're falling,' she told me. I saw her plain as anything. Then the people were screaming everywhere."[22] Charles Alzana reacted quickly, and at the instant before his son and daughter would have hit the ground, he hurled himself at them to break their fall. And he no doubt saved their lives. All three—father, son, and daughter—were hospitalized: Charles with torn neck muscles and Harold and Hilda with broken backs.

If anything, the fall in Miami made the Great Alzana even greater. After four months of recuperation, he was again cavorting on the highwire with his usual flair and dare. Until near the end of the 1948 season, he carried the act alone in what amounted to a center-ring single. Hilda returned for a short while late in the season, but her primary interest was in a French aerialist, whom she married and eventually accompanied to another circus. As a troupe, the Alzanas broke up; but, in the years that followed, Alzana himself continued the act "high and alone." Dale Shaw describes this period:

> Disheartened, Papa Alzana stuck by his son for awhile, and watched with growing fear the chances Harold was taking. A weakness, now that he was alone, was the hypnotic effect the crowd seemed to have for him. Alzana got on the wire, and he stayed too long; his descent down the angled guy wire to the ground could be a masterpiece of quivering uncertainty that was far from phoney. His legs were exhausted. Periodically, he would fall on the incline, but somehow, always manage to nip around and grab the wire in time. When he was up above on the main wire, he used a variety of trick "saves" to avoid taking the big tumble.[23]

Alzana knew that the audiences that watched his act had ambivalent feelings: they wanted to see him "break his neck," yet they did not. There is a thrill in seeing someone "skirt eternity's brink," but there is a sickness in the pit of the stomach at the sight of a crumpled figure on the ground. When he was practicing his wizardry on the wire, spectators may have viewed Alzana as something unreal—not flesh and blood as they were. But someone falling becomes human very quickly. "You have to take chances," he told this author in his backyard that March day in 1981. "If you don't, they won't watch you."[24] They watched Alzana all right.

One of Alzana's most difficult tricks was the rope skip. Because this feat required a wire that had some spring to it, Alzana chose a livelier three-quarter-inch wire over the usual five-eighths-inch one used by most highwire troupes. He started skipping at the center of the wire with a rope six feet long; then he doubled the rope and doubled his skipping. At this point, his hands were so close to his body that they were essentially useless for balance. But also at that point, he would try a reverse skip—an extremely difficult trick to perform. "I never know which way the cable's going to throw me," he once said. "There've been times when I miss and catch it in ridiculous positions, with my hand up behind my head."[25] On several occasions, he even tried a triple skip: "I get close in to the stage. I single skip till I get a level one, and I give a hell of a skip and bang it around three times. It always throws me somewhere, and the people don't realize what I've done. They think it's a double."[26]

One might think, in view of the daredeviltry Alzana displayed on the highwire, that he was a fast liver on the ground also. Not true. If ever there was an athlete who took care of his body, it was Harold Alzana. He ate one meal a day (at noon), with a small snack in the evening, and slept eleven hours each night. At five feet four inches tall and 145 pounds, he was the epitome of muscular agility (and still is). Never a visitor to the pie car or a poker table, the quiet, soft-spoken Alzana spent his free time repairing watches for his fellow performers, and always had a bag full of them during the season. It was a therapeutic release—something as far removed from the wire as he could find.

But he was never very far from the wire. Even between shows during the season, Alzana would go aloft for practice and amusement. While other acts might be practicing on the floor of the big top, Alzana would be in his own high world, putting on, as Bernard Peyton describes it, his own private exhibition:

High overhead, Harold Alzana, inconspicuous in rolled-up jeans and flannel shirt, unattended by spotlights, capers blithely to the center of the wire. He hovers there a second, surveying the patchwork activity below. Then he begins to bounce into a step that might be a Charleston. He stops, retreats to one stage, abruptly runs toward the other, stumbles and catches its railing. He does this perhaps a dozen times, each time stumbling in the same place. Intentional falls are popular, and Harold is proud that even Minnie often cannot tell his fake slips from the real ones.

Back at the center of the wire, he drops to all fours, then tries a one-arm handstand. After this he carefully hooks his toes over the wire, hangs inverted and begins to sway. When his toes tire, he slowly reaches up and pulls himself out of danger. He sits on the wire, stretches and wiggles his toes. After an hour he'll probably come down.[27]

Like anyone who lives with danger, Alzana began about 1955 to worry about falling—something he had never before done. His father had returned to England, where, in a wood-cutting accident, he lost his left hand. Not overly superstitious, Alzana nevertheless saw this incident as a bad omen—and perhaps it was. In 1958, at the Ringling opening in Madison Square Garden, his right knee failed him on the wire, and he fell. Bob Russell, the rigger who, like Charles Alzana, was below to break any fall, did just that; and Alzana suffered only a broken wrist. At a special Ringling opening in Miami in 1960, during the rope-skip, his legs got tangled with the rope, and once more the Great Alzana flirted with death. But Bob Russell was there again to break the fall. A broken collarbone and broken ribs were the only price Alzana paid that time. It was enough, however, for Ringling manager Art Concello. He demanded that Alzana use a net from then on, even though the performer felt that the net was not only useless as a safety measure, but that it also took some of the drama away from the performance.

Alzana was forty-two years old at that time, and he knew it was time to wind down his career. Perhaps, as some said, he was accident prone or he had lost his touch. He would never believe either theory; nevertheless, he and Minnie began a restful life in Sarasota, broken only by occasional bookings for Harold's act. In 1981, in his sixties, he was still in superb physical shape, could still do a handstand with no effort, and could still walk the practice wire in his backyard. He gave up performing, he said, "because they don't want to pay you enough now to take the risks."[28] An opportunity to go to Hawaii several years ago for a two-week booking, for example, would have netted only about two hundred dollars. He once thought that eventually the wire would get him, but it did not. He proved that he was stronger than the wire—that he was the Great Alzana.

The Wallendas—"Aerialists Supreme"[29]

"No, I don't believe I will ever retire," mused Karl Wallenda in December 1970. "To be on the wire is to live. Everything else is just waiting."[30] These words by the patriarch of the Wallenda troupe of highwire-walkers were more prophetic than perhaps even Karl himself ever imagined.

Like Cristiani, Wallenda is a name that is thought by many to be synonymous with the circus. Not so prolific as the Cristianis, the Wallendas were certainly no less talented. Their story has probably been told more than that of any other circus troupe. As the guiding hand behind the achievements of the troupe, Karl Wallenda brought them to the pinnacle of highwire-walking. Not only a daring performer with a flair for showmanship, he was, writes Greg Parkinson, "the greatest innovator of high-wire routines in the nearly 200-year history of the modern circus."[31]

Descended from a Bohemian circus family, Karl Wallenda was born on 21 January 1905. His grandfather Karl, along with two brothers, operated a small circus that traveled the border between Germany and Belgium. The elder Wallenda had four children, three daughters and a son, and all of them were active in the circus. Englebert, Karl's father, was quite versatile, performing as a trapeze artist, an animal trainer, and a clown. He married Kunigunde Jameson, who performed on the slackwire. When Karl was six, his parents separated, leaving Karl and his younger brother Willie at a Catholic boarding school for a year. Karl then joined his mother and older brother Herman, while Willie went with his father. Following her separation from Englebert, Kunigunde had joined her mother's performing arena, where she met George Grotefent. Although he was sixteen years younger than she, they were married. Mounting their own small arena show, the Grotefent Cavalcade of Musical Stars, they loaded Karl and Herman into the wagon and went on the road.

Times were not easy, but, with the coming of World War I, they became even more difficult. George was taken into the army, and Kunigunde and her children stayed in Gros Ottersleben, a small German town of 13,000. By this time, three more children had been added to the family. Karl, now ten, had his own balancing act and was performing in beer gardens and restaurants, sometimes working as many as twenty places in one evening. It was a grueling existence for a youngster, but it did provide Karl the opportunity to sharpen his skills in acrobatics and balancing.

Upon George Grotefent's return from the army, he immediately began plans for a new show, a small circus. Looking much like a band of gypsies, the family took to the road once more. Karl was truly in his element, performing handstands four chairs high and working on the trapeze and the Roman rings. The only problem was a financial one. As a manager, Grotefent left much to be desired, and the show soon folded. Thus it was that Karl went to work in a coal mine—an experience that strengthened more than ever his resolve to get back into show business at the first opportunity.

Fortunately, that opportunity came in the spring of 1921, when Karl, along with Herman and George, signed with the Circus Malve, a show that played the towns of northern Germany. Not only did Karl perform with the circus, he also had to work as a roustabout and travel ahead of the show occasionally to place posters and placards announcing its visit. At the end of the year, Karl was ready for whatever might come his way, as long as it was show business. What came was an advertisement from Circus Busch in Breslau for a young man to do handstands and aerial work. So sixteen-year-old Karl was off to Breslau, unaware that he was about to embark on what was to be his life's career—walking the highwire.

With Circus Busch, Karl met Louis Weitzman, a wire-walker who had just returned from a Russian labor camp in Siberia. When Weitzman told Karl that he was to do a handstand on his, Weitzman's, feet as Weitzman did a handstand on the highwire, the youngster's "heart plummeted to my boots and my appetite promptly sank with it. A handstand on his feet at 60 feet in the air? My god, I did understand. He wasn't kidding when he said *sensational.* That Russian prison had driven the poor fellow crazy!"[32] Crazy or not, Weitzman drove Karl hard in practice on a wire two feet high; and, within two weeks, Wallenda, the wire-walker, was born—sixty feet up in an old Breslau vaudeville house called the Zeltsgarten.

The Weitzman Troupe consisted of Weitzman, Karl, and a nineteen-year-old girl named Margarita—and a successful troupe it was, playing throughout much of Europe. In Budapest, Karl met Magdalena Schmidt (Lena), a woman seven years his senior. They were attracted to each other, so the troupe was expanded to four. Margarita and Lena did not get along, however, and their quarrels soon involved Karl and Weitzman. There was nothing to do but split up, and that is what they did. In Dresden, Karl and Lena struck off on their own, finally ending up with Circus Gleich.

Gleich demanded three people in the act, so an advertisement was placed for an aerialist. Answering the ad was Joe Geiger, who wanted to be a flier but whom Karl transformed into a wire-walker. He was followed by Karl's brother Herman. Now Karl could begin fashioning an act with more spectacular dimensions to it. Among the tricks developed were Karl standing on a shoulder bar linking Joe and Herman; the same trick with Lena standing on Karl's shoulders; and a three-high vertical pyramid. The last was a first for highwire acts.

About this time, Karl met Martha Schepp, a dancer with Circus Busch, and, much to Lena's chagrin, married her. Lena's feelings toward Karl were so strong that she could not possibly remain with the troupe. When she left to return to her home, Helen Kries was added—and the Great Wallendas were on their way, a way that eventually led to Cuba, where their performance not only received a glowing review in the *Billboard* but also caught the attention of John Ringling. Thus on 5 April 1928, the Great Wallendas opened with Ringling in Madison Square Garden—the first of sixteen complete seasons with that show (1928–1938 and 1942–1946).

Given a solo spot in the show—something reserved for only the best of the Ringling performers—the Wallendas were filled with both anticipation and anxiety. Also on the show were such center-ring attractions as Alfredo Codona and Lillian Leitzel, not to mention the many other quality acts that were always a part of a Ringling performance. But the Great Wallendas lived up to their name that opening night and more or less stole the show. As Greg Parkinson notes, "when the Great Wallendas took their last step onto the platform and began to disassemble their three-high pyramid, the New York audience burst forth in a thunderous ovation of cheers and applause that ended only after Equestrian Director Fred Bradna escorted the four back into the ring 15 minutes later for an unprecedented bow."[33] It was one of the proudest moments in Karl Wallenda's life—and one he never forgot.

Probably no other act, before or since, ever received more extravagant praise than did the Great Wallendas. The *Morning Telegraph*'s review of their performance the next day is an example:

> This combination of three men and a youthful looking maiden, billed as the Wallenda Troupe, hold the seventeenth spot and the entire floor to themselves. They also hold the attendance breathless during the short routine, probably the most sensational exhibited here or anywhere. Working on a tight strand of wire, stretched from the base of each gallery row, directly over and across the center ring, high up near the pivot beams of the structure, the Wallendas have nothing beneath them but the tan bark. The slightest mis-cue rated an ambulance call, yet their repertoire of stunts looked difficult enough on the ground.
>
> Working with heavy balancing poles, they offered a chair stand on the wire; a cycle ride across, a head stand and a two-high. The thriller came with a stunt that built into a three-high and walk-off, the latter staged about fifteen feet from the platform. This is probably the most daring specialty ever exhibited and will undoubtedly earn the palm.[34]

From New York, the Ringling show moved to Washington for its first stand under canvas. Martha arrived from Europe and joined Karl in Washington. It was here that the Wallendas were introduced to the real American tented circus—the acres of white canvas, the multitudes of people and animals, and the circus train. Getting used to American ways was no easy matter, and complicating things was the strain that had developed in Karl's relationship with Martha. Not a part of the act, she naturally felt left out. As for Karl, the only place that he found contentment was on the wire. As time went on, the situation improved, particularly when the Wallendas were given a wagon for their dressing room and a private compartment on the train and when Martha began taking part in the show spec and Ella Bradna's Act Beautiful.

In the off-season of that first year in America, the Wallendas toured with a group of performers organized by Fred Bradna to play a number of Shrine Circus dates. In St. Paul, Minnesota, the Wallendas had a brush with tragedy. As Helen was preparing to stand upright on Karl's shoulders as part of the three-high trick, her concentration was distracted by the sound of an explosion. Losing her balance, she fell some forty feet onto a light box, which, because it broke her fall, perhaps saved her life. Helen was bruised and battered but not seriously hurt; and in a shaky but confident voice, she assured Karl that she was not afraid to continue the act.

With the 1929 season, John Ringling hired another wire act—the Gretonas—to feature alongside the Wallendas. If one act was good, he surmised, two would be even better. He forgot, however, the professional jealousy that lurks just beneath the surface in almost every person in show business. Certainly Karl was annoyed at having to share the spotlight, but he was even more annoyed that the Gretonas' act was almost a duplicate of his own. Thus began an almost deadly competition between the two troupes, each trying to outperform the other. "It's fortunate they only lasted a season," said Karl of the Gretonas, "as it was dollars to doughnuts which troupe would first see the emergency ward. We'd experiment with a new trick, they'd attempt to repeat it and we'd ante the danger a notch. It was a murderous poker game played on two strands of cable 40 feet above the heads of an unsuspecting public."[35] For the 1930 season, the Gretonas were assigned to the Ringling-owned Sells-Floto Circus—and the Great Wallendas were once again the solo wire act.

During the 1930s, the Wallendas gained acclaim as a premier highwire act not only in America but also in Europe. Several times Karl booked the troupe for winter dates in England and on the Continent, including a performance before Adolf Hitler in Berlin's Wintergarten in 1933. By this time, virtually the entire family was a part of the troupe. Brother Willie, George Grotefent and his son Artur, Helen's brother Phillip, and Herman's wife, Lu-Lu, made up the second unit of the troupe, the one that replaced the Gretonas on the Ringling show.

Instead of returning to America, Martha remained in Germany with her daughter Jenny. The relationship she and Karl had known earlier had now cooled, writes Morris, "to that of brother and sister. The thrill had gone. The parting was largely unspoken and they remained firm friends. She was a frequent member of the Wallenda Troupe throughout the years, as, happily, was Karl's daughter Jenny and, in turn, her children, Tino and Delilah."[36] The way was now clear for Karl to marry Helen Kries—which he did in 1935.

One of the more exciting tricks added to the Wallenda repertoire in the 1930s—one that many thought could not be done—was called the "Pinwheel of Death." In this trick, Karl and Herman were connected by a shoulder bar to which Helen and Herman's wife held with their hands behind their backs, spinning in synchronized opposite directions. Such a trick is illustrative of Karl's unceasing efforts to keep the act fresh and even on the edge of the impossible.

Bicycles were an integral part of most highwire acts. Although, to a circus audience, pedaling a bicycle across a wire may look very easy, to Karl Wallenda bicycle tricks were among the most dangerous, because in any kind of mishap the performers will fall outward, away from the wire and a possible handhold. Only quick thinking and superior agility and strength can prevent a tragedy—as the Wallendas proved in 1934 in Akron, Ohio, when their rigging slipped during the bicycle three-high. When the wire dropped nearly six feet, bicycles, chairs, and people went flying. Karl grabbed the wire with his hands and miraculously caught Helen, who had been on his shoulders, with his legs. Herman and Joe, too, grabbed the wire. All managed to hold on until a safety net was put in place. Karl had held Helen so tightly with his legs that she was unconscious. Again, the Wallendas escaped serious injury.

After the economically disastrous circus season of 1938, the Wallendas returned to Europe. World War II interrupted what might have been a longer stay, however, and the troupe sailed back to America. For the next couple of years, Karl booked their

act wherever he could—Shrine circuses, fairs, Cuban performances. In 1942, the Wallendas rejoined the Ringling show, then
under the direction of John Ringling North, and remained with
that circus until 1946.

That year, Karl approached North with his idea of a three-
high, seven-man pyramid, a dream that had been with him
since 1938. This pyramid involved four understanders, linked
two each by shoulder bars; two men, linked by shoulder bars,
standing on the bars of the bottom four; and a girl topmounter
standing on a chair—the entire ensemble to move slowly from
one end of the wire to the other. Old John Ringling might have
leaped at the idea, but not his nephew John North. Relations between Karl and North were not of the best anyway, so the latter's
turndown of the new trick was the proverbial straw—and the
Wallendas left Ringling for good. The seven-man pyramid, however, was still in Karl's plans. Driving his troupe harder than
ever in practice, he refused to accept the idea that the "seven"
might be an impossibility. Finally, success! "The Wallendas,"
writes Morris, "repeated the act with total perfection ten times
in two hours. Not a false movement nor one awkward step. Ex-
hilaration overcame them. In the following weeks they pushed
the feat to the unbelievable four levels of humanity—*an eight-
man pyramid upon the wire.* But Herman vetoed it on technical
grounds. The rigging had not been made which would sustain
such stresses."[37]

After a brief and unsuccessful fling at their own circus, the
Wallendas trouped with a number of shows, regularly performing the seven-man pyramid. Even so, times were not easy. The
personnel of the troupe was not stable, and what was once
strictly a family act became a more heterogeneous one—with
names like Mendez, Guzman, McGuire, Murillo, Kinkead, and
Thatcher. The new people required painstaking training. Then,
often as not, they would leave for more lucrative opportunities
to exhibit their talents. Still, Karl went on with his constant and
patient search for the right kind of recruits for the act.

Wherever the Wallendas performed, it was the climactic
seven-man pyramid that received the greatest plaudits of the
crowd. Proud that he had created it and pleased that no other
troupe had duplicated it without a net,[38] Karl was at the height
of his career. Then came the evening of 30 January 1962, at the

Shrine Circus in Detroit—an evening that was to put the name Wallenda on virtually everyone's lips—circus-knowledgeable or not. Since they began performing the "seven" in 1947, the Wallendas had experienced not a single mishap with the trick. On this night, however, the lead understander, Dieter Schepp, a nephew of Karl's first wife, was performing in the pyramid for only the second time. He was followed by Dick Faughman (Karl's daughter Jenny's husband), Mario Wallenda (adopted son of Karl), and Gunther Wallenda (Herman's son). On the bars on their shoulders were Herman and Karl—with Dieter's sixteen-year-old sister Jana on the chair. For some reason, Dieter lost control of his balancing pole, shouting, *"Ich kann nicht mehr holten!* (I can't hold on anymore!)"* His pole bounced off the wire, and he lost his balance, pulling the whole pyramid forward and down. Dieter and Faughman fell to the concrete floor and were killed. Mario, too, fell, suffering severe injuries that left him paralyzed from the waist down. Herman, Gunther, and Karl managed to hang on to the wire—the latter succeeding in grabbing Jana as she fell. She was then dropped into a net, receiving slight injuries when she bounced out of it.

The seven-man pyramid, both a hallmark and a disaster for the Wallendas.
Courtesy of the Pfening Collection.

Of those who did not fall, Gunther was the first down, and the sight he saw was a horrible one: "Dieter lay inches inside the ring curb, blood spurting from his mouth, drenching his costume. Dick was on his back, one knee up, breathing faintly, easily, as though deep asleep. Mario was on his side, doubled in an almost fetal position, his mouth foaming, a piteous gurgling coming from deep in his throat."[39] Man, in his defiance of gravity, had once more suffered defeat. But it was not a defeat that Karl Wallenda was about to accept. Two days later, with Gene Mendez, who had been summoned from New York, Karl, Herman, and Gunther returned to the wire for a performance. "It is, of course, our pride," Karl said, "but more than that. I feel better if I go up again. Down here on the ground I break all to pieces."[40]

And up again they went—throughout the rest of the 1962 season, at fairs and amusement parks and in more Shrine circuses. The Detroit tragedy had made the Wallendas even more of a drawing card. Gunther and Herman, however, were ready to quit. Gunther's nerves were gone, and Herman felt that he was at the age to retire. Obsessed as he was with the act, Karl pleaded with them to do the "seven" one more time. With some trepidation, they agreed; and early in November 1963 in Sarasota, on a twelve-foot-high practice wire, they attempted the "seven" for the first time since Detroit. They failed. The rigging slipped and the wire sagged, sending the whole pyramid toppling. Gunther, with a gashed face and teeth missing from having hit the wire headfirst, decided that he had had enough. Karl's half-joking, half-serious comment that one did not need teeth to walk the wire did not change Gunther's mind.

Karl, however, was not to be deterred from succeeding once more with the "seven." Pushing his troupe with an almost fanatical zeal, he got them ready for one last performance of the trick. The scene was the Shrine Circus in Fort Worth, Texas, in 1963; and the tension was high as the human pyramid began its slow, painstaking journey across the wire—a journey that, though it took only a matter of seconds, seemed to last an eternity. A shaky trick at best, but they had done it. And they were to do it over a dozen times more during that engagement. That, however, was the end of the "seven" for the Wallendas.

With Herman's retirement after the Fort Worth stand, the original Great Wallendas were reduced to the Great Wallenda—

Karl. Other members of the troupe went their various ways, coming together only occasionally for engagements. Even Karl announced his own retirement in 1966, turning his hand to circus management. But he was not content on the ground, and less than a year later he was again performing. With skywalks as his specialty, Karl walked across great distances at great heights, setting a world's distance record with an 1,800-foot walk at a height of sixty feet at King's Island, Ohio.

In February 1978, the movie *The Great Wallendas* was aired by NBC. Although a tribute to a great troupe of wire-walkers and to a great and courageous artist, Karl Wallenda, the movie, as Greg Parkinson aptly points out, "failed to make it known to the viewer that these high-wire performers had challenged death successfully for over 40 years. To the contrary, the movie left the impression that Karl Wallenda's pyramid fell in Detroit after only a few months' practice."[41]

Nor could a movie ever truly capture the essence of a man like Karl Wallenda. Was he the perfect performer, one for whom the performance overshadowed everything else in life? Or was he a man with an unconscious death wish, who could not be happy unless he daily courted disaster? Was he courageous or obsessed? We can never know for sure—and perhaps it is just as well. His accomplishments on the highwire speak for themselves. When, on 22 March 1978 in San Juan, Puerto Rico, a wind blew the Great Wallenda off his wire into eternity, the world lost not only a seventy-three-year-old wire-walker but also one more vital part of what made the American circus great.

6

Send in the Clowns

"THE CLOWN! THE POET! FOR HIM WHO LOOKS SU-
perficially nothing could be less resembling; for him
who knows how to look—to free himself from things apparent—
they are one and the same."[1] So wrote Theodore De Banville,
French essayist and critic. A tribute indeed to those buffoons
who have, through the ages, kept alive a tradition that has provided an antidote to the cares and troubles of the everyday
world. For though man may not die without laughter, neither
will he live very well.

Laughter, in a sense, represents a kind of revolt against, as
well as an escape from, the custom and condition of society.
"What we laugh at," in Edward Haffel's words, "is the unconventional, the indecorous, the disorderly, the unaccustomed, the
unusual, the irregular, the incoherent, the incongruous, the il-
logical, the nonsensical, the eccentric." And those same words
describe best the antics of the myriad of clowns who have ca-
vorted under the big tops of American circuses. "Surely," Haffel
goes on, "there is nothing decorous, orderly, customary, usual,
regular, coherent, congruous, proper, refined, or logical in the
knockabout acrobatics of the clown, the grotesque buffetings to
which he submits, nor, for that matter, in the eccentric attire
which he affects. In fact, his whole art is based on the direct an-
tithesis of these main-pins of the canons of social
conventionality."[2]

The clown, of course, was not born of the American circus.
Even the ancient Greeks and Romans, especially the latter, had
their dancers, jugglers, singers, and clowns. Through history
these wandering entertainers made their livings by amusing

others—in arenas, marketplaces, and banquet halls. Free spirits and unconventional thinkers, clowns found their way to the courts of kings (as jesters or fools), where, even though often the butts of jokes, they were given license to speak more freely than others. Simpletons or true artists, all, says John Towsen, "were viewed as important status symbols; popes and kings had their fools, as did their imitators—aristocrats, city governments, and even tavern owners and brothel keepers."[3] Laughter has never known social distinctions.

As time passed, the clown found his way to the stage of the theater. During the Elizabethan period in England, for example, clowns appeared in plays in which they had little or no direct connections to the plot—ad libbing their own asides to the audience or mimicking the actors in much the same way as many circus clowns in more recent times have mimicked performers. In Shakespeare's plays, on the other hand, clowns (fools) were often given roles to play that were quite significant in terms of plot development.

Whether he be called Snigglefritz or Hansworst (Germany), Jean Potage (France), Pickelherring (Holland), Jack Pudding (England), Maccaroni (Italy), a Kapustnik (Russia), or whatever, the clown is perhaps the only immortal in the world of show business. "Centuries have come and gone, mighty kingdoms have risen and fallen, war, floods, and famine have laid bare the land," notes Haffel, "but nothing has stopped his merry march."[4] Every age has had its clowns; yet, as Paul Eipper remarks, "all of them . . . draw from the same fount of inspiration, today as a thousand years ago. They merely reflect their own time, using the knowledge with which they are endowed to underline the weakness of humanity, and in most cases they secure the greatest applause from their audiences by making them rejoice at the misfortune of others."[5]

That all clowns of modern times have been called Joeys is a tribute to one Joseph Grimaldi (1778–1837), son of an Italian clown. Performing on the stage by the time he was three, Grimaldi's great success as a pantomimist began with his first appearance at Covent Garden in 1805—a success that was eventually to make him beloved by all England. With a face like "Dutch cheese," Grimaldi possessed a dramatic imagination and sensibility that enabled him to play tragedy, comedy, or farce equally well. But it is as a clown—perhaps the archetypal clown—that he is remembered today. A master of body language and disguise (said to have appeared in a thousand faces), Grimaldi seemed to enjoy performing his tricks as much as his audiences did witnessing them—"and whether he was robbing a pieman, opening an oyster, affecting the polite, riding a giant cart-horse, imitating a sweep, grasping a red-hot poker, devouring a pudding, picking a pocket, beating a watchman, sneezing, snuffing, courting, or nursing a child, he was so extravagantly natural, that the most saturnine looker-on acknowledged his sway; and neither the wise, the proud, the fair, the young, nor the old were ashamed to laugh till tears coursed down their cheeks at Joe and his comicalities."[6]

Another European solo clown of note, who contributed much to the clown entree, was Grock (1880–1959), whose real name was Adrien Wettach. A Swiss, he resembled Charlie Chaplin in that he always played the underdog who never gives in to the many ironies of life. "He was," says Alan Wykes, "a pianist whose stool was permanently too far from the keyboard but who ingeniously coped by moving the piano nearer to the stool; he was a violinist continually perplexed by the right way of holding the instrument; he continually sympathized with himself in his distress and warmly appreciated his own felicitous jokes; he challenged gravity by putting his fiddle on the sloping lid of the piano and bidding it stay there, and gleefully discovered that he could stop its downward progress by holding it there with his grotesquely big-booted foot."[7]

Upon his retirement, Grock stated that, though the appreciation of his audience repaid him for his efforts, he was tired of being a clown. Neither would he recommend clowning to anyone as a way of life. "Before the war," he wrote in 1930, "it was comparatively simple to amuse the crowd or make it laugh. At present, the juggler and the clown find it hard work to create an amusing act. People have become too blasé, and they are no longer satisfied with the simple acts which astonished them formerly."[8]

Interesting and colorful as it is, the history of the clown is much too broad to be discussed in detail here. Whatever the past, in recent times the circus has been where the clown's art can be viewed in its purest form.

Whither the Clown?

American circuses utilized clowns from the beginning, or perhaps it was clowns who utilized circuses. Either way, the earliest circus clowns were talking clowns. With the intimacy of small tents that boasted but one ring, a clown's voice could be heard easily by the entire audience. With the ringmaster as straight man, the talking clowns would rely not only on their own spontaneous humor but also on a plethora of borrowed jokes and riddles. "In an effort to disassociate themselves from the 'mere buffoon,'" explains Towsen, "some talking clowns proclaimed themselves to be Shakespearean jesters. Their lofty quotations from the bard were usually combined with less pretentious jokes, conundrums, and witticisms."[9]

Because most early circuses had but one clown, he often had to do more than tell jokes from the ring. John Bill Ricketts's circus, for example, featured John Durang, thought to be the first native American clown. Not only did Durang furnish all the jokes for the ring, but he also performed a number of equestrian clown tricks—including *The Tailor's Ride to Brentford,* a slapstick act that depicted a tailor's unsuccessful attempts to get a recalcitrant horse to carry him somewhere. Durang was the first of a long line of equestrian clowns who performed under American big tops—among whom were the incomparable Poodles Hanneford and one of the greatest of equestrians, Lucio Cristiani.

In addition to *The Tailor's Ride to Brentford,* a number of other humorous sketches were offered by equestrian clowns. One of the most humorous—and most difficult—was the Pete Jenkins act, so aptly described by Mark Twain in *The Adventures of Huckleberry Finn:*

> Well, all through the circus they done the most astonishing things; and all the time that clown carried on so it most killed the people. The ringmaster couldn't ever say a word to him but he was back at him quick as a wink with the funniest things a body ever said. . . . And by and by a drunken man tried to get into the ring—said he wanted to ride; said he could ride as well as anybody that ever was. They argued and tried to keep him out, but he wouldn't listen, and the whole show come to a standstill. Then the people began to hol-

ler at him and make fun of him, and that made him mad, and he begun to rip and tear. . . . So, then, the ringmaster he made a little speech, and said he hoped there wouldn't be no disturbance, and if the man would promise he wouldn't make no more trouble he would let him ride if he thought he could stay on the horse. So everybody laughed and said all right, and the man got on. The minute he was on, the horse began to rip and tear and jump and cavort around, with two circus men hanging on to his bridle trying to hold him, and the drunken man hanging on to his neck, and his heels flying in the air every jump, and the whole crowd of people standing up shouting and laughing till tears rolled down. And at last, sure enough, all the circus men could do, the horse broke loose, and away he went like the very nation, round and round the ring, with that sot laying down on him and hanging to his neck, with first one leg hanging most to the ground on one side, and then t'other one on t'other side, and the people just crazy. . . . But pretty soon he struggled up astraddle and grabbed the bridle, a-reeling this way and that; and the next minute he sprung up and dropped the bridle and stood! and the horse a-going like a house afire, too. He just stood up there, a-sailing around as easy and comfortable as if he wasn't ever drunk in his life—and then he began to pull off his clothes and sling them. He shed them so thick they kind of clogged up the air, and altogether he shed seventeen suits. And, then, there he was, slim and handsome, and dressed the gaudiest and prettiest you ever say, and he lit into the horse with his whip and made him fairly hum—and finally skipped off, and made his bow and danced off to the dressing-room, and everybody just a-howling with pleasure and astonishment.

Then the ringmaster he see how he had been fooled, and he *was* the sickest ringmaster you ever saw, I reckon. Why, it was one of his own men! He had got up that joke all out of his own head, and never let on to nobody.[10]

As American circuses replaced the single ring with three, the days of the talking clown were over. Clowns still shouted at one another and, on occasion, at the audience, but there was no more banter with the ringmaster and no more jokes or riddles to titillate the audience. The Ringling show, by 1885, even had a rule stating that any clown opening his mouth would be fired. Perhaps the European circus could still carry on the tradition of the talking clown, but the American circus, in all of its bigness, was given more to flash and to quick, snappy displays. The result was that the clown became more of a fill-in, someone to distract the audience while rigging was put up or taken down or animals were got in or out of the big top. Arthur Borella, a noted clown, decried, in 1934, the status to which the clown had been reduced:

> Not so much is required of the present-day big-show clown as years ago. Most of the clowning is walkarounds, which do not require special talents as musician, actor, or entertainer. Practically all that is necessary is to get a few good comedy figures, or some burlesque or satire on current events, and walk around. One can never tell. Some time the more simple, least expensive may click and prove an outstanding feature and attract more attention and comment than some number on which another clown might have spent a lot of time and thought to produce, or an act that required years of hard work and practice to accomplish. So a "First of May" clown some time might, in a way, prove as good in this respect as a more experienced clown, who might do an entree, stop and do a number that really required some special talent to put over and fail in its purpose, while a good walkaround done by a novice, one with little or no experience might prove a hit. That's present-day big-show clowning.[11]

The walk-around gave each individual clown—or sometimes pairs of clowns—the opportunity to display his own creativity and ingenuity, as the entire congregation of clowns paraded around the hippodrome track. Walking on stilts, leading costumed dogs, carrying baby pigs, portraying comic-strip characters, or whatever else might come to a clown's mind—all could be seen in a walk-around. Clowns were constantly trying for new and ever funnier walk-arounds. Many walk-arounds, however, were used over and over again, and one can still see them in the circus of today. The levitating clown is an example. In this trick, one clown would lie down on a cot with a sheet over him and appear to be put into a trance. Suddenly he would rise in the air and move away from the cot, his legs sticking straight out and only his feet showing from under the sheet. The trick would be discovered when another clown would pull away the sheet, revealing the first clown holding two sticks in front of him, with a shoe on each. Another example would have one clown chasing his partner with a bucket of water, with which he would eventually douse the latter. Then with another bucket, he would approach the grandstand and, after some threatening gestures, swing the bucket toward the audience. Wood chips would rain down on the cringing audience instead of water.

Clowns in the three-ring circus were not entirely limited to walk-arounds. Most circuses had a producing clown, one who was in charge of, and directed, more elaborate skits that the clowns would present in the rings. He would choose the skits to be presented, build the props, and assign the clowns as he saw fit. Production numbers included clown bands with unusual-looking and strange-sounding instruments; clown weddings, often with a midget bride and a giant groom; clown boxing matches, complete with paddle-sized flat gloves that made low cracks when slapped together between the legs of the clown who appeared to be getting hit by his opponent; clown cars, out of which would appear an unbelievable number of clowns and occasionally even a goat; and the ubiquitous clown fire department that would go through numerous zany actions as they ineptly tried to put out a fire in a prop house.

All of the clowns who took part in these clown tricks (or gags as the clowns called them) fell into three basic classifications. Although all clowns, as previously mentioned, may be called Joeys, Joey may also refer in a more specific sense to that clown who mixed his clowning with an athletic performance—bareback riding, wire-walking, tumbling. Poodles Hanneford, for example, was a talented equestrian who used his clowning to add an extra dimension to the family act. Another type of clown was the Auguste, identified by his white face, huge red spots, pointed hat, and baggy trousers. The Auguste (Berlin slang for stupid) was usually a pretentious fellow, wearing a burlesque version of civilian clothes, who generally got in the way of things. The basic Auguste scenario is described by Towsen: "Rushing into the ring as the circus hands went about the work of setting up the next act, the Auguste would nod his head, shout advice, discuss procedural matters with no one in particular, and offer his help at the most inappropriate moments. As the Auguste tripped over everything and generally got in the way, what should have been a very simple task became utterly complicated."[12] A third type was the Charlie, whose charcoaled face was punctuated by a white mouth that was turned exaggeratedly up or down. Baggy trousers, beat-up derby hat, and ragged overcoat made up his costume. The Charlie was usually seen as a victim of a world in which he was out of place. Try as he might, he never succeeded in getting the audience to feel sympathy with him rather than laughing at him.

So much for that classification of clowns. Ringling clowns Pat Valdo and Emmett Kelly, however, listed eleven more specific categories of clowns: (1) Whiteface, usually with a big, laughing expression; (2) Grotesque, with an overdone mouth, and splashes of makeup for eyebrows; (3) Tramp Clown; (4) Clown Policeman; (5) Slugger, such as an emphatically Irish clown; (6) Rube, usually a thin-faced fellow with chin whiskers; (7) Potbellied Clown; (8) Auguste, featuring a facial makeup of several contrasting colors; (9) Lady Clown; (10) Midget Clown; and (11) European Straight Clown, dressed in knee pants and a halter and playing the part of straight man in a two-clown act.[13] Whatever his type, every clown considered his costume and his makeup a personal trademark, not to be copied by any other clown. Thus, in a large railroad circus, carrying as many as a hundred clowns, the problem of creating a distinguishing clown identity and unique stunts was not an insignificant one. A testament to human imagination and creativity is that clowns, then and now, have continued to find new ways to make people laugh.

One disturbing note regarding contemporary clowning, however, comes from a clown who sees the kids turning away from, even becoming hostile to, clowns: "It's war. They chase us, they spit at us. They've turned hostile. Clowns were the last people that children still respected, but now they don't even respect us anymore. If you're a clown, you're in danger."[14] In an age that needs laughter as much as any—perhaps even more—it would be sad indeed if clowns were to become victims of that pervading cynicism that has debased so many of society's institutions. In the days of the tented circus, happily, such was not the case— and the clown was held in the esteem he so well deserved.

King of American Clowns

The name Dan Rice probably does not ring familiar to many other than circus fans or historians. Yet Dan Rice loomed large during the 1860s as a clown and a circus entrepreneur, and few circus men have ever come close to matching what May has called Rice's "bizarre significance."[15] Animal trainer, equestrian, singer, songwriter, acrobat, ringmaster, circus owner, presidential aspirant, and, above all, clown—Rice was, to say the least, a remarkable personage.

Born Daniel McLaren in New York City in 1823, Rice, by the age of ten, was a professional jockey, riding under the name of Dan Rice—the last name being that of his maternal grandfather. As a jockey, he rode on tracks throughout Ohio and Kentucky, becoming in the process a gambler and part owner in a Pittsburgh livery stable. When weight forced him off the tracks, Rice turned to riverboat gambling and then to circus performing as a strong man and singer and dancer. This latter career took him not only to Barnum's museum in New York but also to several European countries, where he had the opportunity to observe foreign clowns in action. Upon his return to America in 1844, he was discovered by Dr. G. R. Spalding, who immediately signed him as a clown with Spalding's Circus. Dan Rice, at twenty-one, was now on the road to becoming one of the greatest attractions in American circus history.

The association with Spalding continued for several years, culminating in a partnership in 1848, under which the two showmen operated a circus bearing Rice's name but owned by Spalding. The show traveled by steamer and played towns along the Ohio and Mississippi rivers, from Pittsburgh to St. Paul to New Orleans. During this year, Rice made the acquaintance of Zachary Taylor, then campaigning for president. Rice used the circus ring as a forum to argue the virtues of Taylor. The latter, in appreciation, appointed the showman an aide with the title of Colonel.

Rice was, by this time, a most popular talking clown. "Colonel Rice," says May, "was rapidly approaching his zenith. He knew how to meet and perform before all social classes. Backwoodsmen and college professors applauded and pulled for him. Dan began to feel a little heady. He could stand hard liquor but not adulation."[16] An example of Rice's position in the circus world was the unheard-of $1,000 weekly that Spalding paid him the next year. But all was not well between the clown and Spalding, and, amid much ill feeling, the partnership broke up. With the breakup, Rice mounted his own show and began competing with Spalding. What followed was one of the most bitter battles ever fought between two American circuses: "The battlefield was the eastern half of North America. Opponents did not stop at mere casual personalities. Each spent a small fortune distributing rat-sheets ... show bills and heralds in which each accused the other of almost every crime in the calendar. What each said about the other's circus was so scorching that, much as they needed large amounts of money, many newspaper publishers were afraid to accept Spalding's or Rice's full-page advertisements."[17]

The result of this circus imbroglio was a suit for slander brought by Spalding against Rice—a suit that ended with Rice's going to jail for two weeks and losing most of his property. Undaunted, he composed a song called "Blue Eagle Jail," which depicted him as hero and Spalding as villain. Then, borrowing money on his wife's jewels, he started another circus—the euphemistically titled Dan Rice's One-Horse Show. A riverboat show, Rice's outfit worked its way down the Mississippi to New Orleans. The one horse referred to was a most remarkable animal called Excelsior. Prior to the performance of the one horse, Rice and a groom would carry on the following dialogue:

> Rice: We will now have the showing of the steeds. Are the horses ready for the act?
> Groom: That they are, sir.
> Rice: They are properly harnessed, plumed and caparisoned?
> Groom: That's right, sir; they are all ready.
> Rice: You're sure you got them all; you counted them?
> Groom: Yes, sir, I counted them; they are all here and all ready.
> Rice: How many are there, may I ask?
> Groom: One, sir!
> Rice: That's right; lead the animal forth and let the act commence.[18]

The term "one-horse" became, of course, a popular descriptive adjective not only for small circuses but also for small towns. Even the *Billboard*, the famous outdoor-amusement magazine, ran for a number of years a comical column called "The One Horse and Up Show," which detailed the tribulations of a small fictitious circus.

Charles Reed, a member of Rice's small troupe, recalled that season with the "one-horse" show:

> Steamboat days with Rice were perilous, but I didn't realize the danger. Traveling thru the bayous in the Acadia country was comparatively safe, altho the boat ran between close shores in narrow streams. I often used to wake up and hear the boughs of the trees scraping the boat's side as we went crawling thru.
>
> But the Mississippi was really dangerous because of the snags, and Rice's boat was an old stern paddler, with a rotten, leaky hull. The berths were comfortable and I had plenty to eat. So, being young, I would just tumble into my berth and sleep soundly, all unaware of the dangers of the river bed. And they were many.
>
> Rice had a good show. There was no menagerie. We carried tents, seats, stock and performers. Gave a parade at all landings; band rode horseback—horses broken to endure the blare of the instruments. Rice made big money and had a fine show. Later he began to neglect his business. He stayed away from the show, and the public resented this. "Where's Dan?" people would ask. He was very popular and the audience wanted to see him. But he would stay away, week or two at a time. No, it wasn't altogether drink. It was sheer negligence. Then Dan and his wife separated. He married a young chit of a girl, and Mrs. Rice took a young husband. Both had good cause to regret their folly.[19]

Prior to the breakup of his marriage, Rice was on the best of terms with many of the nation's leading political, literary, and military figures—ranging from Abraham Lincoln to William Cullen Bryant to Robert E. Lee. In one sense, he might be seen in the same light as the scholar Ralph Waldo Emerson called for in his "American Scholar" address. Emerson wanted a breaking away from dependence upon European tradition, and Rice, in his own way, exemplified such a breaking away. A folk-humorist and self-made man, he was, in Towsen's view, "a sort of clown equivalent of the cracker-barrel philosopher."[20] Rejecting the use of whiteface, Rice saw himself as more of a jester than a buffoon. Like today's stand-up comedians, Rice utillized every possible subject for his routines. A master of improvisation, a keen observer of human mannerisms, and a skilled mimic, Rice often used impersonation to entertain his audiences. He would also, on occasion, present burlesque verse interpretations of Shake-

speare's tragedies that were very popular. His opening account
of Hamlet is an example:

> Hamlet, the Dane, of him just deign to hear,
> And for the object lend, at least, an ear.
> I will a tale unfold, whose lightest word
> Will freeze your soul, and turn your blood to curd.
> He lived in Denmark, Hamlet did, did he,
> A nice young man as ever you did see.
> Not short, but tall, and rather thin than stout,
> His anxious mother knew that he was out
> Of his head, and rather wise than queer,
> And much in love with Miss Ophelia dear—
> But to my tale, or rather yourn—Shakespeare:
> One night two fellows, standing at their post,
> Beheld—my stars! a real, living ghost—
> Whose ghost was he, so dismal and unhappy?
> It was, my eyes, the ghost of Hamlet's pappy.
> And so those fellows went and told Lord Hamlet,
> Who came to see him in a cloak of camlet
> Toss'd over his shoulders, for 'twas bitter cold,
> While that bad spirit did his tale unfold. . . .[21]

Despite his universal popularity, Rice never succeeded in politics, and his ambition to be president went unrealized. His mag-
netism as a showman, however, put him in great demand. When
his circus was sold for debt, for example, his old enemy, Spalding, offered him a three-year contract at $1,000 per week. Rice
accepted but never fulfilled his obligations. Money, then, was
not the problem; the problem was Rice himself. Drink took its
toll, and the last years before his death in 1901 were lonely and
bitter. Still, May's words might well be a fit epitaph for America's
foremost one-ring clown: "In spite of egotism, dissipation, un-
wise generosity and unreliability, Dan Rice's admixture of
shrewdness, simplicity and grandiloquence have left so many
lasting impressions that as long as there are circus men they
will glory in his many virtues and belittle his few weaknesses."[22]

A Potpourri of Clowns

"The real secret of clowning," according to clown Harry La
Pearl, "is to think up something ridiculous to do and try to do it

in just as serious a way as you possibly can."²³ Having said that, La Pearl pointed to Slivers Oakley, a turn-of-the-century Ringling clown, as one of the best and most serious clowns to perform in an American circus. Nor was La Pearl alone in his estimate of Oakley. Indeed, some of Oakley's contemporaries thought him the very best they had ever seen. The last American clown to have the entire big top to himself for his performance, Oakley was a master pantomimist.

The stunt that made Oakley famous—and for which he was given five minutes alone in the big top—was his one-man baseball game, a "game" that was probably enjoyed more than many a real game. Playing the catcher first, Oakley watched as the batter hit the first pitch high and far—so far that Oakley would pull out a telescope to watch it. He then let the umpire use the telescope and ran frantically after the ball, making a true "circus" catch. With the side retired, Oakley came to bat, hit a long ball, but was thrown out at the plate. Despite his protests, he could not change the umpire's mind and so walked off dejectedly. Towsen reports that Oakley's argument with the umpire was "so funny that it sent the spectators into such a state of hysteria that some required medical attention."²⁴

Because the baseball stunt was so popular in America, Oakley thought it would be in England, too. In London, however, perhaps because the English did not understand the great American pastime, Oakley's baseball game was not so well received; and he returned to America and the vaudeville stage. "He became eccentric," according to Dexter Fellows. "Some say it was because of unrequited love for a great circus rider. Once while I was in Des Moines ahead of the show, he invited me and all the performers on the vaudeville bill to a midnight supper at the city's best hotel. When we sat down we discovered that there was not a single item of food or drink on the table—just papermaché fish, meat, vegetables, and other imitations of the comestibles that would ordinarily appear on a banquet table."²⁵

Deciding to return to the circus, Oakley approached Otto Ringling and asked for his old job back—baseball game and all. What he was offered was a place in the walk-around at fifty dollars a week. More than insulted, Oakley stalked out of Otto's office. Having been a featured clown at as high as $750 per week, Oakley could not see himself as simply a routine clown limited to the walk-around. Shortly afterward, one of the funniest clowns of American circus history played his last trick by taking his own life.

Slivers Oakley might have rejected a walk-around, but interestingly enough it was a walk-around that brought notice to Bluch Landolf, another clown of note. His stunt consisted of his walking along with a long plank balanced on his head. On either end of the plank was a basket of prop tomatoes. Every fifty feet or so, he would do a quick about-face and go in the other direction, but the plank would never move with the turn. The secret was a dome-shaped metal bump on the top of his derby hat that fitted into a socket embedded in the plank. Though Landolf admitted that he had seen the trick done by another clown, he was the one who made it popular. John Ringling was so impressed when he saw Landolf do it in 1928 that he gave him a ten-dollar-a-week raise—not an insignificant amount in those days.

Born Adolph Pelikan in 1878 in Bohemia, Landolf came from a circus family. His father was an acrobat and clown, and his mother was a singer and acrobat. Landolf himself was to become the uncle of one of the greatest aerial performers of all time, Lillian Leitzel. The six Peliken children were apprenticed to various performing troupes. Landolf went to a troup of Hungarian acrobats, but ran away after three years because of the dictatorial leader. He joined an Arab troupe as a broad jumper, staining his body with walnut juice when he went to the interior of Morocco—a place where infidels were frowned upon. After his Arabic adventures, Landolf teamed up with Bud Snyder, an American unicyclist. It was at this point that he took the name Bluch Landolf. He and Snyder performed various unicycle and bicycle tricks, finally coming to the American vaudeville stage.

In 1912, Landolf turned to clowning—because he got bored waiting for Snyder to finish his feature solo tricks before he himself came on. One night, as A. J. Liebling describes it,

> Landolf came onstage during Snyder's act in his oversize corduroys, carrying a lunch pail he had borrowed from a stagehand. He merely gawked at Snyder's tricks, occasionally twisting up his mouth and loosing a loonlike laugh. The audience, at first mistaking him for a real stagehand, was so interested in watching him that he stole the act. In succeeding performances he added more

business, stumbling over his feet to get out of Snyder's way or becoming preoccupied at the disappearance of his right foot in the folds of his corduroys. Having rediscovered the foot after an anxious moment, he would wave a hand triumphantly and seem to lose a finger. Frantically he would count his fingers over his pantomime and never came out with the right answer—sometimes nine, sometimes eleven, then nine again.[26]

Landolf's new act was so well received that it became a feature, and he was in great demand until vaudeville collapsed in 1928. It was then that he turned to the circus—the Ringling show, where his niece, Leitzel, was a star. Always imaginative in thinking up gags for walk-arounds, he was more or less a producing clown for Ringling. One idea that he had came from the huge-lipped Ubangis whom John Ringling had brought from Africa. Landolf fashioned a saucerlike lip for himself and, blacked up, followed the Ubangis as they were paraded around the hippodrome track. To complete the gag, he would squawk in what he felt sounded like Ubangi. The audience loved it, but John Ringling stopped Landolf's gag because he felt that the people might think that the real Ubangis were also fake.

As ingenious as Oakley and Landolf were, neither had the same kind of over-all success in the circus as Pat Valdo, who went from clown to personnel manager for the Ringling show. Born Patrick Fitzgerald, Valdo was being groomed to carry on in his father's cigar-making business when he decided that the circus was for him and signed with the John Robinson Circus in 1902 as an apprentice clown at ten dollars a week—changing his name to Valdo. So good was he at creating clown gags that within two years he was hired by the Ringling show—a big step for someone with so little experience.

An example of Valdo's creativity was the gag he did with a dog that he had got from a hand balancer, who in turn had picked it up as a stray in a small Kentucky town. In what became a staple among clown gags, Valdo taught his dog a number of tricks, the culmination of which came when the dog leaped up and bit Valdo in the pants. He later converted the dog into a miniature elephant, initiating a long line of elephant-dogs that still goes on. Valdo even did this latter trick in the Broadway play *Polly of the Circus*.

Valdo's early career was spent with various circuses—Ringling Brothers, Barnum and Bailey, and Hagenbeck-Wallace. He went wherever the money was best. It was with Barnum and Bailey in 1910 that he met Laura Meers, a member of her father's wire-walking troupe. Despite Robert Meers's efforts to keep his daughter and Valdo apart, the two were married in 1912. "The domestic and professional life of the young Valdo," says Taylor, "excited the admiration of everybody who knew them. Pat was in no way piqued by the fact that his bride, a member of the weaker sex, was able to skip lightly across a ring and ascend to the back of a moving horse [something Valdo had tried valiantly to accomplish in vaudeville but failed]. Mrs. Valdo, for her part, regarded her husband with affectionate seriousness, in spite of the fact he was always clowning."[27]

The big change in Valdo's professional career came in 1923 when Charles Ringling made him the assistant to Fred Bradna, equestrian director. At first, Valdo seemed out of place, especially in the contrast he presented to Bradna, the patriarch equestrian director of American circuses. "As Bradna moved about with a theatrical flourish," observes Taylor, "Valdo jumped up and down like a jack-in-the-box. If an acrobat missed his footing, Bradna presented the audience with a diversionary smile; Valdo, the chances were, was creating a diversion of his own by trying to leap, tailcoat-clad, into the gap."[28]

Whatever the differences between Bradna and Valdo, the latter impressed John Ringling enough that in 1929 the circus king gave the clown a new title—Director of Personnel. This position carried great responsibility, and Valdo was given a free hand in carrying it out. Although he was in charge of all personnel, Valdo never lost his interest in the clowns, often suggesting new routines or listening to ideas from the hundred-odd clowns the Ringling show carried.

A Pair of Charlies

No matter how much they might laugh at the gags of the Joey and the Auguste, circus audiences have always indentified most with the Charlie—the underdog who struggles in vain against the vicissitudes of life. And no two Charlies have ever been more

delightfully funny in their inimitable routines than Otto Griebling and Emmett Kelly.

The son of a grocer, Griebling was born in Coblenz, Germany,
on 28 April 1896. When his father died in 1909, his mother emi-
grated to America, leaving Otto apprenticed to a bareback rider.
In return for his work in the act, Griebling received room,
board, and instruction in riding. Though he and his mentor
were not on the best of terms, Griebling did learn much about
riding. After two years, his mother, who had set up a boarding
house in Brooklyn, sent for him and his brother Emil. In spite of
the difficulty in getting away from his employer, Griebling managed to sail as a messboy on a ship that he thought was bound
for New York. Instead of getting to America, however, he ended
up in Japan. Thirteen months later, he finally joined his mother.
Without any English, the young immigrant, pretending he was a
deaf-mute, learned much about sign language and pantomime
and did his best to make his way in New York. But his real interest was still the circus, and he answered an ad for a bareback
rider with the Albert Hodgini riding troupe, just booked by Ringling. Griebling's American circus career was underway.

Perhaps because Griebling was a bit lazy or perhaps because
he just could not work for someone else in an act, he once again
had trouble adjusting to the position of apprentice. When the
Ringling show arrived in Madison, Wisconsin, the story goes,
Hodgini gave Griebling five dollars and sent him to buy bread
and milk. Pocketing the money, Griebling took a job on a dairy
farm. When the show returned to Madison two years later, Griebling sought out Hodgini and gave him two loaves of bread, a
quart of milk, and some change. Appreciating the humor in the
situation and knowing that Griebling was an excellent bareback
rider, Hodgini welcomed him back into the act. The two-year
stint on the dairy farm was the only time that Griebling was not
with a circus.

About this time, Griebling began developing some comic
stunts as a part of his bareback-riding repertoire. So good was
he that in 1928, with the Sells-Floto Circus, he was asked to substitute for the noted Poodles Hanneford when the latter was out
for several performances because of illness. Griebling did the
act well enough that none of the audience suspected that it was
not really Hanneford.

A fall in 1930 that resulted in a broken wrist, ankle, and leg ended Griebling's equestrian career. While recuperating, he decided that his future lay in clowning. Thus, surrounding himself with all manner of books and articles on psychology and clowning, he began his preparations for a new phase in his show-business career. Bradna describes these preparations: "Remembering his deaf-mute days in Brooklyn, when he had desperately wanted people not to laugh at him, he decided to elaborate this characterization. He would appear to resent the derision and ridicule which accrued to pathetic bits of business such as juggling. Flat on his back, he learned to juggle, to throw a derby hat so that it swept in a circle and returned to him, and other stunts. He studied in texts the psychological elements of pathos, and before a mirror rehearsed embarrassment and anger."[29] In short, he was going to be a Charlie.

With his charcoaled face and white lips, derby hat, baggy pants, and huge shoes, Griebling toured for the next twenty years with a number of American circuses. But it was not until 1951 that he returned to Ringling—this time as a clown. He was ready for the opportunity, and, more importantly, the audiences were ready for him.

Like Emmett Kelly, Griebling preferred to be in the big top while the spectators were entering from the menagerie and finding their seats. During this time he would pretend to be trying to deliver something to a person he could not find. One time he would be a florist's delivery boy with a potted plant for a Mrs. Schultz. As time passed and he could not find her, he grew older and the plant bigger. By show time, he was an old man and the plant ten feet high. Another time he would be a Western Union messenger, who also grew older as he searched for the person for whom he had a telegram. Or he would be an iceman with a huge block of ice on his shoulder. As he again searched for Mrs. Schultz, his block of ice shrank until finally it was just an ice cube, which he would sadly drop and walk away. He and Kelly often cooperated in this latter stunt.

During the show itself, Griebling would wander around the big top—standing beneath aerialists to catch them should they fall, performing juggling tricks, taking bows with performers. His imagination was never at rest, and no one ever knew what the perpetually dour-faced clown would do next. "As a tramp clown," writes Towsen, "Griebling deliberately played on the

Otto Griebling, long a mainstay in the Ringling clown alley. *Courtesy of the Pfening Collection.*

audience's ambivalent attitude toward tramps and performers. He freely toyed with their emotions, sometimes abruptly changing moods, rarely conforming to their expectations. He was perhaps a sad and hapless figure, but he was not to be pitied. Any attempt to cheer him up was a cause for anger. He was downright sassy and might become enraged if the audience seemed to prefer the talents of another performer."[30] Beneath it all was a sensitive man who knew all the ironic subtleties of what it means to be a human being. "If you find yourself able to make people laugh," he said, "it is God's gift. You have to do everything from the bottom of the heart."[31] And Griebling did just that—performing up till his death in 1972.

Less eccentric and perhaps more sentimental than Griebling was Emmett Kelly, probably the one clown whose name is familiar to more people today than any other. A true country boy, Kelly was born (1898) and grew up in rural Missouri. But life on the farm was not for him, so in 1917 he packed a few clothes in a cardboard suitcase and, with twenty dollars in his pocket, headed for Kansas City to look for a job as a cartoonist. Because there was little demand for such, Kelly drifted from job to job—a few of which included working in a creamery, painting kewpie dolls, and running a side show on a carnival. In his autobiography, *Clown*, Kelly says that many "who see my tramp clown routine often conclude that I am probably the laziest fellow in the world. Out of character, I never got the hang of being idle. I was brought up on a farm where everybody worked and I've worked ever since, one place or another."[32]

During this time of many jobs, Kelly developed a cartoon-drawing act, with which he mixed a bit of clowning, and the beginnings of a trapeze act. He managed to place himself and his two acts on the Frisco Exposition Shows for a season—after which he returned to Kansas City. It was then that he finally found a job as a cartoonist, and it was then also, on a cartoon drawing board, that his famous clown character, Weary Willie, was born. "He came gradually, as a forlorn and melancholy little hobo who always got the short end of the stick and never had any good luck at all, but he never lost hope and just kept on trying."[33]

Kelly's first opportunity with a circus came in 1922, when, leaving his cartoon-drawing job, he joined the Howe's Great

London show, owned by Fred Buchanan and managed by Dan Odum. When the latter went over to the American Circus Corporation to manage the John Robinson Circus in 1923, Kelly took his trapeze act to that show. It was there that he met Eva Moore, who also worked on the trapeze, and married her. The second year with the show they worked a double trapeze act under the name of the "Aerial Kellys," and Kelly doubled as a whiteface clown.

The next years saw the Kellys trouping with the Mighty Haag Circus (1925), the John Robinson Circus (1926–1929), and the Sells-Floto Circus (1930–1931). On all of these shows, the Kellys did their double trapeze act. By 1932, however, times were difficult in the circus world, as well as in the world in general. Ringling now owned the former American Circus Corporation shows, so Kelly wrote to Pat Valdo, indicating that he, Kelly, would clown and that Eva would work ladders. The ex-clown, turned personnel director, responded with an offer for the couple to go out with the Hagenbeck-Wallace Circus, a Ringling-owned show managed by Jesse Adkins.

A first-rate show, Hagenbeck-Wallace at that time boasted some excellent acts—Clyde Beatty, the Clarkonians (fliers), Poodles Hanneford, Otto Griebling—and played such major cities as New York, Chicago, Philadelphia, Washington, and Baltimore. Adkins also revived the street parade in 1933.

After the first year with the Wallace show, Kelly decided that if his professional home was to be clown alley, he would try to create something special. "The sad little tramp was nudging my mind again," he says, "and I finally made up my mind that . . . I would bring him to life under the big top."[34] Thus, with the 1933 season, Weary Willie came to the American circus.

Also at this time, however, the Kellys' marriage began to break up. Eva wanted to go where the couple could work trapeze together, but Kelly did not want to give up the security of the Wallace show. A second child was born in 1934, and Eva did not tour again with Kelly. The divorce came in 1935—Kelly taking the older son, Emmett, Jr., and Eva taking Thomas. After the divorce, Kelly became melancholy for long periods of time and this feeling worked its way inevitably into Kelly the clown. "With my family scattered," he says, "I had only the sad-faced hobo and we became at this time indistinguishable."[35]

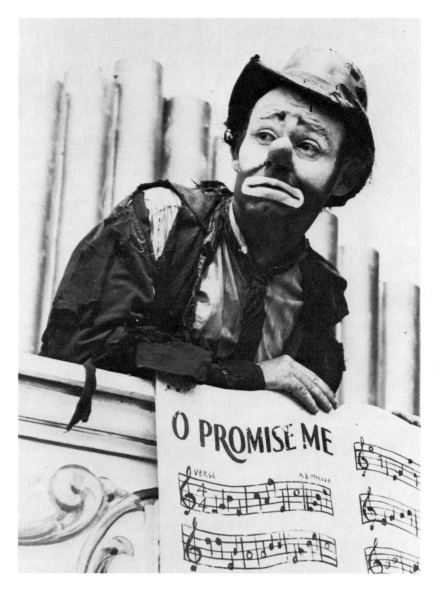

Emmett Kelly, probably the most famous of modern-day
clowns. *Courtesy of the Pfening Collection.*

In the meantime, Kelly had joined the newly formed Cole Brothers Circus and was busy working up new gags: cracking a peanut with a sledgehammer and looking heartbroken when nothing was left; walking into the audience with a board, a saw, and some crumpled blueprints and attempting to saw the board; confronting women in the audience and staring at them while munching on a head of cabbage. Kelly always attempted to suit the action to the mood and to the makeup—both of which, of course, were highly exaggerated. He was, in his own words,

> a sad and ragged little guy who is very serious about everything he attempts—no matter how futile or how foolish it appears to be. I am the hobo who found out the hard way that the deck is stacked, the dice "frozen," the race fixed and the wheel crooked, but there is always present that one tiny, forlorn spark of hope still glimmering in his soul which makes him keep on trying. All I can say beyond that is that there must be a lot of people in this world who feel that way and that, fortunately, they come to the circus. In my tramp clown character, folks who are down on their luck, have had disappointments and have maybe been pushed around by circumstances beyond their control see a caricature of themselves. By laughing at me, they really laugh at themselves, and realizing that they have done this gives them a sort of spiritual second wind for going back into the battle.[36]

"You can troupe all over the world," according to Kelly, "and you can listen to applause in far-away places and you read flattering publicity from hell to breakfast, but when you open with Ringling Brothers and Barnum and Bailey in Madison Square Garden, New York City, you have arrived."[37] Emmett Kelly arrived in 1942. John Ringling North and Pat Valdo had seen him perform with the Cole show and were impressed enough to want him for Ringling.

But it was not so clear that they wanted Weary Willie. Kelly was expected to change costumes for various production numbers, and he knew that the success of Weary Willie depended upon continuity and repetition. He went to John Murray Anderson, who was in charge of production numbers, and asked to be excused from those numbers just for the dress rehearsal so that he could exhibit his individual talent. The plan worked, and Kelly was allowed to free-lance and work throughout the

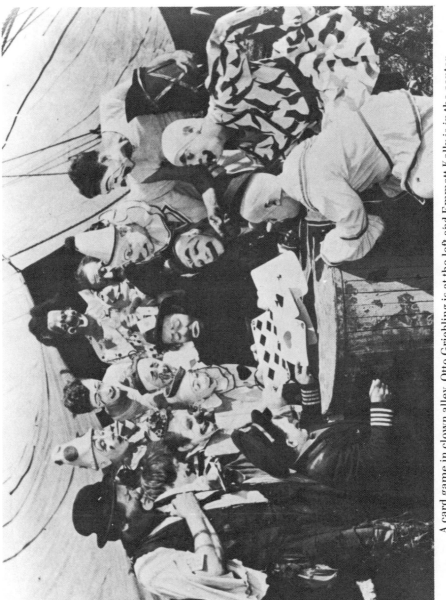

A card game in clown alley. Otto Griebling is at the left and Emmett Kelly is in the center. *Courtesy of the Ringling Circus Museum.*

show—a big step for a circus that had never permitted a clown such freedom. But, as time was to show, it was a wise step indeed.

The one thing that Kelly had to be careful of was not to distract the audience's attention from the featured acts. Eventually, though, almost all of these acts came to Kelly and asked him to prepare a gag that would help focus attention on their performances. When Lucio Cristiani, for example, purposely missed a somersault from one horse to another, Kelly would appear with a ladder and a broom. Placing the ladder against the horse, he would climb up and sweep off the horse's back—to insure better footing for Cristiani.

Kelly's fame as a tramp clown spread, and when the noted film director Cecil B. De Mille began filming *The Greatest Show on Earth,* he wanted Kelly in it—certainly a great tribute to a great clown. Kelly and Willie traveled a long way together and brought much laughter to many an audience, young and old; but for Kelly, it was well worth it, because, he says, "The laughter of children is a sound no circus clown ever can forget. It sticks in his mind and he can still hear the echo warming his heart when he has put aside the motley and quit trouping."[38]

7

Come Fly with Me

ALTHOUGH EQUESTRIANS MAY HAVE BEEN TRADITION-
ally thought of as the foundation of the circus performance, no one ever wrote a song about them. The daring young
man on the flying trapeze, however, has reached at least a lyri-
cal immortality. And well he should, for probably no act—on the
ground or in the air—held the attention of the circus audience
any more than did the flying act. True artists and superb athletes, the men and women of the flying acts appeared near the
end of the show and performed multiple somersaults, dives, pi-
rouettes, twists, and combinations thereof high up in the big top
with a quiet grace that seemed to belie any inherent risk.

The flying act developed over the years from the Frenchman
Jules Leotard's early efforts in the 1870s—relatively late as the
great circus acts go—as well as from those of a troupe of Spanish
casters[1] of the same period. C. G. Sturtevant, in "The Metamorphosis of the Flying Act," points to the Original Silbon Troupe of
five English fliers as the first great flying act.[2] Adam Forepaugh
brought the Silbons to America in 1883, and it was here that Edward Silbon became not only the star of the act, but also one of
the premier fliers of all time. He and Toto Siegrist formed the
Siegrist-Silbon troupe, with Toto Siegrist and Chad Wertz as
catchers and Silbon and Charles Siegrist as fliers. Others were
brought into the act, and it was eventually split into two acts,
both of which were featured in the Barnum and Bailey and the
Ringling Brothers and Barnum and Bailey shows.

Silbon is credited with devising one of the biggest flying acts
ever—the Quadrille of the Air. "This act," says Sturtevant, "had
an immense maze of rigging, with pairs of flying bars set at right
angles to each other. The 41 people in the act executed passing

163

evolutions in one group, while another did likewise across, the whole affording a most intricate and daring display which literally filled the air with flyers."[3]

There is widespread agreement among circus historians and performers alike that Charles Siegrist was the most talented athlete to don a circus costume, be it as a horseman, a tumbler, a juggler, a clown, or a flyer. A mere five feet five inches tall, Siegrist abounded with physical energy, often performing several times during a show. An imitator at heart, Siegrist had a compulsion to duplicate the difficult feats of others—a practice that did little to ingratiate him to his fellow performers, because not only could he duplicate what many of them did, he could often do it better. "As a comedy rider," says Bradna, "he equaled Poodles Hanneford. As a tumbler and wire walker none surpassed him. As a clown teammate of Polidor's he was a vaudeville headliner in winter. As a flyer he was excelled only by Codona, Concello, and Ernie Clarke."[4]

During its European tour, the Barnum and Bailey Circus signed Ernest and Charles Clarke, two Englishmen whose family had a long tradition in show business. These brothers, originally trained as riders, came to America when Barnum and Bailey returned in 1903 and won international fame as the Great Clarkonians. "The striking fact of the Clarkonians' act," according to Sturtevant, "is that it consists of but two people. Ernest Clarke's marvelous aerial evolutions from the swing bar to the catch and back again to his bar are unaided by a third performer releasing the bar to him for a return. It is all a matter of perfect timing by the two brothers."[5]

The Flying Wards were another troupe of aerialists who not only made a contribution to the circus performance, but also trained many fliers in their school in Bloomington, Illinois—including the Flying Concellos, the Flying Thrillers, the Flying Fishers, the Flying Sullivans, the Arbaughs, the Flying Flemings, and the Ward-Bell Troupe. Eddie Ward is credited with popularizing the flying act, and, according to Bradna, inspired the song "The Daring Young Man on the Flying Trapeze."[6] Actually a catcher himself, Ward believed that, if physically possible, all flyers should start out as catchers. With his sister Jennie and his wife, Mayme, Eddie developed the art of flying "to a standard repertoire of the back somersault, the half twist of the body, the forward somersault, and finally the two and a half. This last is a pretty maneuver in which the flyer, leaving the trapeze, turns two and a half backward somersaults and is caught by the ankles. Mayme . . . did the double while blindfolded with a sack on her head."[7]

The three greatest trapeze fliers, in almost everyone's view, were, however, Arthur and Antoinette Concello and Alfredo Codona. This chapter also honors an aerialist who, though not a flier, may have been the greatest of all performers who worked high in the big top—or anywhere in the big top: the incomparable Lillian Leitzel.

The First Family of Flying

Unlike so many stars of the big top, neither Arthur nor Antoinette Concello came from a circus family. Born at opposite ends of the North American continent, both with fathers who were railroad men, they met, as it were, almost in the middle of that continent—at Bloomington, Illinois.

Of Portuguese background, Art Concello was born in Spokane, Washington. When he was three, however, the family moved to Bloomington—a fortunate move indeed for the youngster, who was to become not only one of the top two male fliers in American circus history but also one of the best circus managers. This Illinois town, as noted earlier, was the home of the Flying Wards and the winter quarters for the Sells-Floto Circus. Flying was almost a way of life in Bloomington, and Art Concello, when he reached the age of ten, began following that way. Beginning lessons at the local YMCA under the tutelage of C. D. Curtiss, Art soon displayed a daring talent on the trapeze that, by the time he was sixteen, landed him a job with the Hagenbeck-Wallace Circus.

Strange as it may seem, particularly in light of his achievements on the trapeze, flying was not an obsession with Art. Early in his career he seemed at times to be somewhat indifferent in his attitude toward his profession. A magnificent performer, he often disdained practice. Rather than reporting to winter quarters a month or so before the season for practice, as did the other fliers, Art would arrive perhaps a mere ten days before the show opened. "The manager would raise the devil," according to a co-performer, "but Art would climb up the ladder with a look of great boredom and sail into a two-and-a-half. There wasn't much anybody could say."[8]

Concello himself has admitted that he was more interested in financial success than in artistic success and that he was always thinking of possibilities of increased monetary rewards. But, as Robert Lewis Taylor points out, "the circus pay of that era was skimpy, and he seldom improved his position, so he began, mentally, to branch out. He was considering a number of enterprises, such as training a group of chimpanzees to fly, and opening a filling station, when, at winter quarters, in Bloomington, he met the girl, Antoinette Comeau, who was later to become his wife."[9]

The daughter of a French-Canadian railroad man, Antoinette Comeau grew up in Burlington, Vermont, and, following graduation from the Mount Saint Mary Academy, was headed for higher education at the College of New Rochelle. A visit to her sister Mickey, who was married to Allen King, an animal trainer with the Sells-Floto Circus, changed everything. Just as Art had joined the circus at sixteen, so too did Antoinette. Eddie and Mayme Ward, then with Sells-Floto, took her in hand and taught her how to work on a swinging ladder and how to hang by her teeth (iron jaw in circus jargon). Thus, early on she learned to work at great heights in the big top.

The following winter Antoinette became one of Eddie Ward's students in Bloomington. But that first winter she was not flying; she was catching. This was hardly what she had been hoping for, and it was with some disappointment that she spent many hours hanging head down from a "catch trap" (the catcher's trapeze). While not so glamorous a part of a flying act as the flier's, catching required not only a sure sense of timing but also a strong, well-conditioned body:

> There is a definite technique to catching. The catcher does not see the flyer's approaching hands and feet, merely the mass of the body; he reaches out and grasps by touch. Also, the descending weight of a flyer varies greatly according to the trick he performs, and the catcher must adjust his muscular tensions. A light feminine body, doing a simple trick, may be caught easily by another woman. Only a strong man can catch an athlete after a triple somersault, since the force of momentum generated by the turning

body is sufficient to rip the arms from the sockets of anyone but a perfectly conditioned heavyweight catcher. Here again, just to prove the rule by exception, Mayme Ward is the only woman who ever acted as catcher of the "triple," but she did it infrequently.[10]

Antoinette learned enough that winter to be a catcher of girl fliers on the Sells-Floto show the next year. She also met Art Concello, who had signed with Sells-Floto and was studying at the Wards' flying school. The attraction was mutual. Telling her that she was too small to be a catcher (five feet one, 112 pounds), he convinced Antoinette to let him teach her to fly. She described the experience to Taylor:

> "All I had to do was take orders. He [Concello] and Toughie [another member of Art's act] are the greatest teachers of flyers in the world. There's something about Art—a sense of confidence—that makes you know he can't be wrong. He'd say, 'Antoinette, put on the mechanic'—that's the safety belt—'and try a plange,' and if I missed, he'd call down from the board, 'Now come up and do it again, while you're hot.' Somehow or other, I'd manage to do a plange that day. Art knows exactly when you're ready. All you've got to do is listen." Concello brought Miss Comeau along fast, always watching her carefully to see when she was ready for new moves, and at a propitious time, early in the 1929 season, he married her. "I'd got so used to taking his orders, I just nodded and said, 'Uh-huh,'" she explains. "But I was ready, all right. It was one of Art's best jobs of timing."[11]

And so the Flying Concellos were born.

Working next to the center-ring Wards for the 1929 season, the Concellos did well, both financially and artistically. With the death of Eddie Ward later that year, they purchased the flying school in Bloomington. It was at this time that another purchase took place: John Ringling bought the American Circus Corporation, including the Sells-Floto Circus. And, when Charles Siegrist broke his neck, the Concellos were called to the Big One. Alfredo Codona was working the center ring, but an end ring with the Ringling show was good enough at the time for the Concellos.

Under her husband's excellent guidance, Antoinette was to become, according to Bradna, "the foremost woman flyer of all time. He allowed her to attempt tricks which the Wards had considered beyond feminine strength: the pirouette and the triple. With a fine flair for showmanship, The Flying Concellos dressed their act with graceful flight formations and passing leaps, which employed two flyers working from a single trapeze, one grasping it as the other left it."[12] Their showmanship and talent paid off in 1937, when, with the absence of Codona, they were given the center ring. When told that Codona had done the triple, Art calmly lit one of his ever-present cigars and nodded. Then on their first night in center ring, Art, with an air of nonchalance, did the triple himself.

The great moment for Antoinette came during the same season when Art told her during the act in Detroit that she was ready for the triple. Because she had never performed it even in practice, Antoinette had some misgivings. But after a high swing, at Art's signal, she "dropped the bar and flipped up as high as I could get. I lost track of where I was the second turn—you always do—but I counted three and came out of my tuck, and then I felt Eddie's [Eddie Ward, Jr.] hands smacking into my wrists."[13] She had accomplished what no other woman had—the triple.

While, to the average circusgoer of the time, the triple or any other flying trick may have looked almost easy and completely safe (because of the net stretched below), such was not the case. Falling into the net may have looked comparable to jumping into the hay mow of a barn, but it was not. Knowing how to land in the net without breaking one's neck was as important as any other part of the act. Charles Siegrist, iron man that he was, broke his neck when he hit the edge of the net. Fortunately, he survived to fly another day. In the triple, the danger is greatly increased because of the momentum of the flyer. If the trick misses, says Bradna, "the body hurtles at tremendous speed toward the net—not at its low point over the center of the arena, but at its peak as it sloped upward over the heads of the audience. Thus there is almost no time in which to bundle protectively for the fall. Only superb co-ordination . . . saves the flyer from a broken neck."[14]

Most fliers were, and are, short, lithe people—barely over five feet tall. Antoinette Concello, at the time of her stardom, was a mere five feet one; Art, only an inch taller. As Bradna wryly notes, "a girl must be small-boned, devoid of hips and buttocks:

a heavy posterior does not permit a graceful somersault."[15] Moreover, fliers must be in the very best physical condition. In speaking of the hands that fliers develop, Dexter Fellows, long-time circus press agent, recalled sitting in a restaurant with Tote Siegrist, the catcher in the Siegrist-Silbon troupe: "During the conversation Tote kept his hands under the table, from which came crackling noises. We thought he was shelling nuts, but when he brought his hands up, we discovered to our amazement that he had been cutting calluses from his palms with a penknife."[16]

Always the businessman at heart, Art Concello soon had all of the Ringling flying acts under contract to himself—renting them in turn to the circus. Far from being displeased, John Ringling

Antoinette Concello exhibits the form that made her a premier flier.
Courtesy of the Ringling Circus Museum.

North admired Art's business acumen, as well as his knack for dressing up the acts so as to be more crowd-pleasing. Taylor records an exchange between North and Concello: "North was curious about Concello's training methods. The flying entrepreneur had insisted, modestly, on revising everybody's timing slightly, and whenever possible he or Toughie Genders called the leaps. 'Why do you and Toughie call the leaps, Art?' North asked one day, and Concello, a man of unabashed candor, replied, 'Well, if they get so they do everything on their own, they might leave me.'"[17]

When John Ringling North lost control of the Big One in 1943, Art took the opportunity to venture into the circus business himself, buying the Russell Brothers Circus, a California based operation, for $50,000. Antoinette stayed with the Ringling show for awhile, but a shoulder injury forced her to retire. Besides, flying without Art was not really flying. The next four years were busy enough that it is doubtful that either Art or Antoinette missed performing. A son was born; they merged their show with the Clyde Beatty Circus; and they increased their stable of flying acts, until virtually every flier in the world was under their control.

In 1947, with considerable financial help from the Concellos, John Ringling North regained control of Ringling Brothers. Convincing Art to sell out to Beatty (for $150,000), he made him general manager of the show, an astute move indeed. Art took to the job with relish, as did the show people to him:

> "It's the best move I ever made," North says. "At one time or another, this show's been mismanaged almost to death, but that's all over. Art's finally doing what he always wanted to do—he's in business in a pretty big way." Pat Valdo, who first hired the young, restless, cigar-smoking Concello as a Ringling flyer, thinks that the circus people trust him partly because of his formidable athletic skill. "They know his history and they listen to him," says Valdo. "If Art tells a bunch of Dutchmen to speed up a pony act, they don't argue. Their attitude is, 'It's all right. Concello did the triple.'" Although the circus employees respect him, quite a few of them tend to roll under a tent or secrete themselves in weed patches whenever they see him coming. "The guy's always got something on his mind," said a roustabout one day not long ago at winter quarters.

"He never stops moving or snapping those damned fingers. It ain't human."[18]

Things went smoothly until 1953, when Concello and North had a misunderstanding because the former wanted to reduce the size of the show, with the result that Concello left the show. When North closed the Ringling show in 1956, however, Concello came to him with a proposition: he, Concello, would again manage the show for half interest in it. After much cogitation North and the other executives of the circus accepted Concello's offer. The show would go out noncanvas, showing in arenas and auditoriums—with Art Concello as manager and Antoinette Concello as aerial director. This new circus was different, but, to the Concellos, it was still circus. "I'll take a building . . . any day," commented Antoinette in 1969. "I remember when we used to have to put on tights in a cornfield when it was so cold there was ice in the water buckets, and I remember the top of the canvas tent being so smouldering my makeup ran. But we didn't complain because we didn't know the difference air conditioning could make."[19] Nor did those who sat on so many occasions in the chill or the heat of the big top, watching with wonder and anticipation the study in grace, rhythm, and strength being created so magically above their heads by the Flying Concellos.

Master of the Triple

When Alfredo Codona would swing higher and higher on his trapeze, nearly touching the canvas of the big top, and then at the crucial moment hurl himself into the air and turn three somersaults before his wrists were grasped by his brother Lalo, a circus audience was seeing the triple done by the master. Others could, and did, do it—but none as a routine part of the act and none with the flair and style of Codona. He was in a class by himself.

Unlike the Concellos, Codona was born to the circus, a fact to which he himself attributed his sterling success as a flier. A circus child "learns to walk on his hands or to stand on his head sooner than he does on his feet. While his body is still flexible he

Alfredo Cadona: truly the man on the flying trapeze.
Courtesy of the San Antonio Public Library.

learns to perform minor tricks, aping his elders. Somersaults and cartwheels are almost second nature and as he grows older the trapeze becomes more and more a part of his life, and the more perfect he becomes in execution the higher the bars are raised until he is as much at home in the air as he is on the ground."[20]

Of Irish-German and French extraction, Codona was born on 7 October 1883 in Sonora, Mexico, while his father, Edward (who used the name Eduardo), was leading his troupe, Los Cometos, through Mexico and Central America. An apt learner, Codona was, by the age of five, a part of his father's act, doing simple routines on the trapeze. His sister Victoria and his brother Lalo were also performing, the former presenting a wire act that early in 1909 caught the eye of a Ringling agent in Ciudad Juarez. So impressed was he that, within a short time, she was offered $125 a week and center ring for the 1909 Barnum and Bailey season.[21] Perhaps more or less as an afterthought, Alfredo, too, was offered a job with the show. At any rate, accompanied by their father, the two Codona youngsters joined the Barnum and Bailey Circus. For four seasons, 1909–1912, Alfredo, taking advantage of his sister's good fortune, began his climb toward stardom with a solo trapeze act. In 1911, his brother Lalo joined him as a catcher; and, along with Steve Outch and Ruth Harris, they put together a flying act. From 1913 through 1916, they were with the Wirth Circus in Australia, returning to Barnum and Bailey for the 1917 season. By 1918, with the combined Ringling-Barnum show, Codona was developing into "one of the greatest stars ever seen under canvas. He was also the handsomest man on the circus lot; an Adonis of 155 pounds, perfectly proportioned, with a sleek dark Latin head and crisp black eyes. He moved with the ease of a tiger. Flying develops a muscled, lean, graceful torso, and Codona's naturally classic proportions gave him a god-like look."[22]

In 1922, Codona made his first European appearance in Lisbon, Portugal, and for the next year he performed in numerous continental cities, before returning to America. His growing reputation brought him more offers of European appearances, including the Olympia in London during the 1925–26 winter season. By this time he was well on his way to being considered by many the premier flier of the world.

Codona felt that the secret to success in aerial gymnastics was being "born to it." He may have grown up learning to take bumps and bruises and how to fall without serious injury, but Codona had something else, a touch of élan, perhaps, that led him to contrive the sensational tricks that made up the act of the Flying Codonas and that gave spectators the impression that he was more at home in the air than on the ground. He had what, according to Cosmopolite, all great fliers have—"that wonderful and quite exceptional 'lift' which they possessed owing to the remarkable power and development of the muscles of their arms and back. This 'lift' enabled them to rise materially higher than the ordinary performer when they released their hold of the swinging trapeze, thus affording them a greater space of time in which to finish the remainder of their particular feat."[23]

To perform the triple, Codona, along with the others who were able to do it, needed that exceptional lift, for the triple was indeed an invitation to a disabling accident, even death. Although no accurate record has been kept, it would probably not be an exaggeration to say that during the century fliers struggled to master the triple, scores fell to their deaths in the effort. One manager of a Berlin theater where Codona was performing wrote an article for the program in which he listed a number of fatalities resulting from attempts to do the triple, closing with "Alfredo Codona is now the one living man consistently performing the triple somersault. Sooner or later, of course, he will meet the same fate that has befallen others who have attempted this dangerous feat."[24] The manager was wrong; Codona's fate was not what he predicted.

The essential danger of the triple, as mentioned earlier, lies in the terrific speed necessary to complete it. The body of the flier must travel upwards of sixty miles per hour by the time of the second revolution, a speed that not only prevents control but also causes the brain to fog. It is during the third somersault that the flier must regain his senses in order to avoid a plunge downward to the net or onward beyond it. In such a plunge, the flier has little, if any, time to protect himself. The resulting impact "comes not on his back but at the base of the skull, in as much as the natural whirl of the fall almost invariably carries him toward that position; and the net or mat snaps his neck."[25]

Daring as he was, Codona was not beyond fear. He would sometimes "lie awake at night and find myself thinking how we did our tricks. I would think: I swing so high, then I leap and turn my somersaults, one, two, three, and then I throw myself toward Lalo, waiting for the clasp of his wrists around my hands. . . . I tell you I was scared."[26] Still, even though Codona and the others who worked high in the big top knew that their work was unnatural, that man belonged on the ground, they would forget it all when, in those exhilarating moments of freedom, they defied gravity and floated "with the greatest of ease."

Codona's most spectacular trick, interestingly enough, was not the triple, but one that grew out of a missed attempt at the triple. Heading for the spreader ropes that held up the net rather than for the net itself, he hooked an arm over one of these ropes just enough to break his fall and then went to a sprawled, sliding stop on the track. He was unhurt. The next year in Madison Square Garden, without warning anyone, he did the same thing, purposely this time. Picking himself up and waving away any help, he went to the ladder and climbed back to his trapeze. The applause was thunderous. "It was," he said, "the best trick I ever mastered."[27]

At this point we leave Alfredo Codona's story for a while and turn to that of Lillian Leitzel, the woman he was to marry in 1928.

Queen of the Center Ring

No one familiar with the many center-ring performers who appeared under the big top would question that Lillian Leitzel was the greatest. More than any of the others, she exhibited not merely an astounding physical talent but also a sense of showmanship and charisma that merited for her the title of Queen of the Center Ring. She was, in the jargon, a showstopper—and, indeed, when she entered the big top, for fifteen minutes all else was stopped.

Standing a mere four feet nine inches and weighing but ninety-five pounds, with short legs and overdeveloped arms and shoulders, she was not the image of a Hollywood-type circus aerialist. In fact, she looked almost like a gnome. But, as she fluttered high above the center ring, she was a marvel of supreme beauty and grace—almost something more than human. On the ground, however, she was, in Bradna's words, "the fieriest, hottest-tempered, most furious—and at times the most lovable—individual I ever met."[28] Also on the ground, she could chin herself nineteen times with her left arm and twenty-seven with her right. It is little wonder that band leader Merle Evans, when he saw Leitzel heading for the bandstand after her act with accusation in her eye, would shout, "Drummers take cover! Here she comes!"[29] Her complaints were usually directed to the drummers because drum rolls were essential to her act. Leitzel was indeed a study in contrasts.

Her early background, like Clyde Beatty's, is a bit hazy. She was born Leopoldina Alitza in Breslau, Germany, about 1892. Her father was a former Hungarian army officer who had turned to show business. His idea of family discipline engendered in Leitzel such a complete dislike for him that she refused throughout her life to recognize him as her father, taking her mother's name, Pelikan, as her own. Her mother was a Czech and herself an aerialist. Other members of the maternal side of the family also were (or had been) performers: the grand-mother, Julia Pelikan, had been an aerialist, and an uncle, Adolph Pelikan, became a clown with the Ringling show.

Leitzel and her brother Alfred were reared by their maternal grandparents. Their mother was usually on tour, and the father had more or less faded from the scene. Leitzel attended a girls' school in Breslau and studied music and dancing at conservatories in that city and in Berlin. Although she trained to be a concert pianist, it was not long before her real interests drew her to show business. Her grandparents took her to London, where her mother was performing with an aerial troupe called the Leamy Ladies. Along with continuing her formal education, she began preparing to break into her mother's act—an act that, as Taylor describes it, "was so complex that its like has never been seen again. At one point, the whole gigantic rig revolved in a brisk circle, while one of the ladies rode a bicycle to propel it and her cohorts performed almost unbelievable acrobatics from trapezes suspended beneath."[30]

When the Leamy Ladies came to America in 1911, Leitzel was with them. The act did not catch on, however, and the troupe disbanded. Undaunted, Leitzel, now using as a surname the German diminutive of Alitza (Leitzel), remained in America, determined to create an act of her own, one that was unique and had never been seen before. So, discarding all but the most difficult feats, she began preparing her act, "perfecting each little piece of business, subduing the element of brawn, striving for delicacy, adroitness—something fresh and engaging."[31] It took three years of wandering in the "vaudeville wilderness" before Leitzel was discovered by a Ringling associate at the Orpheum Theater in South Bend, Indiana, in November 1914. Five months later, she opened in center ring with the Ringling show. The *Billboard* review of the show that year commented that her "work as single is so astonishing and so pat for the circus ring, that she will be increasingly a favorite."[32] And that she was—for the next seventeen years.

Leitzel's rise in the circus world was, to say the least, phenomenal. But, as Bradna noted, she was not the easiest person to be around. Jealous of any performer who might be seen as rivaling her dominance (e.g., Con Colleano, May Wirth, Bird Millman), she would seethe both inwardly and outwardly at what she deemed undue applause directed toward an act other than her own. Yet, she conducted a school on the lot for the children of her competitors and, moreover, never failed in giving a birthday party for every circus child, as well as for many of the adults. She would regularly explode at her maid, Mabel Clemings, and fire her, yet she also showered Mabel with affection and money.

Leitzel faced two challenges to her Ringling supremacy in 1920. One came from Marie Meeker, billed as Dainty Marie, a physical beauty whose act consisted of singing while seated on a high perch; the other, from Ruth Budd, whose *piéce de rèsistance* was a slide down a rope on her head. Along with Leitzel, these two prima donnas each wanted top billing. Ruth Budd decided that the whole affair was not worth the trouble and resigned from the show. Leitzel took care of the remaining challenge, Dainty Marie, by marrying Clyde Ingalls, the ring announcer, and convincing him to "forget" to announce the fetching singer. Taylor describes how Dainty Marie reacted to this erratum: "By this point, of course, anyone but a seasoned scrapper would have tossed in the sponge, but Dainty Marie, leading from strength (her bullfrog voice), pranced out and announced herself with a volume that rattled the back seats. Her self-description went, 'I'm Dainty Marie, Unchallenged Queen of the Air,' which everybody agreed was a pretty loose summation of the facts. A direct slap in the face with a sequined brassiere could scarcely have inflamed Miss Leitzel more quickly."[33] Not to be outdone, Leitzel increased the time of her act, remaining in the air to the point that "the other acts all paled into triviality. Short of calling for fire apparatus, there appeared no way of getting her down except to lower the tent."[34] Eventually, Dainty Marie became such a trial to Equestrian Director Bradna that he fired her. Leitzel, never again challenged, emerged as the supreme circus performer—not only in the eyes of the audiences before whom she performed but also in the eyes of the performers with whom she lived and worked.

Leitzel was well aware of her "royal" position in the circus world, and she demanded—and got—more special treatment than any other performer up to that time, eventually convincing the Ringlings to give her a private railroad car, complete with a grand piano, and the most luxurious private tent on the lot. She chose her own "court" of acquaintances, called the "Once in a

While Club." This group was made up of the major figures of the circus, ranging from Charles Ringling to the more distinguished clowns. Everyone else on the circus, says Bradna, "was dirt beneath her feet, to be summoned, charmed, commanded, or ignored, according to her humor."[35]

Although Leitzel and Bradna were not professionally congenial and their association in the circus was marked by one battle after another, the latter recognized the tempestuous aerialist as being "in a class by herself" as a performer. "Not only was she a supreme artist, she was better sold to the public through advertising, exploitation, billing, lighting and presentation, and abler at hypnotizing the audience by projection of her personality, than any other darling of the world of canvas."[36]

Leitzel's act was not a complicated one; on the contrary, it was deceptively simple. But, as she performed it, it became the focus of attention of all in the big top—from awestruck circusgoers to hardened roustabouts who stood deferentially on the ground below. When she entered and moved to the center ring, sometimes with Mosher, her giant male attendant, carrying her, all other activity stopped.

For her performance on the Roman rings, she would ascend a rope in a series of graceful roll-ups, her body extended in a horizontal arc. Grasping the rings with her small hands, she would cavort almost like a child at play. Her efforts seemed not to be efforts at all. "The good fairies," says Taylor, "while giving her the freedom of the upper air, at once lifted from her the tedium of fear, nervousness, oversensitivity, and haunting doubts about failure."[37] Still, like most aerialists, she admitted to having to fight occasionally that inexplicable desire to "let go."

Returning back down the rope to the ground, Leitzel acknowledged the audience's applause; and then, grasping another rope, she was pulled nearly to the top of the tent. Here came that part of her act that had brought her fame as an aerialist—the shoulder-wrenching one-arm plange or swing-over. Slipping her tortured right wrist into a rope loop attached to a swivel, she would, to the roll and beat of a single snare drum, begin throwing her tiny body up and around—sometimes as many as a hundred times. A brutally demanding act, it was made by Leitzel to seem a kind of morning exercise. Her record for the plange was an unbelievable 249.

The incomparable Lillian Leitzel thrilled the hearts of
young and old.
Courtesy of the San Antonio Public Library.

The punishment that her wrist took twice a day left it torn and
raw, so much so that she would, when not performing, keep it
covered by a long-sleeved blouse or a dainty scarf. When asked
once if she could do the act with her left arm, she answered af-
firmatively, but hastened to add that she did not want to ruin the
appearance of her one normal wrist.

As befitted a true "darling of the world of canvas," Leitzel was
hounded by male fans who would haunt the back yard to get a
glimpse of her and adorn her tent with a plethora of floral gifts.
Lavishly entertained by men of wealth, she was deluged with
material offerings, including diamonds and even an apartment
on New York's Park Avenue. To say that she gloried in her power
over men would be something of an understatement. She rel-
ished having them fawn over her; it was her way of enjoying life.
Jenny Rooney, another aerialist and confidante of Leitzel, described the latter's technique:

> She'd stroll up and down, carelessly dressed in her next-to-nothing wrappers, and she didn't give a snap of her fingers what anybody thought. She was a storm center every day she lived. Her tantrums came and went like squalls, but Ed and I noticed she never had one unless there was a good audience around to enjoy it. Now and then I'd say, "Leitzel, you ought to slow down—you're burning up your life in a hurry." Her answer would always be, "Jenny, I'd rather be a race horse and last a minute than be a plow horse and last forever."[38]

Under such circumstances, any marriage would have rough sailing. And Leitzel and Ingalls's surely did. Unable to keep up with a wife who made five times more money than he and who was the idol of virtually every man who met, or even saw, her, Ingalls was not the happiest of husbands. When she threw his clothes off the train one night, he must have known that the end was near—and it was. They were divorced in 1924, and the stage was set for the circus's greatest love story of all time. Or at least its most publicized.

The one person on the Ringling Brothers and Barnum and Bailey Circus equal to Leitzel in every way except education was Alfredo Codona. At the top of his profession, so to speak, he yearned for the cultural background befitting one of his position. He also yearned for Leitzel. His status as the greatest flier of all time gained him admission into the "Once in a While" club, and even more—a club of his own that might have been termed the "All the Time" club. Leitzel, also drawn to Codona, became his tutor. "Her dressing tent," as described by Bradna, "by now an elaborate dwelling spread with Oriental rugs, graced with fresh flowers on elegant tables, dignified by a uniformed maid and a major-domo, was an ideal setting for the afternoon *tete-a-tete* between the two most celebrated personalities of the circus. Here Codona literally sat at Leitzel's feet—the psychological implications of this position did not escape the Bohemian—and caressed Lillian's two Boston terriers, Jerry and Boots, as he listened to her witty chatter. He became a virtual mooncalf in his adoration of her."[39]

But Codona could not bear sharing Leitzel with her army of ardent admirers. His love for her became not only a preoccupation but an obsession. His own marriage collapsed in 1927, when Clara Grow Codona, a member of his act, divorced him. Who acquired whom at this point is unclear, but Leitzel and

Codona were married on 20 July 1928 in a wedding that the newspapers wrote was preordained by the gods of the circus. Perhaps, but they would have had to have been gods with an ironic sense of humor. For this marriage of marriages, the coming together of the circus world's most stellar performers, proved to be a tempestuous affair indeed, alternating between moments of marital bliss and episodes of furious clashes of temperament.

The wedding day itself did not proceed smoothly. The marriage was performed in Chicago between the matinee and evening performances of the circus, with a wedding supper given by one of Leitzel's millionaire admirers, after the last performance. At this supper, Leitzel disappeared for several hours, during which time an enraged Codona searched frantically for her, before she reappeared. Thus was the tone set for the short marriage. Throughout it, Leitzel could not, or would not, turn away from the adulation directed toward her from male devotees. Realizing this, Codona himself, in 1929, became romantically involved with Vera Bruce, a pretty bareback rider who was eventually to join his act as a flier. It was a love triangle to rival that of Barnum's midgets—but it did not last long.

In the winter of 1931, Codona and his flying troupe were booked in Germany, while Leitzel was scheduled to perform in Scandinavia. Shortly after arriving in Copenhagen, she had a dream in which her performing rope began to unravel. Awakening with a scream, she was momentarily unnerved. Later, however, she dismissed the whole thing as nothing more than a bad dream. The more superstitious preferred to see it as an omen—and perhaps it was. On 13 February (Friday) 1931, while performing on the Roman rings in Copenhagen's Valencia Music Hall, Leitzel fell. A ring had broken. Alfredo, upon hearing of the accident, immediately rushed to her side by chartered plane; and for awhile, the plucky aerialist seemed to hold her own. But early on the morning of 15 February she died—bringing to a close one of the most colorful careers in all of show business.

Going Back to Leitzel

Ironically, with Leitzel gone, Codona became the premier performer of the Ringling show. But something was missing. His love for Leitzel, despite the tumultuous marriage, had never

Lillian Leitzel's grave in Inglewood, California.
Courtesy of the Pfening Collection.

flagged, and he was broken-hearted. More than heartbreak, he felt "a blind resentment that he had been conquered for the first time. Somehow the thing he prized most had been taken from him and there was nobody to blame, nothing to do about it."[40] One thing he did do was to commission a sculptor to create a monument for Leitzel's grave on a little knoll in Inglewood, California. The monument has an almost nude statue of Leitzel clinging to an almost nude statue of Codona. Codona's statue has wings, not to make him seem an angel, but to symbolize his life as a flier. Cut into the base of the monument is a pair of Roman rings, with the rope to one broken to show how she died. The monument is titled "Reunion." And it was reunion with Leitzel that Codona desired most of all.

In 1932, the master of the triple married Vera Bruce, perhaps not so much out of real love as to fill the aching void left in his life by the death of his "little Leitzel." But just a year later, Codona suffered another loss—his career as a flier. An injury to his shoulder stiffened his arm in such a way that he could do nothing but the most elementary tricks on the trapeze. For a center-ring star, this was a kind of death in its own way; and Codona was virtually destroyed by it.

While the Codona troupe, with Vera Bruce, carried on in the circus, Codona remained in California, brooding over his fate and performing as a double in several movies, including *Tarzan of the Apes.* This faking before a camera did not compensate for the enthusiastic plaudits he was used to receiving under the big top. Indeed, he resented the accolades that were going to Vera Bruce, with whom audiences readily identified—perhaps because he thought that they should have been going to the dead Leitzel. Codona's moodiness, plus the separations during the circus season, militated against any marital success he and Vera sought; and, in 1937, she filed for divorce, charging cruelty and jealousy. Codona, at this point, seemed not to care, and he did not contest the divorce. At a meeting on 31 July in her lawyer's office, Codona asked to talk with his wife alone. The lawyer left the room, though Vera's mother refused to leave. Codona simply shrugged his shoulders, and, as he lit a cigarette for Vera, he said, "That is the last thing I will be able to do for you." Then, pulling a revolver from his coat pocket, he fired five times into Vera's breast and once into his own head. Both died on the spot.

A suicide note was found that said simply, "I have no home. I have no wife to love me. I am going back to Leitzel, the only woman who ever loved me." Two days later, Codona was buried next to the urn that held the ashes of Lillian Leitzel. So ended one of the greatest love stories of the American circus.

8

All Out and Over

T HE BEGINNING OF THE DECLINE OF THE AMERICAN
tented circus is difficult to pinpoint, but it is safe to say that
when Sam Gumpertz ordered John Ringling from Madison
Square Garden in 1936, that decline was already underway. In
1901, eighty-nine shows were on the road—twenty-two on rails.
As late as 1937, there were still eighty-one on the road, but only
four of those were on rails. And all but Cole Brothers were part
of the Ringling organization. This reduction in railroad circuses
was a significant factor, because, as Stuart Thayer has aptly pos-
tulated, the seventy-eight nonrailroad shows in 1937 "probably
combined did not equal the capital invested, the equipment
owned or the program presented of the twenty-two railers in
1901. It was a decline of style, rather than of number. One could
still see the traditional acts, still feed the elephant, still experience a warm day's entertainment under canvas, but it was done
much less grandly."[1]

Thayer goes on to note that the decline of the circus paralleled
that of the railroads and that each declined for economic, not
geographic, reasons. Increased costs and growing competition
from trucks made it difficult for railroads to raise capital. The
result was consolidation and the shift of control from entrepreneurs to bookkeepers. Like the railroads, railroad circuses, says
Thayer, "faced with higher costs in both movement and equipment, needed more capital to maintain their position. Only
wealthy showmen could get it. The 28 week season could not be
expanded so it became more and more difficult to get a decent
return on investment." Truck shows were an alternative, and
droves of them crisscrossed the country; but the railroad show

"was the penultimate circus and its decline was the decline of the whole genre."[2]

Despite the glamour and romance that surrounded it, the tented circus *was* a business, and, like any other business, it had to adjust to its market. Even John Ringling recognized that the circus had lost its place as the great event of the year to the millions in the hinterlands. Automobiles and movies had seen to that. Still, the tented circus did not go down without a struggle.

Yet More Ringlings

Inevitably, recent circus history is keyed to that of the Ringling Brothers and Barnum and Bailey Circus—probably the only show whose name during the past sixty years has been known to virtually anyone the least bit familiar with the circus as an American institution. As Henry Ringling North describes it, when it was at its height, "it was not only The Greatest Show on Earth but the greatest show there ever had been on this planet."[3]

During the period between John Ringling's being eased out of control of the circus in 1932 and his death in 1936, the fortunes of the show had suffered somewhat. In 1929, still under John's control, the circus netted $1 million from a gross of $2.5 million; between 1932 and 1936, however, under the management of Sam Gumpertz, it netted only $300,000 from a gross of over $20 million.[4] The show itself had become a bit tacky physically, and the performance was, according to some, not up to Ringling standards. It was into this situation that John Ringling North and his brother Henry stepped.

Following John Ringling's death, various factions began contesting for control of his estate and the circus. Without any children, the circus king had drawn up a will on 9 May 1934 that contained the following provisions:

> (1) Funeral expenses were to be paid promptly. (2) His then wife, Emily, was to receive the sum of $1. (3) The Ringling mansion and art museum were to be given to the state of Florida, for the benefit of the paying public. (4) One half of the remainder of the estate was to be held in trust, the income to be turned over to Florida for the purpose of maintaining the house and museum. (5) The sec-

ond half of the residual estate was to go to Ringling's sister, Ida Ringling North, and her heirs. (6) Executors of the estate were to be Ida Ringling North and her son, John Ringling North. (7) The trustees for handling the estate were to be nephew John and his brother Henry, together with their brother-in-law, H. L. Wadsworth.[5]

Because of displeasure with the North family, arising from John Ringling North's recommendation of a rather shady lawyer to help retrieve the circus from Allied Owners' control and from his growing distrust of his nephew, John Ringling signed a codicil in 1935 that left Ida North with only a small annual income and nothing for his nephews John and Henry. He forgot, however, to remove Ida and nephew John as executors of the will. Thus, the control of stock was as follows: Edith Conway Ringling (widow of Charles)—30 percent; Aubrey Ringling (widow of Alf T.'s son)—30 percent; the Estate of John Ringling (voted by John North as executor)—30 percent; Treasury stock (not voted)—10 percent. North, then, was in a position to undertake his mission of gaining control of the circus.

A graduate of Yale University, John Ringling North was a handsome man whose first contact with the circus came as a candy butcher in 1919. Upon his graduation from the university, however, he turned his abundant energies to an investment career on Wall Street, prospering in a modest way. "People who knew him then," says Robert Taylor, "say that as a customer's man he was ideal. His appetite for entertainment was so brisk that many a client, desperate, signed orders for securities simply to be able to leave whatever night club they were in and get some sleep."[6] Not one to miss an opportunity, North knew that now was the time for him to realize his dream of running the Ringling circus.

After much legal maneuvering and a loan from Manufacturers Trust, North was able to arrange for the payment of the note owed Allied Owners; and, in 1938, the circus was indeed back in family hands. Of his brother's efforts, Henry Ringling North says, "Thus, in a few hectic weeks John achieved his first great ambition—absolute control of the management of the circus. And as yet he owned not a share of stock in it. . . . Putting him in charge was a splendid gamble on the part of our relatives and the Manufacturers Trust Company. It was a tremendous challenge to him. His task was to pull a disintegrating, has-been institution out of its doldrums and make it once again The Greatest Show on Earth."[7]

Such a feat was a considerable surprise to the circus world, since North was thought of as more a playboy than a sharp business executive. Both he and Henry, however, knew a few things about the circus. Indeed, according to Fred Bradna, "between them the brothers understood a lot more about circus management than anyone suspected."[8] So, with a five-year contract for him and Henry to manage the show, North refurbished his Uncle John's private railway car, Jomar, stocked it with the best wine and Scotch and went on the road for the 1938 season.

Straws in the Wind

North was to need what solace Scotch might give him during his first season of trying to fill his uncle's shoes. The previous year, Ralph Whitehead, a labor organizer, succeeded in unionizing all the workers of the show, and Carl Hathaway, representing the circus, signed contracts with the American Federation of Actors that were to run for five years. When the 1938 edition of the show opened in Madison Square Garden on 8 April, North bluntly announced that he would not honor any union contracts negotiated the previous summer. The gauntlet was thrown.

Just prior to the evening performance on 12 April, North discovered that he had a strike on his hands. Virtually all the workingmen, from grooms to property men, had walked out. As tradition demanded, the show went on—but it was a show the likes of which sophisticated New Yorkers had never before seen. The spec—Nepal, for example, was carried out on foot rather than on elephants and horses; and the steel arena was erected by North himself, along with other staff members and performers. Members of the audience, too, as they became aware of the situation, rushed to help. Fred Bradna recalls the scene: "I saw many heart-warming sights. The equestrians helped each other get horses into the ring and out again. The Loyal-Repenskys, for example, such bitter rivals of the Cristiani troupe that there was a traditional enmity between the families, put aside their feud and groomed for their competitors. The Cristianis responded by grooming for the Loyal-Repenskys. Nothing I saw that night warmed more than this cooperation."[9]

The next day, North, his hands still sore from rope burns received in the previous evening's efforts to put the show on, entered into negotiations with Whitehead and Arthur Meyer of the Mediation Board. A settlement was reached, and the show finished its stand in the Garden and moved on to Boston. The problem was not over, however, as North and Whitehead continued sometimes heated debate regarding the circus's ability to pay what the union contracts called for. North, in fact, was concerned that the show could not continue the season unless there was a 25 percent cut in wages; and from a raised platform in the big top (at Pittsburgh), he addressed all the personnel of the circus:

> I am speaking to you as the representative of the management of this corporation. I am responsible for the welfare, success and continuation of this organization to its board of directors and to its owners. The purpose of this enterprise, if perhaps some of you have never paused to analyze it, is to bring entertainment to a large cross section of the American public and by doing so to return to the corporation a fair profit. In order to accomplish this purpose, it is necessary to purchase large quantities of materials, employ many men and engage large numbers of performers. The materials must be paid for, the equipment repaired, replaced and maintained, and the employees, workingmen and performers alike, fed and transported from one end of the country to the other. All of this, as you all know, must and does require expenditure of a great deal of money. You also must know that in good times the circus does big business and makes good money, but that should not seem unreasonable for that is its just due. In fact, up to this time the show has made sufficient to winter it. There must be many of you here familiar with the old circus expression that "if a circus hasn't its profits by the 1st of July, it very likely will go home without it." The reason for this is a very simple and sound one. Due to competition, all the shows start out in the territory that seems the best for box office receipts and plays said territory as thoroughly as possible. Then naturally must come many weeks when receipts are far from consistent. In order to play good cities such as the large ones on the west coast, it is necessary to pay high railroad charges and play many towns which the management knows in advance won't bring enough to offset the daily expenses. So even in good normal times a show often considers itself fortunate to get back in quarters still holding the bank balance established way back in July.

And these, gentlemen, are not good times. Prices are high for foodstuffs and materials. Taxes are high and railroad rates are high. Hence the expense of daily maintenance is higher than in good times and the take at the ticket wagons is naturally less than when factories are operating that are now closed and people are working who are now amongst the 12,000,000 or 13,000,000 unemployed.

I sincerely wish it were not my duty to paint such an unhappy picture of current national conditions. I should much rather be appearing before you to offer you a raise rather than asking you to cooperate by taking a cut, for if such were the case it would mean that times were good, that millions were not unemployed and on meager relief and it would mean that the circus was making money and could afford to share more of its profits with you all who certainly share in making them possible. But I would be both a fool and a liar were I to read you figures that would indicate that we can expect big business and big profits. Besides the evidence of bad times ahead is the immediate fact that the circus must meet certain financial obligations. As a result of the preceding depression, it was necessary for my Uncle John to become involved with the bankers. I might say in passing that considerable of his financial grief was caused by his desire to keep as many as humanly possible of the small shows on the road during the depression in order not to throw any people out of work. The Big Show paid for the little shows' losses and still owes money. By careful management this debt and others can and will be paid off, for it is my job to see to it that the great organization which my uncle built doesn't end up under the hammer on some railroad siding.

Last year you men received a raise in pay that, in some instances, amounted to 100 percent. The circus paid that increase last year and has paid it so far this season. I now repeat that I receive no satisfaction from having to ask you to take a 25 per cent reduction, save perhaps the satisfaction of knowing that at least for you here that want to work—I am, I hope, assuring you of work with a fair living wage for the remainder of the season and if I receive your cooperation, I believe this season will be as long as usual and I'd like to think that it might also mark a return to that old order of things around here when many of you who are still here were proud to be working men with the Greatest Show on Earth.[10]

It is somewhat ironic that eighteen years later, in the same city of Pittsburgh, North would change the "old order of things" for good.

The next trouble came at Toledo, Ohio, where all of the circus's teamsters struck, leaving the show's wagons on the lot. North had prepared for such an exigency, however, by purchasing eighteen tractors earlier. "Again the strikers had done us a favor," observes Henry Ringling North, "by forcing mechanization upon us. The circus was operating exactly as it had fifty years before, just as though the internal combustion engine had never been invented. The wagons were still unloaded from the flats by hand and hauled to the lot by horses; and the Big Top was still raised by elephant power. Eighteen tractors replaced three hundred horses with all the problems of transportation, feeding, and handling they involved."[11] But with the horses went one of the more romantic aspects of the circus—and one more nail, as it were, was driven into its coffin.

Tractors might have saved the day at Toledo, but they could not save the season. The pay cuts advocated by North were put into effect on 18 June in Watertown, New York. Four days later, with the show in Scranton, Pennsylvania, a strong union city, Whitehead called a meeting of all the members of the American Federation of Actors. The result of the meeting was a strike by all personnel of the circus—workingmen and performers. The performers changed their minds after a few days of negotiations and tried without success to get the workingmen to agree to work also. During this time, both John and Henry North were, in the latter's words, "virtually barricaded in the Casey Hotel in Scranton. We were in considerable danger. That was an era of labor violence; of sit-down strikes and pitched battles between specially trained labor goons and professional strike breakers hired by employers. Feeling was often bitter. It was very bitter in Scranton."[12]

The last-minute negotiations produced no positive results—with each side trying to outbluff the other. Even the appearance before a group of workingmen in the big top by Mrs. Charles Ringling, widow of one of the founders, in which she pleaded with them to think long and hard before forcing the circus to fold its tents in mid-season, had no effect. North, too, stood his ground, however, and the circus was indeed closed. After arrangements were finally made and the show loaded, it began on 26 June its sad journey to Sarasota, Florida. As for Whitehead, he was seen in much the same light as the Grinch who stole Christmas. Said an editorial in the *New York Herald Tribune,* "A gentleman named Whitehead, who deems himself a labor leader, is responsible FOR ONE OF THE MOST STUPID AND UNPOPULAR BLUNDERS EVER COMMITTED IN THE NAME OF ORGANIZED LABOR. Thanks to his incitement of the roustabouts against any consideration of a pay cut, the Ringling Brothers and Barnum and Bailey Circus has abandoned its tour of the country and is on its way to retirement in Sarasota, Fla. . . ."[13]

Still under the Ringling aegis and touring the western part of the country were the Al G. Barnes–Sells–Floto Combined Shows, and the decision was made to take the best acts and some of the equipment from the Big One and send it on to that show. Thus, just three days after the Ringling trains arrived in Sarasota, Henry North left "with twenty-five railroad cars loaded with motorized equipment, the Big Top, and most of the feature acts—Gargantua, of course, Frank Buck, the Cristianis, Heyer's dressage display and liberty horses, Terrell Jacobs's animals, the Flying Concellos, and Ralph Clark's Jump over the Flaming Automobile."[14] This group joined the Barnes show at Redfield, South Dakota, on 7 July—and, in a sense, a new circus was formed: the Al G. Barnes–Sells–Floto Circus Presents Ringling Brothers and Barnum and Bailey's Stupendous New Features. It was surely a brave-sounding title. The show, as the *Billboard* reported, was going on: "That there are still hundreds of performers and working men who are loyal to the circus and its traditions is being strikingly demonstrated in the new set-up on the Al G. Barnes–Sells–Floto Circus. Despite threats, rumors, and a shortage of help, the show, augmented with many of the feature attractions of the Ringling Bros. and Barnum and Bailey Circus, is moving along with a minimum of difficulties and showing regularly."[15]

Even though dogged by the American Federation of Actors, the new show did passably well, making back the losses caused by the Ringling strike and ending the season with enough profit to get through the winter. The Barnes show did its job in 1938, but was never again to appear on the sawdust trail.

Other circuses were not so fortunate. Colonel Tim McCoy's show closed midway in the season, as did Cole Brothers. The latter, as noted earlier, sent some of its acts to its sister show, Robbins Brothers. Cole manager Zack Terrell summed up the season:

Never had to experience such continual bad business and weather during the 35 years I have been in the circus business. The only cheerful and heartening part of the season was the unselfish loyalty and help furnished by the employees to a man. When salaries fell behind there were no attachments; in fact, the employees acted as if they were all partners in the amusement institution they were seeking to carry through to success.

For weeks the show battled days of rain of torrential proportions. Yet the show moved with marvelous precision and almost invariably opened on time. Thousands of loyal circusgoers greeted us daily, but their attendance with other thousands absent because of non-employment was the difference between a profit and a loss.

Not in any way do I think the permanency of the circus is on the wane. The business grossed by two of the largest circuses on the road last season was greater than the combined gross of all the circuses of 30 years ago. Good times fill the red wagon with bounteous returns but likewise hard times are keenly felt.[16]

And so the 1938 season came to a close—and with it a not-too-happy chapter in the chronicle of the American circus. The circus survived, but the specter of the empty Ringling big top at Scranton was a haunting one—and the straws blowing in the wind outside it were ominous.

A New Look and New Problems

Whatever the previous season was or was not, spring was the time of rebirth for the circus fortunate enough to have had the resources to see it through the winter. And so it was for both the Ringling and Cole shows. Certainly John Ringling North was not to be discouraged by the adversities of 1938.

His circus greeted 1939 with a new big top, "reborn in shades of blue—dark blue at the peaks, paling, down its slopes, to tints of lighter blue. The center poles were gold and the scores of quarter poles were silver. The vast oval of boxes and grandstands were painted a new shade of 'Ringling red,' and the draperies along the entire circumference of the hippodrome track were deep blue with giant gold tassels. . . . Golden stars glittered in the center of the ring carpets, on drapes and on poles. . . ."[17]

The tent was reduced in length and given more of an oval shape, thus improving the view of spectators on the ends. More than that, it was cooled by eight motor-driven blowers.

The performance itself also received North's attention. Using theatrical ideas and techniques, he began transforming the show from "a mere panorama of acrobatics" to "a sort of muscular musicale, with animals."[18] Although he was roundly criticized from many quarters for deviating from the tradition of true circus, North knew that the circus needed change to keep it from withering any more than it already had. Thus, each season was to exhibit a new theme around which the show would be built. Elaborate choreographies were used, complete with bevies of chorus girls. Even Igor Stravinsky was called upon to compose a ballet for elephants—cranking out "a number, filled with whistles, gargles, and moosecalls, that everybody said was among his best works."[19] Eventually, North himself was writing much of the music for the show, but he spared no expense in making the specs and production numbers even more colorful. The result of the new look that he gave the circus was a significant increase in profits. The debt to Manufacturers Trust was reduced, and some of the properties that John Ringling had willed to Florida were bought back.

Because of America's entrance into World War II, the Norths questioned the advisability of sending the show out in 1942. Not only acquiring materials and arranging transportation were problems, but also the hiring of enough personnel to operate the show efficiently and safely. Because the government was strongly in favor of keeping the circus on the road, however, North issued the following statement: "The Management of Ringling Brothers–Barnum and Bailey Circus thinks it timely and fitting to state its policies and hopes for the future at this critical period in our national history. Through letters from many individuals, wide editorial comment . . . and direct expressions from the country's Army, Navy, and political leaders, it has been made clear that the public wants The Greatest Show on Earth to carry on during wartime. . . . President Roosevelt personally has expressed his appreciation of the fact that the Show is Going On. . . ."[20] And the show did go on, realizing one of its best seasons in terms of attendance. But it was a season not untouched by tragedy.

Fire was always something feared by the tented circus, for obvious reasons. Fire-proof canvas, though developed by the 1940s, was unavailable to circuses because of government priorities. The big top of the Ringling show was flame resistant, but the other tents, waterproofed with paraffin and benzene and dried out by the sun as they were, were dangerously flammable. And it was one of these—the menagerie—that on the morning of 4 August 1942 in Cleveland, Ohio, inexplicably burst into flame. Within a few minutes the tent was gone, and with it some sixty-five animals—four elephants, twelve zebras, two giraffes, thirteen camels, an ostrich, four lions, three tigers, four pinzgavens, three pumas, sixteen monkeys, two black bucks, and a sacred cow from India.[21] Fortunately, no people were injured.

More trouble awaited North at the end of the season, and it had nothing to do with fires, train wrecks, blowdowns, or any other of the dangers faced by the circus. This trouble came in the form of some of his Ringling relations. His five-year contract for running the circus at its end, he had to face the opposition of Robert Ringling, Edith Ringling (Robert's mother), and Aubrey Ringling. At the directors' meeting in January 1943, he proposed either operating the circus under the sponsorship of the government as a morale booster for service men, thus giving it higher priority for materials and train transportation, or putting it into quarters for the duration of the war. He lost in the voting and immediately resigned his position, remaining as a minority director with no power. Henry North went to war. Thus, the North faction of the Ringling family was essentially out of show business for awhile.

Under the leadership of Robert Ringling, the show went out with a shortened train and a more traditional program. It enjoyed a profitable year in 1943 and opened the 1944 season with high hopes. Robert Ringling left the show early that year for health reasons, putting Jim Haley (Aubrey Ringling's new husband) in charge. Even with wartime restrictions, the show did well enough—until 6 July. On that day, in Hartford, Connecticut, the big top burned, killing 168 people, mostly women and children, and injuring 487 others. From a tiny orange flame at its top, the huge tent became a ceiling of fire for the 6,789 patrons who scrambled in wild confusion to escape. Merle Evans and his big band played "The Stars and Stripes Forever" march, the

traditional circus disaster signal, "until the six center poles began to sway dangerously, giant trees of flame with no lines or
canvas to support them. Then the world's largest single spread
of canvas settled to the ground like a cloud of fire, smothering
and burning everything beneath it."[22]

The Hartford fire was the worst single disaster to strike a circus, and its reverberations were felt nationwide. Cities and
towns quickly adopted more stringent fire ordinances and codes
for circuses and other outdoor amusements. The Ringling show
itself was held in Hartford as the clamor for retribution was
heard from all corners. Only by posting $1 million was the cir-
cus able to move. Six circus officials, including Jim Haley, were
charged with criminal negligence but were permitted to help
get the show back to quarters in Sarasota. In late 1944 they were
found guilty and were sentenced the following April to jail terms
of up to a year and a day. The circus itself was back on the road
in less than a month, reopening in the Akron, Ohio, Rubber Bowl
and continuing to show in open-air stadiums, ball parks, or fair-
grounds. Once again the show went on.

The fight for control of the Ringling show also went on. The
family did agree on one thing, however, and that was that they
would not file for bankruptcy to avoid the horrendous lawsuits
facing the circus, but would pay its just debts—which they did
over the next decade. John Ringling North's desire to regain
control of the circus was not diminished by the show's problems. Haley, upon his release from jail, told North that, in exchange for being president of the circus for one year, he would
help him in his efforts. Henry Ringling North's description of the
1946 stockholders' meeting gives some indication of the intra-
family struggle:

> This time it was Aunt Edith and Robert who got the surprise. Au-
> brey was ill—either really or diplomatically—and was not present.
> Jim Haley, holding her proxy, voted her stock with Brother John.
> What an unholy row ensued! Robert and Edith in outraged voices
> demanded that the stock be voted in accordance with the Ladies'
> Agreement [a previous agreement made among the Ringling
> women]. The arbitrator, Carl Loos, ruled that this must be done.
> Jim Haley told Loos where to go and voted with John. A new board
> of directors was elected, which named Haley president and John
> Ringling North executive vice-president of Ringling Brothers–
> Barnum and Bailey Combined Shows.[23]

Thus, North was once more in control of the circus.

His problems in this area, however, were not over. The alliance with Jim Haley was an uneasy one and soon began to splinter. Both men wanted a larger say in the operation of the circus. After much bickering and maneuvering, North, in 1947, finally gained control of 51 percent of the total shares of stock. Assured of his position, he and Henry began a further modernization of the circus, in an effort to reestablish its image as The Greatest Show on Earth.

Auld Lang Syne

That these latter-day Ringling brothers did not succeed was not a comment on their abilities or efforts so much as on the institution of the tented railroad circus itself. Like the dinosaur, it could not adapt to a changing environment. The very things that the circus needed were becoming scarcer and harder to obtain. With unionization, labor grew increasingly more expensive. The railroads, running into economic problems of their own, gave less efficient service to the circus, at ever higher costs. Audiences, once eager for circus day, were now finding entertainment from other sources (movies, television, sports, travel). Food for the personnel and the animals was more expensive. Skilled department bosses, so important to the efficiency of moving and setting up the circus, were becoming extremely difficult to find.

Despite efforts at modernization and mechanization, the large tented circus could not operate profitably in light of these problems. By 1955, for example, the Ringling show was grossing $5 million but still losing $1 million. In its heyday, under the original Ringlings, the show would net $1 million on a $2.5 million gross. By the start of the 1956 season, then, the Norths suspected that the end was near; they knew it by July, when they had already lost over $1 million. Thus, on 16 July, in Pittsburgh, after the evening performance, the band played "Auld Lang Syne," and The Greatest Show on Earth folded its tents for the last time.

For Henry Ringling North, the problem was strikingly simple. It was a matter of space and distance:

> Then I realized the final basic reason why the road show had to go; why the people no longer came to see it. They simply could not get

there. It took a fifteen-acre lot to hold the forty-one tents in which the circus lived and showed. And you needed another big lot to park three thousand cars. With suburbs ringing every city in America from three to thirty miles in depth, where on earth could you still find a fifteen-acre lot that could be reached by public transportation or even conveniently by automobile? The answer was: virtually nowhere. Thus we had been gradually pushed farther and farther from the urban centers until we were practically pitching our tents in the sticks. It was not the American people who were forsaking us. We had forsaken them.[24]

As he watched that last performance under canvas of his circus, John Ringling North's mind may have been looking to the future and envisioning in that future a new kind of show. Indeed, he did succeed in mounting that show—one that would perform only in the great auditoriums of the land; and, in that sense, the show did go on. But, in another sense, what remained was not nearly so significant as what was lost; 16 July 1956 not only marked the closing of Ringling Brothers and Barnum and Bailey under canvas, it also marked the end of a long and glorious tradition—that of the tented railroad circus. A handful of motorized tented circuses may still, under one title or another, wend their way across the country in a nostalgic effort to keep the tradition alive, but probably Joe McKennon says it best at the end of his *Logistics of the American Circus:* "Yep, my friend, tears drop on my typewriter as I reach this conclusion. IT'S GONE, AND WE AIN'T EVER GONNA BRING IT BACK."[25]

What is it that "we ain't ever gonna bring back"? Surely the animal trainers, acrobats, aerialists, equestrians, and clowns who constitute the performances of the two units of the Ringling Brothers and Barnum and Bailey Circus today are masters of their art. And surely the animals are just as intriguing and captivating as they are put through their paces. Yes. But the auditoriums in which the performances take place, though they may offer air conditioning, comfortable seating, and elaborate lighting, cannot supply that magic of the tented city that arrived and departed with so much color and excitement. Important as it certainly has always been for the circus, the performance itself was only one part of the tented railroad circus. The other part—and in its way just as important—was that undefinable something that made circus day a day eagerly awaited and long re-

The circus as it was—a sight no more to behold.
Courtesy of the Pfening Collection.

membered. Perhaps R. M. Harvey was right when he suggested in 1934 that it was the rough, crude side of the circus that appealed to the American public, that if the circus were made too classy, too grand, then its basic appeal would be lost.[26]

"The circus, at its best," wrote a *New York Times* editorialist when the Ringling show closed in 1938, "is a first-class example of the old American way of doing things—noisy, blaring, rich with color, rolling all history into a hodgepodge, smelling of prairie earth and New England barnyards, yet redolent of the perfumes of Araby. We didn't invent it, but it is steeped in our tradition. Streamlined or knobby, may it recover from its slump and once more come into its own—the delight of youth, the solace of old age. We need circuses as well as bread."[27]

The circus did recover, but probably not in the image that the editorialist had in mind. Although, in reality, the tented railroad circus is gone, it will, as a part of American tradition and nostalgia, always remain very much alive.

Notes and References

Chapter 1

1. George L. Chindahl, *A History of the Circus in America* (Caldwell, Idaho, 1959), p. 8.

2. For a detailed discussion of the various structures used by Ricketts's circus, see James S. Moy, "A Checklist of Circus Buildings Constructed by John B. Ricketts," *Bandwagon,* September-October 1978, pp. 21–23.

3. C. H. Amidon, "Behind the Scenes with John B. Ricketts," *Bandwagon,* November-December 1974, p. 17.

4. Ibid.

5. Ibid., p. 19.

6. For a brief discussion of each of these figures, see Chindahl, *History,* pp. 33–67. Chindahl also presents an exhaustive list of American circuses in his appendix.

7. P. T. Barnum, *Struggles and Triumphs; or Forty Years' Recollections of P. T. Barnum* (Buffalo, 1875), p. 26.

8. Ibid.

9. Ibid., p. 33.

10. Ibid., p. 52.

11. Ibid., p. 61.

12. Ibid., p. 65.

13. Ibid., p. 74.

14. Ibid., p. 76.

15. Ibid., p. 80.

16. Ibid., p. 104.

17. Ibid., p. 133.

18. Ibid., p. 134.

19. Charles Stratton was not a dwarf, but a perfectly formed midget. Barnum changed the age in order to make him more of a curiosity.

20. Irving Wallace, *The Fabulous Showman* (New York, 1967), p. 88.

21. Ibid., p. 112.

22. Barnum, *Struggles,* p. 341.

23. Wallace, *Fabulous,* p. 177.

24. Barnum, *Struggles,* p. 395.

25. Ibid.

26. Wallace, *Fabulous,* p. 294.

27. Barnum, quoted in Wallace, *Fabulous,* p. 295.

28. August Rungeling Americanized his name when he moved to Baraboo.

29. Gene Plowden, *Those Amazing Ringlings and Their Circus* (Caldwell, Idaho, 1968), p. 21.

30. Earl Chapin May, *The Circus from Rome to Ringling* (New York, 1932), p. 140.

31. Alvin F. Harlow, *The Ringlings, Wizards of the Circus* (New York, 1951), p. 100.

32. Henry Ringling North and Alden Hatch, *The Circus Kings—Our Ringling Family Story* (Garden City, N.Y., 1960), p. 88.

33. Ibid., p. 103.

34. Harlow, *Ringlings,* p. 122.

35. Although Baraboo no longer serves as winter quarters for any circus, the Circus World Museum, with its many fine exhibits and research library, is located there.

36. North and Hatch, *Circus Kings,* p. 197.

37. In "How Ringling Made the Greatest Show Greater," *Literary Digest,* 5 October 1929, p. 38.

Chapter 2

1. The "nut" refers to a circus's daily expenses. Depending upon its size, a major railroad circus could have had expenses ranging from $2,000 upward.

2. Charles P. Fox, *A Ticket to the Circus* (New York, 1959), p. 174.

3. Joe McKennon, *Logistics of the American Circus* (Sarasota, 1977), p. 16.

4. For a detailed description of the Cole Brothers' winter quarters in Rochester, Indiana, see Joseph Bradbury, "The Cole Bros. Winterquarters at Rochester, Indiana," *Bandwagon,* May-June 1972, pp. 18–26.

5. See Tom Parkinson and Charles Fox, *The Circus Moves by Rail* (Boulder, 1978), pp. 75–96, for many photographs of advance cars, as well as a discussion of their function.

6. See Fred D. Pfening, Jr., "Circus Bill Posting and Advance Advertising Cars," *Bandwagon,* November-December 1975, pp. 33–43, for some interesting anecdotes on opposition.

7. Parkinson and Fox, *Circus Moves,* p. 77.

8. McKennon, *Logistics,* p. 19.

9. A. Morton Smith, "Forty Years of Circus Advertising," *Billboard,* 29 December 1934, p. 127.

10. William B. Reynolds, "Barrymoring Circus Publicity," *Billboard,* 7 April 1928, p. 45.

11. See Copeland MacAllister, "The First Successful Railroad Circus Was in 1866," *Bandwagon*, July-August 1975, pp. 14–16.

12. Parkinson and Fox, *Circus Moves*, p. 23.

13. For a complete list of the railroad circuses in 1911, see Parkinson and Fox, *Circus Moves*, p. 26.

14. For a fascinating view of the small truck circus of modern times, see Fred Powledge, *Mud Show: A Circus Season* (New York, 1975).

15. See Fred D. Pfening, Jr., "Circus Train Wrecks," *Bandwagon*, September-October 1975, pp. 18–22, for pictures and commentary on various circus train wrecks.

16. Quoted in Warren A. Reeder, *No Performances Today* (Hammond, Ind., 1972), p. 60.

17. Ibid., p. 100.

18. Ibid., p. 118.

19. For an excellent discussion of the circus cook house, see Kenneth D. Hull, "The Flag's Up, Let's Make the Cookhouse," *Bandwagon*, May-June 1981, pp. 23–27.

20. Thomas Wolfe, "Circus at Dawn," in *From Death to Morning* (New York: Scribner's, 1935), p. 209.

21. In the 1920s, the Ringling show had as many as 1,000 men working under Happy Jack Snellen, the boss canvasman.

22. At each end of the big top were the blues, cheaper seats that were simply boards placed across stringers. On each side were reserved seats with backs. These latter were called starbacks.

23. George Speaight, "The Origin of the Circus Parade Wagon," *Bandwagon*, November-December 1977, p. 37.

24. Charles P. Fox and Beverly Kelley, *The Great Circus Street Parade* (New York, 1978), p. 2.

25. See Gordon M. Carver, "Sparks Circus Season of 1928," *Bandwagon*, May-June 1979, p. 6.

26. Fox, *Ticket*, p. 108.

27. A. Morton Smith, "Spec-ology of the Circus," *Billboard*, 31 July 1943, p. 51.

28. Fred Bradna and Hartzell Spence, *The Big Top* (New York, 1952), p. 102.

29. For a complete list of these rules, see Fox, *Ticket*, p. 129.

30. Courtney Ryley Cooper, *Under the Big Top* (Boston, 1923), pp. 214–15.

31. Sarah Comstock, "Circus Folks Are Folks," *Harper's Magazine*, August 1924.

32. North and Hatch, *Circus Kings*, p. 91.

33. John Francis O'Connell, "The Circus Working Crew," *Billboard*, 24 March 1928, p. 54.

34. See *Billboard*, 24 October 1931, pp. 3, 63.

Chapter 3

1. Joanne Joys, *The Wild Animal Trainer in America* (Boulder, Colo.: Pruett, 1983), p. 7.

2. John and Alice Durant, *Pictorial History of the American Circus* (Cranbury, N.J., 1957), p. 32.

3. Fred D.Pfening, Jr., "Masters of the Steel Arena," *Bandwagon*, May-June 1972, pp. 4–5.

4. Ibid., p. 5.

5. Ibid., pp. 4–5, 11.

6. Gardner Wilson and Robert Hickey, "The Circus Program Metamorphosis," *Billboard*, 12 April 1924, p. 51.

7. Maurice B. Kirby, "The Gentle Art of Training Wild Beasts," *Everybody's Magazine*, October 1908, p. 445.

8. Joys, *Wild*, pp. 54–55.

9. Peter Taylor, "Training Wild Animals for Circus and Stage Not Cruel," *Billboard*, 30 June 1923, p. 66.

10. Courtney Ryley Cooper, "Inside the Training Den," *Billboard*, 30 June 1923, pp. 67–68.

11. Ibid.

12. Ibid.

13. Joys, *Wild*, p. 61.

14. Alfred Court, *My Life with the Big Cats* (New York, 1955), p. 2.

15. Ibid., p. 9.

16. Ibid., p. 11.

17. Ibid., p. 20.

18. Joys, *Wild*, p. 159.

19. *New York Times*, 31 March 1940, n.p.

20. Pfening, "Masters," p. 13.

21. North and Hatch, *Circus Kings*, p. 299.

22. Court, *My Life*, p. 30.

23. Bradna and Spence, *Big Top*, p. 207.

24. Court, *My Life*, p. 33.

25. Ibid., pp. 29–30.

26. Ibid., p. 102.

27. Bill Ballantine, *Wild Tigers and Tame Fleas* (New York: Rinehart, 1958), p. 86.

28. Courtney Ryley Cooper, "The Lady of the Steel Arena," *Ladies Home Journal*, July 1921, p. 94.

29. Ballantine, *Wild Tigers*, p. 90.

30. Joys, *Wild*, p. 74.

31. Cooper, "Lady," p. 94.

32. One obvious reason for the scarcity of tiger acts—and of tigers in menageries—is that, being Asiatic animals, tigers cost more than did lions or other cat animals.

33. Francis Beverly Kelley, "Snarling Devils," *Collier's,* 8 February 1930, p. 58.

34. Mabel Stark, quoted in Earl Chapin May, "This Lady Wrestles a Tiger," *Physical Culture,* August 1923, p. 119.

35. Mabel Stark, *Hold That Tiger* (Caldwell, Idaho, 1938), p. 13.

36. Ibid., pp. 86–90.

37. Ballantine, *Wild Tigers,* p. 94.

38. Stark, *Hold That Tiger,* p. 22.

39. Ibid.

40. Ibid., p. 17.

41. See Dave Price, "Clyde Beatty: Man or Myth." *White Tops,* July-August 1974, pp. 13–20, for an enlightening discussion of the building of the legend of Clyde Beatty. Price is probably the best authority on Beatty.

42. Clyde Beatty (with Edward Anthony), *Facing the Big Cats* (Garden City, N.Y., 1965), p. 266.

43. Ibid., p. 268.

44. Both titles were owned by the American Circus Corporation, mentioned in chapter 1. Beatty stayed with Corporation shows under one title or another until they were bought by John Ringling in 1929.

45. Price, "Clyde Beatty," p. 14.

46. Ibid.

47. Beatty tried to mate lions and tigers in an effort to get what he would have called a tigron. Although he did have a lion and a tigress who became quite fond of each other, there was no issue.

48. Quoted in Ballantine, *Wild Tigers,* p. 138.

49. E. W. Ritchey, "Clyde Beatty . . . As I Knew Him," *White Tops,* November-December 1965, p. 23.

50. "King of the Beasts," *Time,* 30 July 1965, p. 55.

51. Unidentified clipping, Clyde Beatty file, Circus World Museum Library, Baraboo, Wisconsin.

52. Ballantine, *Wild Tigers,* p. 127.

53. Beatty, *Facing,* p. 199.

54. Quoted in Ballantine, *Wild Tigers,* p. 124.

55. Beatty, *Facing,* p. 10.

56. I remember as a child being taken by my uncle, who was with Cole Brothers Circus when Beatty was, to the practice arena at winter quarters in Rochester, Indiana, where Beatty was working. The racket from the whip and pistol was so frightening that I wanted to leave. Beatty gave me a dime to stay.

57. Quoted in "How the Cat Man Fights Off Claws and Fangs," *Literary Digest,* 24 January 1931, p. 33.

58. Beatty, *Facing,* p. 195.

59. Beatty appeared with the Ringling show at its opening in 1931,

1932, 1933, and 1934, returning afterward to Hagenbeck-Wallace for the regular season. It should be noted that the Wallace show was now owned by Ringling, having been purchased by John Ringling as part of the American Circus Corporation.

60. Beatty also appeared in *In Darkest Africa* (1936) and *Perils of the Jungle* (1939).

61. Beatty, *Facing*, p. 193.

62. Quoted in Charles Sprague, "The Clyde Beatty Jungle Zoo," *Bandwagon*, September-October 1973, pp. 13–14. I know the place myself, for when I was eleven years old, I spent a summer with my aunt in Beatty's house in Fort Lauderdale. She was in charge of the zoo during the summers when Beatty was on the road with his act. The zoo was a virtual wonder-world of palm trees, lakes, and animals.

63. Ibid., p. 15.

64. Quoted in "King of the Beasts," p. 55.

65. Beatty, *Facing*, pp. 1–2.

Chapter 4

1. For a discussion of these acts, see Iles Brody, "Horses, Riders, and Circuses," *White Tops*, December 1939–January 1940, p. 12.

2. Bradna and Spence, *Big Top*, p. 154.

3. Brody, "Horses," p. 12.

4. Courtney Ryley Cooper, "Under the Horse Tents," *Saturday Evening Post*, 10 January 1925, p. 65.

5. Ibid.

6. See L. B. Yates, "Circus Horses," *Saturday Evening Post*, 12 November 1921, p. 32.

7. John D. Draper, "May Wirth," *White Tops*, March-April 1979, p. 16.

8. Quoted ibid., p. 17.

9. Ibid.

10. Bradna and Spence, *Big Top*, p. 308.

11. Quoted in Draper, "May Wirth," p. 18.

12. Bradna and Spence, *Big Top*, p. 155.

13. Ibid., p. 156.

14. Ibid., p. 157.

15. Ibid., p. 159.

16. Ibid., p. 20.

17. Quoted in Gail L. Mann, "Life with the Circus, A Memoir," *Belair Road Booster*, 11 November 1981, p. 18.

18. Quoted ibid.

19. Quoted in Fred Phillips, "The Riding Rudynoffs," *White Tops*.

20. Quoted in Mann, p. 18.

21. Ibid.
22. Ibid.
23. Ibid., p. 19.
24. Ibid., pp. 19–20.
25. Ibid., p. 20.
26. Fred Phillips, "The Big Top," *Courage,* n.d., p. 12. See Rudynoff file at Circus World Museum Library, Baraboo, Wisconsin.
27. Richard Hubler, *The Cristianis,* (Boston, 1966), p. 4.
28. Ibid., p. 77.
29. Ibid., p. 54.
30. Quoted ibid., p. 152.
31. Quoted ibid., p. 117.
32. Ibid., p. 156.
33. Quoted ibid., pp. 213–14.
34. Quoted in John Kobler, "Don't Tell Them the Circus Is Dead," *Saturday Evening Post,* 21 September 1957, p. 41.
35. Ibid.
36. Quoted in Hubler, *Cristianis,* p. 315.

Chapter 5

1. Vivienne Mars, "Before Blondin," *White Tops,* January-February 1953, p. 18.
2. Vincent Starrett, "Blondin—Prince of Manila," *Saturday Evening Post,* 22 October 1929, p. 133.
3. Quoted in John Lentz, "Protesting the Perilous Performances," *Bandwagon,* May-June 1977, p. 29.
4. Dixie Willson, *Where the World Folds Up at Night* (New York, 1932), p. 151.
5. Quoted in "Bird Millman," *White Tops,* June-July 1940, p. 17.
6. Bradna and Spence, *Big Top,* p. 307.
7. Quoted in "Bird Millman," p. 19.
8. Unidentified typescript in Circus World Museum Library, Baraboo, Wisconsin.
9. Edward Howe, "Toreador of the Tight Wire," *Cole Brothers Circus Program,* 1950, p. 30.
10. Bradna and Spence, *Big Top,* p. 313.
11. Quoted in J. Bryan, "Castle in the Air," *Collier's,* 27 June 1942, p. 55.
12. Quoted ibid.
13. Ibid.
14. Quoted ibid., p. 38.
15. Bernard Peyton, "He Just Loves to Scare You," *Saturday Evening Post,* 12 August 1950, p. 110.

16. Quoted ibid., p. 107.

17. Greg Parkinson, "They Walk Above the Crowd," *Bandwagon,* July-August 1976, p. 12.

18. Quoted in Peyton, "He Just Loves," p. 110.

19. Quoted in Dale Shaw, "Alzana, the Accident-Prone Aerialist," *Argosy,* n.d., p. 108.

20. Peyton, "He Just Loves," p. 30.

21. Ibid.

22. Ibid., p. 107.

23. Shaw, "Alzana," p. 109.

24. Conversation between Alzana and author, March 1981.

25. Quoted in Peyton, "He Just Loves," p. 106.

26. Quoted ibid., p. 107.

27. Ibid., p. 110.

28. Conversation between Alzana and author, March 1981.

29. Inscription on Wallenda family burial stone.

30. Karl Wallenda, quoted in the *St. Petersburg Times,* 13 December 1970, p. 31.

31. Greg Parkinson, "A Legend Is Born," *Bandwagon,* May-June 1978, p. 15.

32. Quoted in Ron Morris, *Wallenda* (Chatham, N.Y., 1976), p. 30.

33. Parkinson, "Legend Is Born," p. 16.

34. Morris, *Wallenda,* pp. 94–95.

35. Quoted ibid., pp. 109–10.

36. Ibid., p. 120.

37. Ibid., p. 148.

38. The Bob Gert troupe performed the seven-man pyramid in 1952–53 in England, using a net.

39. Bill Ballantine, "The Wonderful Wallendas," *True,* April 1963, p. 4.

40. Quoted in Bill Ballantine, "War of Nerves on the High Wire," clipping in Wallenda file, Circus World Museum Library, Baraboo, Wisconsin.

41. Parkinson, "A Legend Is Born," p. 21.

Chapter 6

1. Quoted in Edward J. Haffel, "The Art of the Clown," *Billboard,* 23 March 1929, p. 59.

2. Ibid.

3. John H. Towsen, *Clowns* (New York, 1976), p. 22.

4. Haffel, "Art," p. 59.

5. Paul Eipper, *Circus!* (New York, 1931), p. 90.

6. Raymond Mander and Joe Mitchenson, *Pantomime* (London: Peter Davies, 1973), p. 20.

7. Alan Wykes, *Circus!* (London: Jupiter Books, 1977), p. 41.

8. Quoted in "A Word to Boys Who Want to Be Circus Clowns," *Literary Digest,* 5 April 1930, p. 56.

9. Towsen, *Clowns,* p. 117.

10. Mark Twain, *The Adventures of Huckleberry Finn* (New York: Holt, Rinehart and Winston, 1967), pp. 148–49.

11. Arthur Borella, "Why Circus Clowning Lags," *Billboard,* 1 December 1934, p. 35.

12. Towsen, *Clowns,* p. 210.

13. Robert Lewis Taylor, *Center Ring: The People of the Circus* (New York, 1956), p. 152.

14. Quoted in Bob Greene, "Sad Saga When Kids Turn Against Clowns," *Des Moines Tribune,* 18 August 1980, p. 2.

15. May, *Circus,* p. 59.

16. Ibid., p. 63.

17. Ibid.

18. Towsen, *Clowns,* pp. 138–39.

19. Townsend Walsh, "Oldest Living Bareback Rider," *Billboard,* 23 March 1929, p. 65.

20. Towsen, *Clowns,* p. 134.

21. Quoted ibid., p. 135.

22. May, *Circus,* p. 67.

23. Harry La Pearl, "This Clown Business," *Billboard,* 29 March 1930, p. 16.

24. Towsen, *Clowns,* p. 268.

25. Dexter Fellows and Andrew Freeman, *This Way to the Big Show* (New York, 1936), p. 210.

26. A. J. Liebling, "Here Come the Clowns," *White Tops,* April-May 1939, p. 16.

27. Robert Lewis Taylor, *Center Ring: The People of the Circus* (New York, 1956), p. 146.

28. Ibid., p. 148.

29. Bradna and Spence, *Big Top,* p. 227.

30. Towsen, *Clowns,* p. 301.

31. *Toronto Star Weekly,* 27 October 1962, n.p.

32. Emmett Kelly (with F. Beverly Kelley), *Clown* (New York, 1954), pp. 40–41.

33. Ibid., p. 49.

34. Ibid., p. 113.

35. Ibid., p. 124.

36. Ibid., pp. 125–26.

37. Ibid., p. 175.
38. Ibid., p. 269.

Chapter 7

1. Casting, as described by Fred Bradna, consisted of two men hanging heads down from a stationary rigging and casting a third back and forth between them.
2. C. G. Sturtevant, "The Metamorphosis of the Flying Act," *Billboard*, 8 December 1928, p. 105.
3. Ibid.
4. Bradna and Spence, *Big Top*, p. 177.
5. Sturtevant, "Metamorphosis," p. 105.
6. Bradna and Spence, *Big Top*, p. 168.
7. Ibid., p. 169.
8. Quoted in Taylor, *Center Ring*, p. 168.
9. Ibid., p. 169.
10. Bradna and Spence, *Big Top*, p. 171.
11. Taylor, *Center Ring*, pp. 170–71.
12. Bradna and Spence, *Big Top*, pp. 172–73.
13. Quoted in Taylor, *Center Ring*, p. 173.
14. Bradna and Spence, *Big Top*, p. 173.
15. Ibid., p. 174.
16. Fellows and Freeman, *This Way*, p. 226.
17. Taylor, *Center Ring*, p. 175.
18. Ibid., p. 176.
19. Quoted in *St. Louis Globe-Democrat*, 30 August 1969, n.p.
20. Louis Zara, "The Flying Codonas," *Esquire*, July 1937, p. 94.
21. Greg Parkinson, "Poster Princess-Victoria Codona," *Bandwagon*, July-August 1980, p. 11.
22. Bradna and Spence, *Big Top*, p. 192.
23. Cosmopolite, "Alfredo Codona and the Art of the Aerial Acrobat," *White Tops*, December 1938–January 1939, p. 21.
24. Alfredo Codona, "Split Seconds," *Saturday Evening Post*, 6 December 1930, p. 76.
25. Ibid., p. 75.
26. Quoted in Zara, "Flying," p. 153.
27. Alfredo Codona, "Taking the Fall," *Saturday Evening Post*, 28 February 1931, p. 88.
28. Bradna and Spence, *Big Top*, p. 179.
29. Taylor, *Center Ring*, p. 216.
30. Ibid., p. 225.
31. Lillian Leitzel, quoted in untitled article in Leitzel file at Circus World Museum Library, Baraboo, Wisconsin.

32. *Billboard,* 24 April 1915, p. 54.
33. Taylor, *Center Ring,* p. 237.
34. Ibid.
35. Bradna and Spence, *Big Top,* p. 183.
36. Ibid., p. 179.
37. Taylor, *Center Ring,* p. 217.
38. Quoted ibid., p. 239.
39. Bradna and Spence, *Big Top,* p. 190.
40. Unidentified clipping in Codona file, Circus World Museum Library, Baraboo, Wisconsin.

Chapter 8

1. Stuart Thayer, "A Note on the Decline of the Circus," *Bandwagon,* July-August 1972, p. 17.
2. Ibid.
3. North and Hatch, *Circus Kings,* p. 214.
4. Ibid., p. 251.
5. "Ringling Wrangling," *Fortune,* July 1947, p. 161.
6. Taylor, *Center Ring,* p. 31.
7. North and Hatch, *Circus Kings,* p. 255.
8. Bradna and Spence, *Big Top,* p. 137.
9. Ibid., p. 141.
10. Quoted in Robert Hasson, "A Very Turbulent Circus Season, 1938," *Bandwagon,* November-December 1980, pp. 24–25.
11. North and Hatch, *Circus Kings,* p. 282.
12. Ibid., p. 283.
13. Quoted in Svere O. Braathen, "The Sheet Anchor Failed," *Bandwagon,* May-June 1972, p. 28.
14. North and Hatch, *Circus Kings,* p. 285.
15. See Hasson, "Very Turbulent," p. 31.
16. Zack Terrell, quoted ibid., p. 34.
17. North and Hatch, *Circus Kings,* pp. 290–91.
18. Taylor, *Center Ring,* p. 43.
19. Ibid., pp. 43–44.
20. North and Hatch, *Circus Kings,* p. 315.
21. Ibid., p. 319.
22. Plowden, *Amazing Ringlings,* pp. 281–82.
23. North and Hatch, *Circus Kings,* p. 335.
24. Ibid., pp. 367–68.
25. McKennon, *Logistics,* p. 111.
26. R. M. Harvey, "The Circus That Was, Is and Will Be," *Billboard,* 29 December 1934, p. 126.
27. *New York Times,* 6 August 1938, p. 12.

Selected Bibliography

Bibliographical Note

The definitive study of the American circus has yet to be written. When—and if—it is, it will no doubt be a multi-volume work. In the meantime, we must be satisfied with the numerous books and articles that have been written and hopefully will continue to be written. The following bibliography is a mere sampling of the books that, in one way or another, treat the American circus. I have not included articles simply because there are too many of them. Yet, it is probably in the hundreds of articles in such magazines as the *Billboard* (through the 1950s), *White Tops* (Circus Fans of America), and *Bandwagon* (Circus Historical Society) that one must search for the many pieces necessary for a complete picture of the American circus. Fortunately, there are many toilers in the "circus vineyard"—Charles Fox, Tom Parkinson, Stuart Thayer, Chang Reynolds, Fred Pfening, Jr., Robert Parkinson, Greg Parkinson, Sverre Braathen, Antony Coxe, Robert Hasson, Gene Plowden, Joe McKennon, George Speaight, and Joanne Joys, to name only a very few; and it is through their painstaking efforts that the history of the American circus is recorded.

Ballantine, Bill. *Clown Alley.* Boston: Little, Brown, 1982. Offers good insights into clowns and clowning by the dean of the Ringling clown college.

Barnum, P. T. *Struggles and Triumphs; or Forty Years' Recollections.* Buffalo: Courier, 1875. A fascinating, though not always objective, autobiography of the great showman's career.

Beale, George B. *Through the Backdoor of the Circus.* Springfield, Mass.: McLoughlin Bros., 1938. A good glimpse of the life of a large tented circus.

Beatty, Clyde, with Anthony, Edward. *Facing the Big Cats.* Garden City, N.Y.: Doubleday, 1964. Hoked up a bit, like his act, but still a valuable book for anyone interested in Beatty and his methods of training.

Bradna, Fred, and Spence, Hartzell. *The Big Top.* New York: Simon & Schuster, 1952. Very informative book, with keen insight into the circus and its people from the vantage point of equestrian director.

Chindahl, George L. *A History of the Circus in America.* Caldwell, Idaho: Caxton Printers, 1959. A good place to begin a study of the American circus. Good references.

Cooper, Courtney Ryley. *Under the Big Top.* Boston: Little, Brown, 1923. An inside view of the circus by a person who knew it well.

Court, Alfred. *My Life with the Big Cats.* New York: Simon & Schuster, 1955. Traces the career of Court from its beginning to his retirement from Ringling.

Coxe, Antony H. *A Seat at the Circus.* Hamden, Conn.: Archon Books, 1980. Covers the history of virtually every circus act.

Durant, John, and Durant, Alice. *Pictorial History of the American Circus.* New York: Castle Books, 1957. Excellent for pictures and general history.

Eipper, Paul. *Circus!* New York: Viking Press, 1931. A picture of the small circus in Europe—on a day-to-day basis.

Fellows, Dexter, and Freeman, Andrew. *This Way to the Big Show.* New York: Macmillan, 1936. Another book by an insider—a press agent. Entertaining and informative.

Fenner, Mildred S., and Fenner, Wolcott. *The Circus, Lure and Legend.* Englewood Cliffs, N.J.: Prentice-Hall, 1970. Many good illustrations, along with a collection of essays and articles on the circus. Impressionistic.

Fox, Charles, and Parkinson, Tom. *The Circus in America.* Waukasha, Wis.: Country Beautiful, 1969. Good for illustrations and general background.

Fox, Charles P. *A Ticket to the Circus.* New York: Bramhall House, 1959. Good for general background. Black and white illustrations.

———, and Kelley, F. Beverly. *The Great Circus Street Parade.* New York: Dover, 1978. The best work yet on the street parade. Lavishly illustrated.

Hammarstrom, David L. *Behind the Big Top.* New York: A. S. Barnes, 1980. Excellent coverage of recent circus history.

Harlow, Alvin F. *The Ringlings, Wizards of the Circus.* New York: Julian Messner, 1951. Story of the Ringlings and their rise in the circus world.

Harris, Neil. *Humbug.* Boston: Little, Brown, 1973. A study of Barnum that relates the showman's career to the cultural milieu of his times.

Hubler, Richard. *The Cristianis.* Boston: Little, Brown, 1966. A history of the Cristiani family—one of the great families of the circus.

Joys, Joanne. *The Wild Animal Trainer in America.* Boulder, Colo.: Pruett, 1983. The best study to date on the wild-animal trainer in America.

Kelly, Emmett. *Clown.* New York: Prentice-Hall, 1954. An autobiography that is well written and informative on clowning.

May, Earl Chapin. *The Circus from Rome to Ringling.* New York: Duffield & Green, 1932. One of the basic works on the history of the circus.

McKennon, Joe. *Circus Lingo.* Sarasota, Fla.: Carnival Publishers, 1980. Extensive list of circus slang terms.

————. *Logistics of the American Circus.* Sarasota, Fla.: Carnival Publishers, 1977. Excellent description of the logistics of a large railroad circus—the most complete yet.

Morris, Ron. *Wallenda.* Chatham, N.Y.: Sagarin Press, 1976. Traces Karl Wallenda's career from its beginning till just before his death.

North, Henry Ringling, and Hatch, Alden. *The Circus Kings: Our Ringling Family Story.* Garden City, N.Y.: Doubleday, 1960. Personal view of the Ringling family—biased in places, but quite informative.

Parkinson, Tom, and Fox, Charles P. *The Circus Moves by Rail.* Boulder, Colo.: Pruett Publishing, 1978. Excellent book on circus rail travel—many pictures and informative commentary.

Plowden, Gene. *Merle Evans: Maestro of the Circus.* Miami: E. A. Seeman, 1971. Traces career of Ringling band leader and provides anecdotal information of circus life.

————. *Those Amazing Ringlings and Their Circus.* Caldwell, Idaho: Caxton Printers, 1968. An informative history of the Ringlings—with some fresh angles of inquiry.

Powledge, Fred. *Mud Show: A Circus Season.* New York: Harcourt Brace Jovanovich, 1975. A penetrating treatment of life on a modern truck show—a pleasure to read.

Reeder, Warren A. *No Performances Today.* Hammond, Ind.: North State Publishers, 1972. Thorough coverage of the Hagenbeck-Wallace train wreck in 1918.

Speaight, George. *A History of the Circus.* New York: A. S. Barnes, 1980. Concentrates on great performers and their acts. Thorough and well documented.

Stark, Mabel. *Hold That Tiger.* Caldwell, Idaho: Caxton Printers, 1938. Autobiography of Stark. Many anecdotes.

Stott, R. Toole, ed. *Circus and Allied Arts—A World Bibliography.* Derby, England: Harpur & Sons, 1958. A most useful source for anyone doing research on the circus.

Taylor, Robert Lewis. *Center Ring: The People of the Circus.* New York: Doubleday, 1956. Excellent information on various performers—a collection of essays that first appeared in the *New Yorker.*

Towsen, John H. *Clowns.* New York: Hawthorn Books, 1976. A complete and authoritative history of clowning.

Wallace, Irving. *The Fabulous Showman.* New York: Alfred A. Knopf, 1967. A well-documented examination of the career of P. T. Barnum.

Willson, Dixie. *Where the World Folds Up at Night.* New York: D. Appleton, 1932. Another inside view of the circus and its people. Good for anecdotes and background.

Index

Adam Forepaugh Circus, 29, 52
Ade, George, 20
Adgies, M'lle, 52
Adkins, Jesse, 77, 78, 157
Agee, John, 86
Al G. Barnes Circus, 21, 53, 55, 62–66, 69, 105, 117
Al G. Barnes-Sells-Floto Circus, 192
Alitza, Alfred, 176
Alitza, Leopoldina, 175; *See* Leitzel, Lillian
Allied Owners, Inc., 187
Alzana, Charles, 123, 125; *See* Davis, Charles
Alzana, Elsie, 123; *See* Davis, Elsie
Alzana, Harold, 118–26; *See* Davis, Harold
Alzana, Hilda, 122, 123; *See* Davis, Hilda
Alzana, Minnie, 119, 122, 123, 125
Alzanas, The Great, 119
American Circus Corporation, The, 21, 26, 97, 167
American Federation of Actors, The, 119
Amidon, C. H., 2, 3
Anderson, John Murray, 159
Angelo Troupe, The, 44
Antaleks, The, 43
Arbaughs, The, 164

Bailey, Hackaliah, 5
Bailey, James A., 13, 19, 41

Ballantine, Bill, 63, 73
Ballard, Ed, 21
Baraboo, Wisconsin, 15, 20, 22, 25, 26, 38
Barnum, Phineas T., 5–14
Barnum and Bailey Circus, The, 13, 19, 20, 32, 52, 87, 93, 163, 164, 172, 173
Barnum's American Museum, 8
Bates, Jacob, 1
Beatty, Clyde, 55, 57, *70–82*, 157, 175
Beatty, Harriett, 78
Blackpool Tower Circus, 120
Blondin, The Great, 110, 111, 119; *See* Gravelet, Jean Francois
Bloomington, Illinois, 164, 165
Boone, Edgar Daniel, 52
Borella, Arthur, 142
Bottari, Anna, 101
Bowers, Bert, 21
Bradna, Beata, 91
Bradna, Charles, 92
Bradna, Ella, *91–94*
Bradna, Fred, 44, 60, 70, 84, *90–94*, 116, 129, 152, 164, 167, 168, 175–78, 188
Bradna, Johan, 91–93
Bradna, Josephy, 90
Bradna, Katha, 91
Bridgeport, Connecticut, 14, 20, 25
Bruce, Vera, 182, 183
Bryant, William Cullen, 147
Buchanan, Fred, 157

217